CURSE OF THE GIANT MUFFINS

And Other Washington Maladies

MICHAEL KINSLEY

SUMMIT BOOKS

NEW YORK • LONDON • TORONTO • SYDNEY • TOYKO

DESIGNED BY JAMES F. BRISSON
MANUFACTURED IN THE UNITED STATES OF AMERICA

1   3   5   7   9   10   8   6   4   2

LIBRARY OF CONGRESS CATALOGING IN PUBLICATION
DATA

Kinsley, Michael E.
Curse of the giant muffins, and other Washington
maladies.

1. United States—Politics and government—1981—
2. Reagan, Ronald.   I. Title
E876.K54   1897   973.927   87-10202
ISBN 0-671-64092-5

ACKNOWLEDGMENTS

The following articles are reprinted by permission of *The New Republic*:
"Got a Match?" July 30, 1984
"We Wuz Robbed," June 9, 1986
"Take Two Aspirin and Avoid Nuclear War," Feb. 25, 1985
"Away with a Manger," October 31, 1983
"The Double Felix," March 26, 1984
"Mixing Dog and Politics," October 15, 1984
"Blaming America First," July 29, 1985
"Back to Nature," May 7, 1984
"Manila, Managua, Pretoria," March 24, 1986
"Still Chosen," December 3, 1984
"No White Feather, Please," June 16, 1986
"The Case for Glee," December 22, 1986
"Jerkofsky & Co.," September 9, 1981

(continued at the back of the book)

CONTENTS

PREFACE

First of all, I don't want any grief about throwing together a bunch of old articles and calling it a book. If you think that's cheating, don't buy it. For myself, I like reading old magazine articles—my own, of course, but even other people's. Among other things, it's a way to recapture the flavor of the recent past. If this collection has any lasting value, it's as a survey of the political moods and obsessions of the early and mid-1980s—the Reagan era.

For that reason, in putting together this book, I've tried hard not to cheat by editing or updating what I've written (except in footnotes and introductory remarks). In a few cases, it was impossible to pass up the chance to rewrite some clumsy phrase that's been gnawing at me for years, or to delete some observation that strikes me now as exceptionally stupid. I'm also ashamed to admit that in going through my old stuff, I caught myself repeating myself several times and decided there was no point in letting you catch me at it as well. Finally, although, as an editor who believes in heavy editing, I try to follow the golden rule (let others do unto you what you spend all day doing unto others), I couldn't resist restoring a few phrases and paragraphs to their original, unmolested form.

Some of these pieces are fairly nasty. People sometimes ask, "Aren't you worried that you're going to run into him/her some day?" Well, I do worry. In the world of journalism, there are two approved alternative solutions to this problem. The high-minded alternative is: Stick to your principles. Avoid socializing with people you write about. If you run into one, be coolly polite. The low-minded alternative is: We're all people of the world. Washington's a small town. You've got to be able to savage a guy in print one day and go drinking with him the next. My own solution for dealing

9

with people I've written negatively about is to run the other way
when I see one coming.

But it's not always necessary. I once wrote a column (not included
here) about a small political scandal involving Charles Wick, head of
the USIA (U.S. Information Agency) and a close friend of President
Reagan. Although the piece basically came to Wick's defense, it did
contain the line, "By all accounts, Wick is a jackass." A couple years
later, to my surprise, Wick invited me to lunch at the Metropolitan
Club. With some trepidation, I went, but it seemed he had no
memory of this crude public insult. I was just one man on a list of
journalists he wanted to inform about USIA's magnificent accom-
plishments. Toward the end of lunch, I couldn't resist saying, "It's
nice of you to have invited me here, Mr. Wick, considering that I
once wrote that you're a jackass." Wick paused, then replied with
great dignity: "I don't mind criticism from the press, as long as it's
accurate."

Writers always praise the vital contribution of their editors, but it
probably takes an editor to really mean it. I've been associated with
The New Republic for more than a decade, which makes me the
senior employee, so I hardly know where to begin listing the valued
associates I've had the pleasure of working with over the years. Of
course I do know: the place to begin is with my friend, colleague,
and boss Marty Peretz. In addition, thanks to Dorothy Wickenden,
Jeff Morley, Rick Hertzberg, Morton Kondracke, Ann Hulbert,
Charles Krauthammer, Mickey Kaus, Leon Wieseltier, Fred Barnes,
Chuck Lane, Luke Menand, Jim Glassman, Leona Roth, Bruce
Steinke, Karen Watkins, Gwen Somers, Elisabeth Brandner, Laura
Obolensky, Roger Rosenblatt, Jack Beatty, Steve Chapman, Jamie
Bayliss, Jeff Dearth, Eliot Marshall, and Ken Bode.

From the golden age at *Harper's*, thanks to Helen Rogan, Louisa
Kearney, Jan Drews, Jeff Morley (again), Jamie Bayliss (again), Erich
Eichmann, Mickey Kaus (again), Bob Asahina, Tamara Glenny, Jeff
Schaire, Jim Wolcott, and David Owen. At *Fortune*, thanks to Dan
Seligman, Bill Rukeyser, Betty Morris. At the *Wall Street Journal*,
thanks to Robert Bartley, Tim Ferguson, John Fund, and Jeane
Leung. At the *Washington Post*, thanks to Meg Greenfield, Ken
Ikenberry, Steve Rosenfeld, Dave Gunderson, and Jamie Bayliss

(again!!). At the *Washington Monthly*, thanks to Charlie Peters, Carol Trueblood, and Tim Noah.

And thanks, of course, to Jim Silberman of Summit Books and my agent, Rafe Sagalyn. I thought Rafe was crazy when he left *TNR* many years ago to become a literary agent, and now he can buy and sell scribblers like me.

This book is dedicated to my parents, George and Lillian Kinsley. Any factual errors or lapses of judgment are strictly their fault.

LIBERALS

INTRODUCTION

Just as I sat down to write this introduction, my friend Maureen Dowd of the *New York Times* called in search of evidence for an article about "the return of Liberal Chic." Can it be true? Of course it's a sign of how far the political pendulum has swung the other way that the term is "liberal chic." The return of "radical chic" remains nearly unthinkable. In any event, I like to think of myself as a liberal (although I don't like it enough to waste time in tedious arguments with people who think I don't deserve the label). So I hope it's true, as Maureen says, that liberals are being invited to parties again. My address is in the phone book.

In American politics, unlike (say) in Britain, political party platforms aren't supposed to be taken seriously. So "Got a Match?" might be seen as cheating. Nevertheless the Democratic platform of 1984 is a pretty authentic document of the condition of American liberalism at the peak of the Reagan era, and not a cheery one.

Little has been heard lately from the party's Fairness Commission ("Preferences"), which was essentially a sop to Jesse Jackson. As far as I know, the final breakdown of its membership by sexual preference has never been announced. The complete revision of the Democratic party rules has been a quadrennial tradition for two decades now. These days, the trend is back toward the back-room arrangements that earlier reforms were supposed to eliminate.

I see that in "We Wuz Robbed" (which argues that moving the Democratic Party "back toward the center" is not the right cure). I assert that "politics is not a game," whereas in "The Case for Glee" (see page 87) I state that "politics *is* a game." I guess that's inconsistent. Well, Mr. Know-It-All, is politics a game? Fortunately, the columnist has a ready answer for this sort of question: yes and no.

International Physicians for the Prevention of Nuclear War, which I wrote about shortly after its founding in 1981 ("Take Two Aspirin and Avoid Nuclear War"), went on to win the Nobel Peace Prize in 1985. So much for my influence. You probably couldn't win the Nobel Prize for Medicine by announcing your earnest intention to cure cancer without actually making any progress toward that end. But apparently standards for the Peace Prize are not so unreasonably high. Or perhaps the group's copresident, Dr. Eugene Chazov, allegedly Leonid Brezhnev's cardiologist, deserves some credit for his contribution to world peace in helping to kill off his star patient. The antinuclear fever these doctors began spreading in 1981 reached epidemic proportions the next year with the publication of Jonathan Schell's comic masterpiece, *The Fate of the Earth* (see page 23).

The resignation of Chief Justice Warren Burger, the ascension of Justice William Rehnquist, and the appointment of Justice Antonin Scalia are three more nails in the coffin of *Roe* v. *Wade*, the abortion decision. As argued here ("Abortion Time Bomb"), that may be no bad thing for American liberalism, or even necessarily for women's right to choose abortion.

Please know that I am a card-carrying member of the American Civil Liberties Union, even though I think its annual Christmas crèche hunt is insane. In the Rhode Island case discussed in "Away with a Manger," the court ultimately held that the city-sponsored nativity scene was not a violation of the First Amendment, since it was part of a larger display involving Santa Claus, reindeer, and other secular manifestations of the season. Partly in response to this annual controversy, some cities have taken to putting up Hanuka menorahs as well (or "Passover menorahs," as President Reagan referred to the one in Lafayette Park across from the White House). In a fine impartial spirit, the ACLU is suing over these as well, leaving Jewish communities split and city officials ready to tear their hair out. Merry Christmas.

The long review of the life and thought of investment banker Felix Rohatyn ("The Double Felix") might have gone in the business section, but the cult of Rohatyn among liberals and Democrats is a telling indication of the state of American liberalism. The glory days of the cult may be over. Talk of Felix for president has died out. But Rohatyn's *pronunciamientos* are still treated with excessive respect. In 1986 he and his wife made a splash in New York by proclaiming that elaborate charity fund-raising balls had become unseemly. This was after years of skilled social climbing by the Rohatyns through the world of charity balls. Likewise, Felix is now quoted regularly warning about the dangers of corporate merger mania. Few people have done more to feed the merger boom—both its first wave two decades ago and its second wave of recent years—than Felix Rohatyn. As far as I know, he hasn't offered to give his fees back.

Got a Match?

THE NEW REPUBLIC, *July 30, 1984*

My favorite line in the 1984 Democratic platform declares, "We know more about the number of matches sold than about the number of children across the country who die in fires while alone at home." The indignant tone suggests this is a bad thing, but the matter is not pursued. The moving finger points, and having pointed, moves on to motor vehicle crashes ("the leading cause of death and serious injury among children between the ages of six months and five years") and teen-age suicide ("We support the creation of a national panel . . .").

Much of what Democrats find endearing and exasperating about their party is in this sentence. You can just see it bubbling up from some earnest social welfare academic at Hunter College, through a Washington lobbying group, and straight into the platform because it's on someone's agenda, and no one else took offense. (The Matchworkers Union must have been asleep at the switch when this one came barreling past.) Through an initial impression of sourness, the sentence shines with generosity and optimism. Republican platform writers have been debating whether to narrow their definition of who should get government help, from "the truly needy" to "the very truly needy." ("Truly nutty," the *Washington Post* remarked.) But no human sorrow is alien to the Democratic Party. First we need to "know more." Knowing more will lead to a government program, and soon the problem will be solved.

And yet, if we don't even know how many children die in fires while alone at home, how do we know it's such a terrible problem? There's a characteristically Democratic inverse complacency in the assumption that knowing more is bound to reveal that a problem is even more pressing than previously supposed. Is this liberalism, or is it social hypochondria? "Oh, doctor, we need a cure. But first, we need a disease." Yes, of course, even one death of a child in a fire while alone at home is too many. But the lunatic specificity of this complaint is itself a comment on such open-ended compassion. Is the Democratic Party turning its back on children who die in fires while at home but not alone, or while alone somewhere else, or—crowning irony—neither at home nor alone?

The Democratic platform goes into more detail about children than about any other subject. This may be because, as the platform says, "Simple decency demands that we make children one of our highest national priorities." Or it may be that children are the only thing Democrats can really agree on these days. We forthrightly favor children, and we dare the Republicans to criticize us for it. On a similar note, we are the party that opposes "violent acts of bigotry, hatred, and extremism." Wanna make something of it? On most other matters, however, we are less forthright. Geraldine Ferraro, the head of the platform committee, said she wanted "themes" and "directions," rather than specifics, and that's what she got. But producing a platform full of generalities is not a simple matter of turning on the fog machine. It's a delicate exercise in writing in code.

For example, the skilled platform writer can appear to endorse a controversial position, and then use generalities to render that endorsement meaningless: "We affirm our strong commitment to Irish unity—achieved by consent and based on reconciliation of all the people of Ireland." (See also, "We favor cheap air fares—

achieved by the suspension of gravity.") On the other hand, a platform can use generalities to endorse a controversial position while appearing not to: "We believe it is a sound principle of international trade for foreign automakers which enjoy substantial sales in the United States to invest here and create jobs where their markets are," which is code for the domestic content bill. A promise to "honor the principles of residency in taxation" means tax breaks for prosperous Americans living abroad. I have no idea what it means to pledge to "address all facets of our maritime industry . . . in an integrated matter." But I bet it means something specific, and nothing nice.

The domestic content example illustrates another platform technique, which might be called "flag-wrapping": take an unassailable high-minded principle, such as "international trade," and use it to package something of less universal appeal. Calling the notion that cars sold in the United States should be made in the United States "a sound principle of international trade" is preposterous, since the whole idea of international trade is to make something in one country and sell it in another. Consider also the phrase, "Medicare, Social Security, federal pensions, farm price supports and dozens of other people-oriented programs," as if paying farmers not to grow food were on a par with guaranteeing health care to old people.

If you're serving up something soft and bland, try garnishing the dish with a spicy sense of urgency: "It is time that a national Economic Cooperation Council was created." This council is supposed to address "several particularly important functions that today are poorly performed or poorly coordinated by the government," including "coordination and policy coherence," so you can see why time is of the essence.

On the other hand, if you know that what's cooking is truly indigestible, try slathering it with mayonnaise. Don't say you're against deregulation; say, "the country should take a careful look at the direction deregulation is taking." If you're not sure whether you want to serve a particular dish at all—or even what, exactly, it is ("an independent criminal justice corporation"?)—just say it should be "considered."

The organization of a platform is a subtle business. A pledge of more research money for AIDS goes in the paragraph that starts, "We reaffirm the dignity of all people." A pledge of more research money for sickle-cell anemia, by contrast, belongs in the department, "Economic Justice: Keeping Our Commitments." Measles vaccines go under "Investing in Children." I seem to have missed all the references to dreadful diseases that strike without regard to race, age, or sexual preference. But I'm damned if I'm going to read the thing again.

Preferences

THE NEW REPUBLIC, *August 6, 1984*

> Be it resolved that the Democratic National Party
> shall, during the 1984 Democratic Convention,
> create the Fairness Commission which shall be
> responsible for the review and revision of the
> Democratic Party Rules. . . . The Commission
> shall consist of at least fifty members equally di-
> vided between men and women, and shall in-
> clude fair and equitable participation of Blacks,
> Hispanics, native Americans, Asian/Pacifics,
> women, and persons of all sexual preference con-
> sistent with their proportional representation in
> the party.
> —*resolution adopted by the Democratic Party Rules*
> *Committee*

Okay, let's see.

Twenty-six women and twenty-four men.

Twenty blacks, fifteen Hispanics (five Puerto Rican, five Mexican, five other Latin), five native Americans, ten Asian/Pacifics. What? Oh, right. So make it ten whites, take five from the blacks, three from the Hispanics, and one each from the native Americans and Asian/Pacifics. No sweat.

Ten gays, thirty-five straights, three celibate/onanists, and two pedophile/beastiophile/miscellaneous. Beastiophile? Note to liaison staff. What is value-free term for animal lovers? Ck with Humane Society.

Thirteen who prefer the lights on and thirty-seven who prefer the lights off.

Twenty-four at night, twenty in the morning, six between noon and 4 P.M.

Thirty-one one partner or less, twelve two, seven three or more.

Twenty-seven on top, twenty-one underneath, and two standing up. What? You're kidding. Well, if Yankelovich says so, eight on top, twenty-nine underneath, and thirteen standing up.

Eighteen rock, eleven classical, twelve country-and-western, five jazz, nine "All Things Considered."

Fourteen a cigarette afterward, ten a long talk, nine an old movie on TV, eight a shower, six chocolate-chip ice cream, three cab fare home.

Fifty who prefer no sex at all to any cuts in Social Security.

We Wuz Robbed

THE NEW REPUBLIC, *June 9, 1986*

A good test of political seriousness is whether anyone opposes what you have to say. The Democratic Leadership Council, a group founded last year with the mission of moving the Democratic Party back toward the political center, wants the party to be "a force for advancing the common interest; for spurring growth, creating jobs and opportunity, and defending freedom." According to former Virginia governor Charles Robb, one of the DLC's founders, "The Republicans have . . . appropriated themes which used to belong to the Democrats: keeping our economy healthy and our defense strong. Democrats need to reclaim these bedrock issues."

I suppose there are people who oppose growth and strength. And I suppose it's a good thing that the Democratic Party not be dominated by Club-of-Rome antigrowth loonies and weak-kneed appeasers, if it ever was. It may even be true that growth and strength were once associated in the public mind more with the Democrats than with the Republicans. Of *course* the Democrats should be for growth and strength. Also for public sanitation and child safety. But what is the point of trying to rebuild the party on such unobjectionable themes?

First, it probably won't work. If these issues were once thought of as Democratic, the Republicans stole them fair and square (in Senator S. I. Hayakawa's famous formulation about the Panama Canal). Perhaps these issues can be neutralized, but it will be a long time before growth and strength alone will be perceived as reasons to vote Democratic.

More important, though, why bother? Politics is not a game of capture-the-flag. If all the important things Democrats would like to say are already being said by Republicans, it's hard to see why stealing them back is worth the trouble.

The big question for Democrats—especially for groups like the Democratic Leadership Council and the Coalition for a Democratic Majority, which want to nudge the party toward the right—is what the party should do differently that doesn't amount to simply becoming more conservative. "We're just like the other guys, only somewhat less so" is not a very inspiring slogan. "What really distinguishes us from the Republicans is the breadth of our vision," says Robb. Another would-be centrist, Senator Joe Biden, says that in foreign policy the party must adopt a "common-sense" approach, avoiding "the ideological demons of both the right and the left."

But politics is about ideology, and the Democratic Party might as well fold up and go away unless it has the courage to present itself as forthrightly to the left of the Republicans. "To the left" needn't mean a rejection of growth and strength. But it must mean a demonstrated greater concern for the have-nots of our society and a greater skepticism about military adventure. Euphemisms like "breadth of vision" and "common sense" are timorous and demeaning.

In the present gilded-age atmosphere, calls for greater sacrifice by the haves on behalf of the have-nots may seem like an unpromising strategy. But sharper marketing minds than mine or yours disagree. Why else have the Coca-Cola Company and other large corporations been spending millions of dollars to associate themselves with the ridiculous "Hands Across America" campaign? They must be convinced that unselfishness can sell. And these are people who know what sells.

The only prominent Democrat attempting to peddle forthright progressive rhetoric, with some success, is Governor Mario Cuomo of New York. "Today the American scene is rife with contrasts . . . contrasts of need and plenty," and so on. This is great stuff. Unfortunately, Cuomo is disingenuous about which side of the great divide his listeners are on. In a recent speech, after charging that "our prosperity has been purchased at the expense of the well-being, the hopes and expectations of a large part of our nation," he subtly switches gears and defines the exploited element as "moderate-income households and the poor." Moderate-income households means you, the typical voter. What begins as an inspiring appeal to Americans' sense of generosity ends as a bilious appeal to their sense of grievance.

Much of what the Democratic Party currently stands for domestically is nothing more than an expression of Cuomo's ideological sleight-of-hand: peddling selfishness as progressivism. Programs and policies like Social Security, farm price supports, IRAs, and trade protection all benefit people at least as well off as those who are paying for them in taxes or higher prices. There is nothing progressive about these government initiatives in their present form. DLC types talk bravely but vaguely about "new departures." Robb says that "for Democrats, reducing the deficit is more important than preserving individual programs." The double test for would-be reformers of the party is to specify what old programs they are actually prepared to abandon, and what new initiatives they propose that can truly be called progressive.

Take Two Aspirin and Avoid Nuclear War

THE NEW REPUBLIC, *April 11, 1981*

The medical profession performed miracles last week in Washington, working with great skill and speed to save the lives of

President Reagan and three other victims of a nut with a revolver. But this was trivial compared to the medical triumph that occurred the previous week at a conference center out in the Virginia countryside, where a group of doctors from around the world, led by a team from Harvard, developed a cure for nuclear war. Oh, there are a few kinks to be worked out, but the report on the proceedings of the First Congress of the International Physicians for the Prevention of Nuclear War is cautiously optimistic. The cure consists of persuading everyone that nuclear war is a medical problem, about which one naturally should follow the advice of one's doctor. The doctors, based on their expert understanding of human physiology, have concluded that the best medical advice about nuclear war is: "Don't have one. It is bad for your health. Believe me, I'm a doctor." Soon, nuclear war will be as obsolete as smoking.

Well, I am not a doctor, so perhaps it is presumptuous of me to interfere, but I think that this cure may not work. Speaking strictly as a layman, I see three difficulties.

First, these doctors seem to think that nations build nuclear weapons because they don't realize how unpleasant a nuclear war would be. The "Statement of the Problem" in their prospectus begins: "There is a profound lack of understanding worldwide of the consequences of nuclear war, as evidenced by the enormous nuclear weapons arsenals of the superpowers and the rapid proliferation of nuclear weapons around the world." At their Virginia conference, the doctors addressed their special expertise to this problem. In a closing statement, they report:

> As physicians and scientists, we have for the past several days reviewed the data on the nature and magnitude of the effects that the use of nuclear weapons would bring. We have considered independently prepared medical and scientific analyses from many sources. Our unanimous conclusions are:
> (1) Nuclear war would be a catastrophe with medical consequences of enormous magnitude. . . .

So now you know. In fact, anticipating the results of last month's scientific study, members of Physicians for the Prevention of Nuclear War have been publishing articles for many months in both the specialist and the lay press, describing the gory results of a nuclear exchange. These articles tend to emphasize the effect on doctors and hospitals. "When we contemplate disasters," says the conference report, "we often assume that abundant medical resources and personnel will be available." But the report argues otherwise. Following hair-raising accounts of deaths by the million, colossal fires, widespread famine, generations of genetic mutants, not to mention "grave psychological trauma," the report reveals that "neither doctors nor the hospitals in which they work will be spared." Perhaps there is someone somewhere who had thought that medical care would be unaffected by a nuclear war. And perhaps there are people who can contemplate with relative equanimity the loss of their own lives and those of their family and friends but sicken at the thought that the Harvard Medical School and its affiliated hospitals could be blown away. These people should take heed.

But if we do have nuclear Armageddon, it won't happen because somebody believed that it would be no big deal. Everyone with access to the button realizes that there is no rational reason actually to start a nuclear war, because the result would be dreadful for all sides. The problem for a generation has been that no major power has been willing to give up the ability to *threaten* nuclear attack, and indeed would be foolish to do so as long as an adversary retained it, and there is a risk the game of chicken will get out of hand. A newer problem is that nuclear weapons are getting into the hands of people who aren't rational at all. Graphic descriptions of Boston in flames are unlikely to have a sobering effect on Colonel Qaddafi.

And then there's the disconcerting thought that only the existence of nuclear weapons has prevented a major conventional war between the superpowers for the past thirty-five years. Surely the United States would not be so reluctant to encourage the Poles in their present, obviously sympathetic, rebellion if it weren't for the fear of descent into nuclear catastrophe. Some might find this forced acquiescence in Soviet tyranny unfortunate. But few activists in the campaign against nuclear weapons, I presume, are motivated by a desire to make the world safe for conventional warfare.

The doctors, judging from their literature, have no new prescription for these basic dilemmas of the nuclear age. This is the second difficulty with their cure. Utterly lacking anything constructive to suggest, they simply repeat that "as physicians" they have a special role in preventing nuclear war. The founder of the group, Dr. Bernard Lown of Harvard, wrote last month in the *New England Journal of Medicine*:

> It may be argued that nuclear war is an issue in the political and social domain and that physicians need confront it only as concerned citizens. But on closer examination, it is apparent that the danger of nuclear war in undermining health, fomenting disease, and causing the death of untold millions is an unprecedented threat to humanity.

Dr. Howard Hiatt, dean of the Harvard School of Public Health, has called nuclear war "the last epidemic." A resolution from last month's conference declares that international cooperation among doctors can cure nuclear war, just as it cured smallpox.

But how? The doctors are fond of quoting Einstein, who said that because of nuclear weapons, "We shall require a substantially new manner of thinking if mankind is to survive." Not one of his most brilliant insights, perhaps, but the "new thinking" of these doctors is contained in a handout entitled, "What Physicians Can Do To Prevent Nuclear War." It recommends: "review all information"; "provide information by lectures" and other means; "bring to the attention of all concerned with public policy the medical implications"; "seek the cooperation of the medical and related professions"; "develop a resource center"; "encourage studies of psychological obstacles" to thinking about nuclear war; "initiate discussion of development of an international law" banning nuclear war; "encourage the formation in all countries of groups of physicians and committees"; "establish an international organization to coordinate the activities"; and so on. In other words, "as physicians" they have no better idea about how to prevent nuclear war than anyone else.

Dr. Robert J. Lifton, the mass horror specialist from Yale and a member of the physicians group, goes further. Writing March 28 on the *New York Times* op-ed page, he endorses the action of the "Plowshares Eight," led by Daniel Berrigan, who broke into a nuclear weapons factory last fall, damaged two nose cones, and poured blood on some documents and tools. Lifton complains that, at their trial, he was denied the right to testify as an "expert witness" that their action was exculpable under the legal doctrine of "necessity" because nuclear war would be so awful. "How far should one go in one's actions to prevent nuclear war?" he asks. "The need now is to convert these fragmentary efforts into a deeper awareness that, in turn, leads to a genuine change, to nuclear-arms control—and, yes, disarmament." How a universal awareness even as profoundly deep as his own about the likely effects of nuclear war can actually prevent nuclear war, Dr. Lifton does not reveal.

But let us suppose that universal revulsion, on the advice of doctors, could lead the nations of the world to lay down their nuclear weapons for good. There is a third difficulty. How is this medical education campaign to be conducted in the Soviet Union (let alone Libya, Pakistan, South Africa, and so on)?

The structure of Physicians for the Prevention of Nuclear War, and the publicity the group has cultivated, posits a loony international symmetry. Dr. Lown of Harvard is only co-president of the group. The other co-president is Dr. Eugene I. Chazov, Soviet deputy minister of health and reportedly Chairman Brezhnev's own cardiologist. The group's prospectus balances a list of participating U.S. doctors with a list of participating members from the USSR Academy of Medical Sciences. Yet I can't help feeling that these Soviet doctors may have difficulty applying their chosen therapy of getting "respected and well-informed people to discuss publicly the facts about nuclear war" in a society where the tradition of the op-ed page is not highly developed. The recommendations for "resource centers," public lectures, and so on suggest that, however international the membership list, the real movers behind Physicians for the Prevention of Nuclear War are more familiar with life in Boston than with life in the Soviet Union.

And I wonder if the fact that physicians "are widely respected as scientists" and are "identified with human life and health" will carry as much weight with Soviet leaders as these physicians hope. The last time a Soviet party chairman thought he noticed physicians developing an interest in political matters, he arrested nine of them. All were tortured, two died, and the other seven were saved only by the timely failure of the chairman's own medical treatment. Things have changed in Russia since the days of Stalin and the "Doctors' Plot." But somehow, even today, I can't see Dr. Chazov whipping out his prescription pad and saying, "Now, Comrade Brezhnev, take this for your nerves, and remember: *no nuclear war!*"

But this may not even be necessary, because Brezhnev is already a convert. On March 20, 1980, he wrote to the physician group's American organizers that "the Soviet Union consistently stands for banning these and all other types of weapons of mass destruction and annihilation." And, "You may rest assured that your humane and noble activities aimed at preventing nuclear war will meet with understanding and support in the Soviet Union. With best wishes of success, L. BREZHNEV." As for our side, Representative Hamilton Fish has submitted a proposed concurrent resolution, "expressing the sense of the Congress that all nuclear weapons in the world should be eliminated." Unfortunately, the bill got stalled in committee. If we had a political system as efficient as the one enjoyed in the Soviet Union, all the nuclear weapons in the world would be gone by now.

Abortion Time Bomb

THE NEW REPUBLIC, *February 25, 1985*

One of the worst things that ever happened to American liberalism was *Roe* v. *Wade*, the 1973 Supreme Court case announcing a constitutional right to an abortion. Almost overnight, it politicized millions of people and helped create a mass movement of social-issue conservatives that has grown into one of the most potent forces in our democracy. Although it was written by a Nixon appointee, Harry Blackmun, and supported by two others, including Chief Justice Warren Burger, *Roe* became a symbol of "liberal" judicial excess and cast a retrospective shadow of illegitimacy on all the important cases of the Warren era.

Roe declared that the constitutional right to privacy "is broad enough to encompass a woman's decision whether or not to terminate her pregnancy." After the first "trimester" of pregnancy, the court said, states may regulate abortion for the purpose of protecting the mother's health. After the second trimester, states may take a legitimate interest in the "potential life" of the fetus, and "may go so far as to proscribe abortion . . . except when it is necessary to preserve the life or health of the mother."

The reasoning in *Roe* was, in a word, a mess. There was almost no effort to explain where this "right" to an abortion came from. Previous "privacy" rulings had involved protecting the exercise of political freedom or controlling the police, both matters that feature prominently in the Bill of Rights. Abortion doesn't. As for those trimesters, the court reasoned that abortion during the first trimester is safer for the mother than normal childbirth, whereas the beginning of the third trimester is when "the fetus becomes 'viable' . . . outside the mother's womb." But why should the fact that abortion is safer than childbirth mean the state can't regulate abortion to make it safer still? Why is "viability" the magic point at which the fetus's potential life becomes a legitimate concern? Why, even at that point, should this potential life be held constitutionally less important than a woman's "health," defined in a companion case to include "all factors—physical, emotional, psychological, familial"? The court never said.

The *Roe* opinion placed great weight on giving doctors the freedom to exercise their best medical judgment. But most abortion decisions are for personal reasons and don't depend on doctors' expertise. On the other hand, Blackmun's biggest concession was authorizing state interference to protect the mother, which is odd since the issue is the mother's own right to be free of state interference. This aspect of *Roe* has become an invitation to hypocrisy. States keep trying to make abortion more difficult, ostensibly to protect the health of the mother, and the court keeps playing doctor and saying these measures aren't really necessary.

In subsequent cases, the court has made it next to impossible for states to exercise their ostensible right to protect the fetus after "viability." In 1976, it ruled against specific definitions of viability in terms of gestation time or fetal weight. Then in 1979, it ruled that a statute simply defining viability as "the capability . . . to live outside the mother's womb albeit with artificial aid"—words lifted almost directly from *Roe*—was "void for vagueness" (one of my all-time favorite legal expressions).

But there is a time bomb ticking away inside *Roe* v. *Wade*. Scientific developments of the past decade, allowing us to peer into the womb, have affected the emotional climate and a lot of people's thinking about abortion. Less widely noted outside legal circles is how other medical developments have started to undermine abortion's legal basis.

Justice Blackmun wrote in 1973, "Viability is usually placed at about seven months (twenty-eight weeks)." He conceded that it "may occur earlier, even at twenty-four weeks," but went on to declare twenty-eight weeks—the beginning of the third trimester—as the definite cutoff. He later defined viability as "a reasonable likelihood" of survivability outside the womb, "with or without artificial support." Who knows what "a reasonable likelihood" means, but according to Dr. Michael Epstein, a neonatologist at Harvard Medical School: "If you go back ten years, the babies with a fifty-fifty chance were about thirty weeks. Now that's down to twenty-six or twenty-seven weeks." A study cited by Justice Sandra Day O'Connor in a 1983 abortion case reported a 20 percent chance of survival for infants born at twenty-five weeks. Babies born as early as twenty-one to twenty-two weeks have been known to survive. Dr. Epstein feels that twenty-four weeks may be the lower limit of regular survivability, but others are more optimistic. Meanwhile, of course, "test-tube baby" experimenters are burrowing in from the other side. It's not wild to suppose that the two medical expeditions will meet in the middle some day.

Five of the seven justices who concurred in *Roe* twelve years ago are still on the court. The future of abortion may depend on whether developments in gerontology can outpace developments in neonatology. But the present Supreme Court cannot remain intact forever. Already there is one new justice who has made plain her opposition to *Roe*. Add the two who voted against it originally and a chief justice who seems eager to undermine it, and that's four. Five is a majority.

Supreme Court justices are deeply reluctant to overturn decisions of their predecessors, even decisions they disagree with. (That's because if their predecessors were wrong about something, why, even they themselves might . . . no, no, it doesn't bear thinking about.) But advances in medical technology might give a future court just the opportunity it needs to repeal the result of *Roe* v. *Wade* without brazenly rejecting its logic.

The court already has cited medical advances to undermine its own "trimester" analysis. In 1973, "whether [abortion] must be in a hospital" was offered as a specific example of something the state could regulate after the first trimester. In 1983, noting that "the safety of second-trimester abortions has increased dramatically," the court rejected such a regulation. As O'Connor pointed out in a dissent, improvements in abortion safety are pushing forward the court's "maternal health" dividing line at the same time as developments in the care of premature babies are pushing back its "viability" dividing line. "The *Roe* framework . . . is clearly on a collision course with itself."

What this saga of judicial folly makes clear is that abortion just doesn't belong in the Constitution. There are no neutral principles that can be applied, or "bright lines" that can be adhered to. There is only the tragic trade-off between society's understandable desire to protect human life and a woman's understandable desire to control her own body and life. The absolutist claim of the right-to-lifers is superficially more plausible than that of the pro-choicers, but only superficially. Unless you are prepared to protect the fetus from the moment of conception against all claims of the mother—even her own right to life (because the law does not permit you to take an innocent person's life, even to protect your own)—you are back to the tragic trade-off.

The decision about where on the spectrum of weighty and trivial reasons for an abortion, and when in the growth of the fetus, that trade-off should occur cannot be made by reference to eternal values. It must be made through social consensus, so that a particular society at a particular time can live with it. In other words, it ought to be made democratically. In thinking about the trade-off, I am not overly impressed by the recent spate of grotesque demonstrations that ever-younger fetuses can smile or wave their limbs. So can dogs.

Until you prove to me that a three-month fetus has a greater sense of itself than, say, a cow, I am going to continue thinking that the best solution to this impossible problem is to leave it in most circumstances to the woman who's got to live with the result.

Polls show that most people favor legal abortion. This majority isn't as politicized as the anti-abortion minority, but that might change if the Supreme Court overturns or eviscerates *Roe*. Within five years of such a ruling, I predict, legal abortion would be widely available again—just as it was getting to be widely available before the court swept politics aside. What's more, the campaign for abortion could become the cornerstone of a liberal revival based on the issue of personal freedom.

The greatest danger is a future Supreme Court ruling that legal abortion not only is not required by the Constitution, but actually is forbidden as a denial of due process to the fetal "person." Many conservatives would cheer. This certainly would not be an example of "strict construction" based on the "intent of the founders," since abortion was widely legal when the Bill of Rights was written. But abortion is another area of the law where conservatives are discovering the joys of "judicial activism," and liberals may soon discover the virtues of "judicial restraint." If it happens, that will be *Roe* v. *Wade*'s worst legacy of all.

Away with a Manger

THE NEW REPUBLIC, *October 31, 1983*

It's getting to be that time of year again, and Christmas just wouldn't be Christmas without the American Civil Liberties Union's annual campaign to rid the nation of religious displays on government property. (Mary McGrory once accused the ACLU of

"pursuing the spirit of Christmas across the land like a thief.")
Washington got a foretaste of this beloved seasonal rite, like a
snowstorm in October, when the Supreme Court, on day two of its
new term, heard oral arguments about a nativity scene in Pawtucket,
Rhode Island.

According to the ACLU brief, the offending tableau is ten by
fourteen feet and "includes a stable approximately four and one-half
(4-1/2) feet high, together with thirteen to fifteen figures ranging in
height from one (1) foot"—guess who?— "to five (5) feet. The figures
include a baby lying in a manger, arms outstretched, two angels,
several animals, and several figures kneeling in a posture of worship."
This threat to our freedom was purchased in 1973 for $1,365.

The ACLU may be right that government-sponsored nativity
scenes violate the First Amendment's injunction against the "establishment of religion." Past Supreme Court rulings about the establishment clause have been a bit confusing. When I was studying for
the bar exam, we were taught that the best way to guess which
pro-religion government activities pass muster was the mnemonic
device of the letter "t": *text*book subsidies for parochial schools,
charitable *tax* deductions, and so on. Parochial school lunches
("*tuna* fish") are okay, too. On the other hand, the court ruled in
1980 that posting the *Ten* Commandments in public schools is
unconstitutional, so my education is clearly out of date. Recreating
a central moment of Christianity in the center of town does seem to
imply some sort of endorsement, despite comic claims by the Justice
Department (which supports Pawtucket) that it merely recognizes the
religious element in a secular folk tradition.

Nevertheless, it wearies me to see the ACLU expending its limited
resources of money and good will playing the Grinch like this.
Obviously the mere fact that its position is unpopular is no reason for
the ACLU to shy away. Unpopular causes are the only ones that
need civil liberties protection. The ACLU's greatest glory of recent
years was defending the right of Nazis to march in Skokie, Illinois.

But that was a defense of free expression—the ACLU's central
mission—and a rejection of intolerance. The anti-crèche campaign
has nothing to do with free expression (of religion or speech), and in
a funny way it reflects a spirit of intolerance. What, after all, is wrong
with a publicly sponsored crèche? It's obviously not the money,

which is trivial compared to other ways government supports religion (tax deductions, for example). The problem is the appearance of official sanction, which is taken as an affront.

"On a practical level," the ACLU writes, "a child whose family does not believe in the Divinity of Christ must view the public crèche as a symbolic representation of his or her status as an outsider. The child will question . . . his identification with the American culture."

I think that's right. But I also think this child had better learn early on to question his identification with the American culture, because it's a tough question that will follow him all his life no matter how successful the ACLU is in banning nativity scenes. There *is* a majority culture in this country. It is Christian, white, middle-class. Jews and nonbelievers (I am both) *are* outsiders to some extent in that culture. So are blacks, homosexuals, Orientals, and so on. This is so even though we are a society that is constantly remaking itself, and a society committed to protecting the civil rights and economic opportunities of minorities. The battle for minority rights goes on, of course, but does final victory require eradication of the majority culture? And is every manifestation of that culture an insult to those who aren't fully a part of it?

People who want to go through life with nothing to remind them of their minority status ask too much. They will not get it, and full civil equality does not require it. Furthermore, in the name of ethnic or religious or racial or sexual awareness, they would impose a vast unawareness on national life in which, for official purposes, most Americans are of no particular race or religion (or equally divided among all).

In theory, there is a difference between the society and the polity. In practice, the difference is impossible to police. The majority culture needs some degree of government sanction, and attempts to prevent the government from recognizing this are futile. December 25 has to be a national holiday. If we are going to get any work done at all we can't add Hanuka and Ramadan.

Anyone who is truly affronted by the sight of a publicly sponsored crèche is (to repeat Joel Sayre's famous crack about John O'Hara) "a master of the fancied slight." This official recognition of the majority culture totally lacks the unnerving gratuitousness of, say, the late Interior Secretary James Watt's terminal asininity about women, blacks, Jews, and cripples. What was so chilling about this remark?

The labels themselves, except for "cripple," were not insulting. What shocked, I think, was the unwitting revelation of how aware a man like Watt is of the "otherness" of people around him, and the implicit contrast to himself as a whole, white, male, Christian American. It reminded me of an eerie occasion in high school when I went to dinner at a friend's house and his mother told me, apropos of nothing, that she didn't know how to make chicken soup.

Far from being a handicap, a sense of "outsiderness" can be a great asset in a society that does, in the end, try to protect the rights of cultural outsiders. It energizes, promotes skepticism, gives perspective. I would not want my child to grow up completely comfortable in his surroundings, never forced to "question . . . his identification with the American culture." The enormous literary contribution of homosexuals, the prominence of Jews in courageous social causes of all sorts, the creation of jazz by blacks all derive in part from the discomfort of being outside the majority culture. I am happy to be a bit of an outsider in my own country. I am no less an American for it, and may even hope to be a better one as a result.

The Double Felix

THE NEW REPUBLIC, *March 26, 1984*

Felix Rohatyn, the little stock-jobbing fixer from ITT who went to Kleindienst to get an ant-trust break for his wee, tiny, multi-billion dollar conglomerate . . .

Nicholas von Hoffman
Washington Post, March 10, 1972

Rohatyn was architect of the various schemes that held New York from default. That [1975] crisis left him with the nickname "Felix the Fixer" because of his arm-grabbing style of diplomacy and legendary powers of persuasion.

Robert Kaiser and William Claiborne
Washington Post, February 9, 1977

> I am, by temperament, a fixer of things.
> *Felix Rohatyn, The Twenty-Year Century*
> (advance review copies)

> I am, by temperament, an active negotiator.
> *Felix Rohatyn, The Twenty-Year Century*
> (final bound edition)

Rohatyn's progress from Felix the Fixer to Felix the Philosopher is one of the great public relations ascents of our time. The transformation has been so complete that even the *Washington Post* forgot along the way that he first hove into view (and got his nickname) as a minor figure in the Watergate scandal.

Rohatyn, then as now an investment banker at the firm of Lazard Frères, was the key adviser to ITT Chairman Harold Geneen in the 1960s merger blitzkreig that turned ITT into the king of the conglomerates. ITT's crowning acquisition was the Hartford Fire Insurance Company, but in 1969 the Justice Department filed suit to undo this deal. It was to be a test case of conglomerate merger. Then, in July 1971, the Justice Department unexpectedly announced a settlement that allowed ITT to keep Hartford.

Remember Dita Beard? She was an ITT Washington lobbyist. In February 1972, columnist Jack Anderson revealed a memo she had written shortly before the surprise settlement. The memo credited the happy ending to a $400,000 ITT contribution to the Republican Party. Acting Attorney General Richard Kleindienst immediately denied any connection between the payment and the settlement. He insisted that the head of the antitrust division, Richard McLaren, had handled the negotiations without interference. But Anderson then revealed that Rohatyn had met half a dozen times with Kleindienst himself to discuss the ITT settlement. It later came out that, during this period, Rohatyn also had met four times with Attorney General John Mitchell and twice with White House aide Peter Flanigan, sometimes on the same day as his meetings with Kleindienst. Mitchell implausibly insisted that the ITT case never came up in these talks. About this time, the *Washington Post* reported that Dita Beard and Felix Rohatyn were both on a Nixon reelection committee list of major Republican contributors.

When Jack Anderson's story broke, Dita Beard quickly fled, ostensibly for a vacation in Yellowstone National Park. She mysteriously took ill on the plane and ended up in a Denver hospital, complaining of chest pains and conveniently incommunicado. This is where E. Howard Hunt showed up in his famous ill-fitting red wig, to get a statement from her declaring that the memo was a fraud. With this, Dita Beard disappeared from history. Since Beard was unavailable, the Senate committee investigating the affair had only Rohatyn to rake over the coals. They never found any evidence connecting Rohatyn with the controversial payment, though his firm later signed a consent decree with the SEC over another smelly aspect of the Hartford settlement. After the Nixon tapes came out (Nixon to Kleindienst: "The ITT thing—stay the hell out of it. Is that clear?"), Kleindienst ultimately pleaded guilty to misleading the senators by denying White House interference in the ITT deal.

I. F. Stone, covering Rohatyn's Senate testimony for the *New York Review of Books*, complained that this notorious corporate operator "might have been Joe Blow off the sidewalks of New York as far as the senators seemed to be aware." That was 1972. In 1982 Senator Thomas Eagleton introduced a constitutional amendment to allow foreign-born citizens to become President. He was moved by "my unbounded admiration for the intellect and skills of Felix Rohatyn," born in Vienna. By then, testimony from Rohatyn had become a regular feature of Senate hearings on crucial issues. Even more amazing, verbatim reprints of Rohatyn's testimony had become a regular feature of the *New York Review of Books*.

Chuck Colson put Watergate behind him by finding religion. Felix Rohatyn has gone further: he has become a secular saint. He is simultaneously a leading member of the business community and the official investment banker of the New York left-wing intelligentsia. Colleges give him honorary degrees, politicians seek his advice, and columnists cite his pronouncements with reverence. His presence at a party is a social coup. (Charlotte Curtis in the *New York Times*: "The first course was caviar, and along about salad, Felix Rohatyn suggested that women might be smarter than men.") Only a very prestigious thinker indeed gets a major publishing house to put

out a volume like the one under review* preserving in hard cover
Rohatyn's articles, speeches, congressional testimony, and sundry
pensées of the past few years.

Rohatyn's reputation as more than just another investment banker
has paid financial dividends, too. Lazard was "written off by its Wall
Street competitors" in the mid-1970s, according to a recent biography of Rohatyn's mentor, André Meyer. Rohatyn's high profile has
revived the firm's prestige and brought in new business. In particular,
based on Rohatyn's role as head of the team that guided New York
through its fiscal crisis, Lazard has developed a specialty in crisis
management for troubled municipalities and corporations. Desperate
officials scrape the bottom of their depleted treasuries to pay for a bit
of Rohatyn's magic.

Rohatyn's fame as a financial alchemist has become a self-
fulfilling prophecy. The city of Detroit, for example, was in such
desperate straits a while back that no one would buy its bonds.
Bankruptcy loomed. A "trauma team" from Lazard was hired to help
the city reorganize its finances. "Not that they come up with
anything different" from what the city might do on its own, said one
Detroit official, "but their very presence at the table lends credibility." Another official said, "There's no question the association with
Lazard Frères helped convince banks" to buy Detroit's tattered
bonds. It's almost a high-class protection racket: "Nice little bond
issue you've got here. Sure would be a pity if no one would buy it."
Governments commonly lend their credibility to private business
ventures, but it's the rare individual who can personally lend
credibility to sovereign governments. Rohatyn can.

How has he done it? Obviously his role in "saving" New York
played a part, as do his proposals for saving the rest of mankind,
which impress some people. But his reputation among literary
intellectuals and journalists, at least, has other sources as well.

First, Rohatyn has diligently curried favor with these people,
flattered them, invited them to his house in the Hamptons, and so
on. It works. Shocking, but true. Many of these people are naive

---

* *The Twenty-Year Century: Essays on Economics and Public Policy*
[Random House, 1984].

about financial matters, and easily dazzled. In a slavish *New Yorker* profile a year ago, Rohatyn described his first dealings with journalists during the New York fiscal crisis.

> *A very interesting thing happened, which was very important to us, namely, the New York daily papers, which had the choice of putting their financial reporters or their political reporters on the story, put their political reporters on it. This meant that they had to be taught about finance, and I was the person they turned to to teach them.*

Rohatyn's campaign got a boost from a changed attitude toward money, over the course of the 1970s, among the people he was trying to impress. Put simply, money became fashionable again. The longing Tom Wolfe had described as *nostalgie de la boue* (nostalgia for the mud) was replaced by something more like *nostalgie de l'argent*. Black Panthers out, investment bankers in. After all, imagine: here you are, used to being awestruck at somebody's $100,000 book advance, and you find yourself seated at dinner next to a man who just closed a deal worth $3 million in fees. And *he's* sucking up to *you!*

Another laughably easy way to help get yourself a reputation as a philosopher is to use the word "philosophical" a lot. Also "profound" (as in, "Today I am neither liberal nor conservative, but profoundly skeptical") and, for that matter, "skeptical." ("Skepticism is what is needed today—skepticism of easy solutions, of cant, of ideology of the left or right.") Refer to your own writings as "essays," not articles. Call other people "brilliant." The "essays" in *The Twenty-Year Century* reveal that Rohatyn has mastered all these techniques of literary social climbing.

But if you wish the *New Yorker* to say of you, "His articles [sic] have a casual eloquence, and convey the impression that a vast degree of cultivation and much careful thought underlie them," you must do more. It is not enough to merely say you are philosophical. You must be philosophical. You must write: "I am convinced that we can deal with our problems; in fact, I believe that in dealing with them we shall find our greatest opportunities." You must list "the basic issues for the future of the world." You must bemoan "the snapshot quality of television news." Although your book has nothing to do with the subject, you must declare in the introduction that "the notion that nuclear war is 'winnable' strikes me as utterly demented." And, just to be safe, you'd better stick in a warning near the end that, "The recent sharp increase in black and Hispanic voter registration . . . could have serious repercussions," though you needn't say what these are or what connection this thought has to those preceding and following it.

In fact, "Serious Repercussions" is the name of the game. Rohatyn sees them everywhere, which makes him seem very philosophical indeed. The very title of this book oozes foreboding. (It's misleading, though. The actual reference is not to the remainder of the twentieth century, but rather to Rohatyn's mundane observation that the "American Century," which Henry Luce predicted in 1941, pretty much ran its course between 1945 and 1965.) "I believe that what is at stake here," he writes, "is the future of democracy. We have tried liberalism; we are now trying conservatism. If we continue to be frustrated by the results, this could lead to political experiments much more extreme than anything we have witnessed so far."

Rohatyn's "philosophy," in a nutshell, is this. Life is like the New York City fiscal crisis. And doom is imminent on all fronts unless the normal processes of democracy and capitalism are suspended and someone like Felix Rohatyn is put in charge—temporarily. This is essentially what happened in New York. But Rohatyn didn't exactly save New York from bankruptcy. What he did (put in its best light) was skillfully administer a bankruptcy, to minimize the pain and spread it fairly. The city was already bankrupt in all but name, so there was no need to argue whether desperate measures were justified: they were inevitable. In these "essays," Rohatyn argues that the same is true of American basic industry, the banking system, the Northeastern and Midwestern states . . . in fact, the whole damned country, if not the world.

Unfortunately (for him, fortunately for the world), Rohatyn has weakened, rather than strengthened, his case that the end of the world is at hand by collecting his writings into a book. For example, according to Rohatyn:

> The United States today, like New York City in 1975, is on the edge of crisis. Financially, militarily, spiritually, we are like an airplane about to stall. . . . I do not believe that our society will

stand the strain over the next four years. Our next President will
face an emergency during his term of office, either internationally
or domestically, possibly both.

It requires a special kind of credulity to read, in 1984, these words
written in 1980 (from a New York Review piece entitled "The
Coming Emergency and What Can Be Done About It") and to
believe them. In an introductory note, Rohatyn argues rather lamely
that his prediction of an "emergency" came true when Mexico and
Brazil almost defaulted on their bank loans. Were you hoping for
something more sensational? Don't despair. In another piece,
written just last August, Rohatyn promises disaster if the budget
deficit isn't reduced before the 1984 election.

Through an excess of either hubris or humility, Rohatyn reprints
various of his predictions that have turned out flatly wrong. He
predicted in 1980 that another oil price rise "inevitably will result
from the Iran-Iraq war." He predicted in 1981 that "the so-called
rescue of Chrysler . . . is nevertheless doomed to failure, at a heavy
cost to the taxpayers," because it was not part of a Rohatyn-style
gargantuan industrial restructuring. At a press conference in February of this year, Rohatyn hailed Chrysler as "a spectacular success"
and therefore proof that his kind of plan can work.

No change of circumstance allays Rohatyn's panic. Every development makes drastic action even more urgent. "At the time I wrote
this essay," he says in his introduction to "The Coming Emergency"
of 1980, "the value of the dollar was too low; now it is too high."
Whatever. In 1979 he worried about inflation. Now, he says in
reprinting that piece, it's "slow growth and deflation in the Third
World." Today's problems are serious, of course. But you wonder
about a doctor who prescribes the same cure, no matter what the
disease.

And what about a doctor who insists that the cure is even more
urgent if you're no longer sick? In 1981, Rohatyn worried that a
feeble economy would erode the nation's commitment to social
justice, with explosive political consequences. He wrote, "The
'zero-sum society' can be neither free nor fair." In 1984, he wrote,
"I believe that economic recovery will bring the issue of fairness to
the fore more starkly than in times of recession."

Rohatyn's cure is well known. He would create a "tripartite" board composed of leaders of labor, business, and government to supervise the revitalization of the American economy. The board's main tool would be a government agency, modeled after the old Reconstruction Finance Corporation, to invest in the private economy. The agency might start with $5 billion from the federal treasury and raise $50 billion in capital of its own. Its "expert staff" would decide which companies ought to get the money, and what conditions ought to be imposed. Conditions would include an equal amount of new investment by private capital, management changes, and labor concessions on wages and work rules. Besides providing money, this agency would be empowered to assist by "adjusting taxes and helping with international trade problems"—that is, by reducing taxes and restricting foreign competition.

The name for this is "industrial policy." The main difference between Rohatyn's industrial policy and other schemes carrying that label is where the money would go. Unlike the "Atari Democrats," Rohatyn is not interested in searching out "high-tech" or "sunrise" industries. Unlike Lester Thurow, he doesn't want to grease the wheels of change by helping workers to move and retrain for new jobs in different locations. Quite the opposite. Rohatyn's targets are America's war-horse industries and oldest regions: autos and steel, the Northeast and Midwest.

Rohatyn figures his scheme would requisition no more than $150 billion a year in public and private funds. "In a $3 trillion economy," he writes, "this hardly amounts to socialism." Hardly is right. This is the socialism of investment bankers.

There are two standard objections to this sort of thing, one from the right and one from the left. The objection from the right is that Rohatyn's arrangement would override the judgment of the market. If certain companies are in trouble and can't attract new capital, maybe there's a reason. Why should government "experts" be better at predicting what investments will pay off than people with their own money on the line?

Rohatyn insists that his plan "does not consist of either 'picking winners' or 'bailing out losers,' " but this is disingenuous. He is allocating capital. If the companies he helps don't turn out to be profitable "winners," then he will have been bailing out unprofitable "losers." Nothing in his plan increases the supply of credit available in the economy. It merely directs up to $150 billion a year of this credit (which would have been half of all business investment in 1983) to places it would not go if left alone. Someone—lots of someones—won't get that money who otherwise would have. The most likely squeeze-out victims are small businesses with ideas promising enough for the market to take a risk on but too modest for Rohatyn's government agency to spot. If the capital markets think that a small entrepreneur is a better bet than U.S. Steel, why should the government interfere?

Rohatyn has an answer to this. "The answer is that the capital markets do not negotiate concessions among the various parties." He thinks his government agency can *make* its wards into profitable investments by forcing changes they would not make on their own, such as wage reductions. But forcing necessary changes in return for infusions of capital is exactly what investment bankers like Felix Rohatyn do much of the time, quite profitably. You don't need the government for that. You do need the government if you'd like to offer extra carrots like protectionism. But all experience and logic suggest that foreign competition is a better disciplinarian than the promise of protection from it. Lane Kirkland supports Rohatyn's scheme, but not because he thinks it will lead to wage reductions.

The main objection to Rohatyn's proposal from the left is that it is antidemocratic. It would give unprecedented power to an unelected group of dignitaries chosen from established elites. Rohatyn finds the accusation a joke:

> *This type of cooperation does not imply a sinister corporate-statist conspiracy at the expense of the public or of democratic accountability. Preserving the environment, occupational safety, consumer protection, affirmative action—these and many other issues central to the public interest can and should be an essential part of any arrangements by which business, labor, and government cooperate to save the economy.*

. . . a response that misses the point thoroughly enough to prove it. In a democracy, the public interest is not supposed to be entrusted to distinguished worthies, however high-minded. It is supposed to be entrusted to elected officials. Everything is wrong with Rohatyn's "tripartite" equation. The American body politic is not composed of equal parts business, labor, and government. The heads of the largest corporations don't represent the true interests of American capital. The heads of the big unions don't represent the interests of all workers. Since when does capital get to vote anyway, let alone get an equal vote with the people? And, most especially, why should elected government be reduced to one-third of any power-sharing arrangement intended to protect "the public interest"?

Am I off-base to wonder what royalist language like this is doing in a supposedly left-wing journal like the New York Review?

> The fact of the matter is that our country today cannot muster a majority for anything except complaint. The body politic is so splintered and Balkanized that the impotence of the political establishment is a perfectly valid reflection of the negativism and lack of interest of the electorate.

Rohatyn has an answer to this one too. "To the cries of elitism or the fear of creating a new 'establishment,' I say that where we are going otherwise is infinitely worse." Sans moi, le deluge.

Rohatyn warns that "the automotive, steel, glass, rubber, and other basic industries" are collapsing. America will "become a nation of short-order cooks and saleswomen, Xerox operators and messenger boys." He asks: "Is it rational, in the name of the mythical free market, to let our basic industries go down one after the other, in favor of an equally mythical "service society" in which everyone will serve everyone else and no one will be making anything?" Rohatyn worries equally about the regional shift from Snowbelt to Sunbelt. He calls it "one of the gravest events in our history," and warns that "half of this continent is turning into an underdeveloped country." He attributes "blame for these trends" to everything from "government regulation" to "a culture that idolizes rock stars." Pretty philosophical!

Rohatyn naturally exaggerates. America's basic industries are going through some rough times, but they are not collapsing. Charles Schultze of the Brookings Institution, the most prominent liberal critic of "industrial policy," points out that U.S. manufacturing output increased 37 percent during the 1970s, compared to a 33 percent average for the Western industrial democracies. With the economic recovery, the prospect for slimmed-down auto and steel companies is pretty good. Likewise, nothing is happening that will "divide the country into 'have' and 'have-not' regions." In fact, several Southern states remain the poorest in the country, while New England enjoys a remarkable boom.

Nevertheless, there are some big changes going on in the American economy. More interesting than the way Rohatyn exaggerates the trends is the way he exaggerates the dangers they pose. The terribly conservative essence of Rohatyn's philosophy is fear of change. He would invest the leaders of today's elites with extraordinary power and money in order to preserve the industrial, geographic, and financial status quo.

Rohatyn's fashionable critique of the "service society" is a good example of needless scaremongering. The shift into services is a sign of prosperity: services are what people want to buy. Rohatyn should look at his own life. As he became richer, did he buy more products made of steel, rubber, and glass, or did he go in for more restaurant meals, vacations, and personal attention? Rohatyn is right to deplore the waste of human brainpower in fields like law (and investment banking?), which shuffle paper and add nothing to general well-being. But a lot of crap comes out of factories, too. There is nothing inherently unproductive about services as opposed to manufactured items.

Productivity growth is slower in the service sector than in manufacturing, because it's not as easy with services to increase output by adding capital. But the shift of labor and capital from manufacturing to services clearly increases their productivity. It wouldn't be happening if the payoff weren't better. National prosperity is bound to improve as a result. There is legitimate reason to worry about how that prosperity will be distributed, if the effect of the shift is to eliminate middle-class blue collar jobs and to replace them with a few high-paid glamour spots and lots of drudgery at the minimum wage. But thwarting economic growth in the name of economic justice is always self-defeating. Indeed, this is one of Rohatyn's themes: "Without the capacity to create wealth, it is impossible to deal with the issue of fairness. . . . Only with sustained economic growth . . . will [economic] disparities disappear."

It is harder to be cheerful about the regional shift, which is causing a lot of local tragedies and brings no obvious net benefit to the country as a whole. Rohatyn is right that we make the problem worse with an insane federal system that allows people and companies to molt their social obligations as they slither off to new places. All we can say for sure is that America's growth has been a series of wrenching transformations, and cries of alarum usually seem foolish in retrospect. Seventy years ago, Rohatyn would have been denouncing the migration from farms to cities. How can we abandon an industry that employs half the population and produces the very stuff of survival? Where will these people get jobs and housing? How can America build its future on frivolities like automobiles when it won't even be able to feed itself? And so on.

An odd item on Rohatyn's agenda is the plight of international banks. "This was a subject that had troubled me for some time, but about which I was loathe to write," he explains. "I decided, however, that the problem would not go away" without his intervention. Failure to solve it, he concluded, could lead to (what else?) "serious repercussions."

The problem is that the major banks have ineptly loaned billions of dollars to nations in the Third World and the Eastern bloc which will never pay them back. If this brute fact were acknowledged on their books, many of the banks would be bankrupt. To prevent this, Rohatyn proposes that his American redevelopment agency, or an international equivalent financed by the Western governments, should supply the banks with extra capital and/or take over some of these bad loans. The loans would be stretched out and the banks would fess up to some serious losses, but the taxpayers would swallow some of the cost in order to avoid the risk that a default or two could set off a dangerous spiral of chaos.

So far, this is vintage Felix: for God's sake, keep all the balls in the air at any cost. Some people (capitalists and anticapitalists alike) may think it's unhealthy to save capitalists from their own stupidity, but these people don't recognize the Serious Repercussions.

What's odd is that in an article on Polish debts, Rohatyn pulls a great switcheroo. He urges the West to declare Poland's overdue loans in default and force the nation into bankruptcy. His very sound reasoning is that this is the best way to stop subsidizing Soviet repression. In making this case, though, Rohatyn accidentally refutes his adjacent case that disaster waits if we don't bail out the banks.

"The arguments against default . . . do not withstand scrutiny," he writes. "The fact is that Poland is bankrupt, with no visible hope of meeting its future obligations." He more or less says the same of some Third World countries and the banks that have lent to them, but in those cases Rohatyn puts a great premium on preventing the appearance of bankruptcy from catching up with the reality. "What of the possible danger to Western banks?" Well, the biggest suckers were German banks, and even they "clearly have no liquidity problem, since the Polish loans are paying interest late and paying no principal at all." That is, the loans are bad and the banks are still in business, so where's the crisis? "What is involved here," Rohatyn says with an airy dismissive wave, "is . . . essentially accounting problems." Yes, there will have to be large write-offs. "But the Polish loans already are bad loans; declaring Poland in default will not make them worse." Exactly.

In the course of a chapter that appeared previously as a commencement address, as congressional testimony, *and* as an "essay" in the *New York Review*, Rohatyn endorses that most boring of all political ideas, "four to eight years of a bipartisan Administration in which a Republican or a Democratic President would include opposition leaders in his cabinet and would appoint a genuinely representative group" of distinguished leaders to direct the economy. He is sincere. He thinks that if all the top people can sit around a table "allocating sacrifice" (the title of that hagiographic *New Yorker* profile), they can prevent things from getting out of hand. Twelve years ago, Rohatyn only hung around with corporate types. But now, he's come to treasure the wisdom of the best people in all walks of life. And with that, his journey from fixer to philosopher is over.

CONSERVATIVES

INTRODUCTION

My colleague Fred Barnes says that what he dislikes most about journalists is their incessant bragging, "I wrote that first." Nevertheless, we are all sinners (as I believe I am the first to point out). Therefore, I can't resist observing that "Mixing Dog and Politics" was published a year and a half before George Will's influential 1986 column noting the same similarity between George Bush and man's best friend. Will's devastating slap echoed through Washington and signaled Bush's official transformation into a figure of fun.

Whatever happened to Lenny Skutnik ("Waiting for Lenny")? I was sure he'd be popping up in American Express commercials, but he's sunk from sight. As for President Reagan's effort to replace government programs with "private sector initiative," it suffered an embarrassing setback with the revelation that his "private" supply effort for the Nicaraguan contras was getting government money on the sly.

" 'Penumbras,' Anyone?" is about conservative hypocrisy on the subject of "judicial activism." For liberals, though, the nightmare prospect of right-wing judges with lifetime appointments imposing their ideology on an unwilling nation is a case of chickens coming home to roost. (See "Abortion Time Bomb," page 28). Reagan's first Supreme Court appointee, Antonin Scalia, has been fairly scrupulous so far. But depending on how many judges and justices Reagan gets to appoint, and who wins in 1988, liberals may soon find themselves arguing for "strict constructionism" and "judicial restraint," while conservatives promote exotic constitutional theories.

"Dining on Red Herrings" and "Blaming America First" are about the neoconservatives. The first piece concerns their effort to make something out of nothing (the notion of "moral equivalence"), the second concerns their effort to make nothing out of something (the value of American democracy). With a bombardment of news clips,

51

Norman Podhoretz has forced me to back down from my assertion that "I don't know *anyone* who believes that the U.S. and the Soviet Union are 'morally equivalent.' " But I still contend it's laughably far from a widely held view. The title of the second piece refers, of course, to Jeane Kirkpatrick's famous refrain about the "San Francisco Democrats" in her speech at the 1984 Republican convention: "They always blame America first."

The Reagan administration has virtually abandoned any effort to justify its Nicaraguan policy under international law ("Back to Nature"). The "Reagan Doctrine" (a phrase coined by my colleague Charles Krauthammer) dismisses international law as the illogical elevation of sovereignty over more important values such as democracy and freedom. Put that way, it sounds hard to argue with, but this is my attempt to do so. The essential argument is the same as for any other procedural rules: life is messier than theory.

"Manila, Managua, Pretoria" is actually stitched together from parts of two different columns: one on President Reagan's false analogy between American policies in the Philippines and in Nicaragua; the other on the analogy the Reaganites ignore between our policies in Nicaragua and in South Africa.

The abandonment of Reagan by Jews in the 1984 election ("Still Chosen") may have been an early sign that the new majority alliance Republicans thought they were forging—similar to the Democratic alliance that dominated American politics for half a century—was not to be. The final, analyzed results of the election, by the way, confirmed the early data on which this piece was based.

A few decades from now, somebody will write a great book about the changing meaning of the Vietnam War in the minds of the baby-boom generation ("No White Feather Please"). Undoubtedly there will be some surprising variants we can't even imagine now. But so far, at least, the memory of Vietnam remains a powerful force for antiwar sentiment—even, indeed especially, among veterans—despite conservative efforts to turn it to exactly the opposite end.

"A 'Public Choice' Analysis of 'Public Choice' Analysis" was widely disliked and misunderstood among some people I respect, so I guess that's my fault. You judge. My purpose was not to suggest that Nobel Prize economist James Buchanan is a fraud. It was only to note that this is the conclusion you might reach using Buchanan's own sort of analysis. Actually, cynicism about people's motives—the essence of "Public Choice"—is a vice of mine as well, and I'm being disingenuous when I label it a vice. My complaint about conservatives is that they carry cynicism to extremes when analyzing the behavior of public servants (and journalists). They can dish it out, it seems, but they can't take it.

"The Case for Glee" was also widely disliked, indeed widely denounced, to my surprise and (on balance) delight. I almost didn't publish it because I thought the point—that it's okay for liberals to relish the Reagan Iranamok scandal—was hardly worth making. Thanks to Dorothy Wickenden, *TNR's* managing editor, for changing my mind. Not only did this column incite a vicious attack from David Broder, who everyone agrees is the nicest journalist in Washington. It also produced my first anonymous phone call, at 2 A.M., in which some fierce-sounding fellow barked the last three words of the piece ("Ha. Ha. Ha."), followed by an unprintable obscenity, followed by the click of the phone being hung up. In fairness to me, the piece is not just a naked gloat—it has some serious points—and many people also said they liked it.

In fairness to Meg Greenfield, editorial page editor of the *Washington Post*, she says she was being ironic when she described anyone who dared to enjoy the scandal as "reprehensible."

Mixing Dog and Politics

THE NEW REPUBLIC, *October 15, 1984*

VICE PRESIDENT BUSH: You're asking my opinion?
MS. STAHL: Yes.
VICE PRESIDENT BUSH: Forget about it. I don't
worry about it.
—*"Face the Nation,"* August 19

*E*very great leader needs a loyal friend who will chase a stick wherever he throws it, a source of uncritical affection he can count on to be there, no matter what, barking approval and wagging his tail. FDR had Fala, Nixon had Checkers, Reagan has George Bush.

Loyalty is a fine quality in a dog, and not a bad one in a person. Bush's loyalty is so dogged, though, that it raises doubts about his ration of other desirable qualities in a national leader, such as principles, depth, and an interest in communicating with others through use of the English language.

In 1980 Bush said he could tolerate government financing of abortions in cases of rape and incest, or to save a woman's life. Since then, he has heard his master's voice. George now has "no recollection" of having taken this minimally humane position. His stand today? Easy. "My position is like Ronald Reagan's. Put that down. Mark that down. Good. You got it." In 1980 Bush supported the Equal Rights Amendment. Today, "I'm strongly supportive of the tack we're on," which tack is to oppose it.

Bush also had no recollection of his famous remark that Reagan's fiscal plan was "voodoo economics," until Ken Bode of NBC News dug up the videotape. Today, Bush can hardly contain his enthusiasm for Reaganomics, or his contempt for "the liberal Democrats" and their "philosophy of tax and spend, tax and spend." For Pete's sake, George, get it right: it's "tax and *tax, spend* and spend."

Poor George. Looking to 1988, he wants to disguise his mutt bloodlines as a moderate Republican and acquire a conservative pedigree. But he can't pass. I think the rabid right admissions committee misreads Bush slightly. They see him as a closet moderate, still secretly fantasizing about tax increases and abortions for rape victims. In fact, Bush is a man of no discernible political passions, beyond a passion to win political office, which itself doesn't seem to run all that deep. His is a free-floating ambition that went into Republican politics mainly because of family tradition.

One reason Bush is unconvincing as a right-wing zealot is that he is so obviously not neurotic, as any zealot (or, perhaps, anyone who's really serious about politics) has to be. No one is going to believe that George Bush lies awake at night in bug-eyed alarm about Soviet designs, or about anything else. Bush gives every appearance of being a happy man without a serious care or grudge in the world. Recently he went to North Carolina to campaign for Jesse Helms, a man who viciously opposed his selection as Vice President.

This thesis helps to explain Bush's bizarre way of talking. Consider his amazing disquisition, on "Meet the Press" September 16, about the fashionable topic of mixing God and politics:

> *I think in politics there are certain moral values. I'm one who—*
> *we believe strongly in pluralism, we believe in separation of*
> *church and state, but when you get into some questions there are*
> *some moral overtones. Murder, that kind of thing, and I feel a*
> *little, I will say, uncomfortable sometimes with the elevation of*
> *the religion thing—not that I don't feel strongly—I've been*
> *blessed by faith, my own family and a family that's been very*
> *close and all of that. . . .*
>
> *We don't believe God is a Republican, but they're elevating it,*
> *they're on the wrong side of the issue. Now let—I have respect for*
> *what Mr. Cuomo tried to do, but that is his religion. Catholi-*
> *cism. Let them sort it out, and I'll do my thing as Episcopalian,*
> *and you and Marvin do your thing. . . .*

Bush is not stupid. But who can believe that a man who talks this way ("all of that . . . my thing as Episcopalian") wastes an ounce of unnecessary energy thinking about either politics or religion, let alone both at the same time?

When Geraldine Ferraro stumbled over the theological distinction between a "first strike" and a "first use" of nuclear weapons, she stirred up talk that she is a lightweight. Meanwhile Bush sails through the campaign babbling things like, "I believe in unions and I believe in non-unions." Remember his moronic toast of Philippine dictator Ferdinand Marcos in 1981? "We love your adherence to democratic principles."

Here is Bush's summary of the Nicaraguan revolution: "The Sandinistas came in. They overthrew Somoza, killed him, and overthrew him. Killed him, threw him out." Told that Somoza had been killed while in exile, and not by the Sandinistas, Bush said he was using the term Sandinista in a "generic" sense. Pressed further, he abandoned words completely. "I will just stay with what I said yesterday." ("I'll freeze, Bill," as they used to say on "The Price Is Right.") Can you imagine the scathing reviews if Ferraro performed like this?

What protects Bush from the lightweight charge is his résumé—
"all these marvelous credentials," as he himself put it in 1980. In the
1960s Bush served two terms in the House of Representatives and lost
two races for the Senate. (In his second Senate race, he took
$106,000 from a secret Nixon slush fund, something else that's not
on Geraldine Ferraro's résumé.) It's his glittering series of appointed
posts in the 1970s, second only to Elliot Richardson's, that give Bush
that statesmanlike glow.

Bush's puppydog qualities are what have led Presidents to seek him
out. Bush's main accomplishment as U.N. Ambassador in 1971 was
to lead the lonely American campaign against admitting Communist
China. He called it "a day of infamy" (good line) when he lost.
Meanwhile, unbeknownst to George, Henry Kissinger was in Peking
arranging Nixon's breakthrough visit. Oh well.

Next, Bush became Republican national chairman. This episode
is misrepresented in the only full-length biography of Bush, which
happens to be a recently published memoir by his own dog—*C.
Fred's Story: A Dog's Life* by C. Fred Bush, edited by Barbara Bush
(Doubleday, $13.95). C. Fred is a real dog's dog. As he recalls it,
during Watergate, "Bar [Mrs. Bush] taught me how to sit up, roll
over, catch biscuits, walk like a man—in fact, a whole bag of tricks.
Speaking of tricks, George spent that whole year fighting a whole bag
of 'Dirty Tricks' that had taken place the year before." In fact,
George, too, spent much of that year rolling over, if not walking like
a man. He ardently defended Nixon throughout Watergate until the
emergence of the "smoking gun" tapes, when, like England's famous
Vicar of Bray, he had another timely change of faith. (*And this is
law, I will maintain,/Until my dying day, sir,/That whatsoever king
shall reign,/I will be the Vicar of Bray, sir!*)

For his loyalty, President Ford threw George another biscuit, the
job of America's first special envoy to Communist China, no longer
a nation of infamy. Next, it was head of the C.I.A. (Good dog!) Like
his other big bowwow jobs, Bush held this one just long enough to
update the résumé before moving on, this time to chase the biggest
biscuit of all. "Would I be a good President?" he asked in 1980. "I'd
be crackerjack. I'd do it with style, dignity, feeling, strength. . . . I
have a conviction. I know I'd be a better President than Reagan."

Republican voters disagreed and, on reflection, Bush disagrees

too. Ronald Reagan is the greatest President the world has ever
known. He will work even more wonders in the next four years. And
George Bush? "For my part, I'll talk about leadership—Ronald
Reagan's leadership. America's back, and Ronald Reagan's leadership has brought it back." Slurp, slurp. Down, boy! Down!

Waiting for Lenny

HARPER'S, *March 1982*

On January 13, Lenny Skutnik dived into the icy
Potomac and saved the life of a woman from the Air Florida plane
that crashed after takeoff from Washington's National Airport.
Skutnik was acting in a private capacity, not in his official government role as a $14,000-a-year gofer at the Congressional Budget
Office. Speaking to some business executives in New York the next
day, President Reagan praised Skutnik's courage. "Nothing had
picked him out particularly to be a hero, but without hesitation there
he was and he saved her life." Reagan offered Skutnik as an
illustration of his theme that the proper way to solve our country's
problems is through private initiative. By "private initiative," Reagan
means two different things: the free-enterprise system of private
capitalism, of course, but also private good works and charity. These
latter activities are often grouped under the rubric "voluntarism," in
implicit contrast to the compulsory nature of the government's
financing arrangements.

Reagan has struck the chord of voluntarism a lot recently, as the
federal social-welfare cutbacks have begun to take effect. In December, he announced the formation of a "President's Task Force on
Private Sector Initiatives." Its purpose, says a task force handout, is
to demonstrate the President's "concern for those people affected by

58 MICHAEL KINSLEY

the fundamental change now occurring in the servicing of social programs" by encouraging private citizens and corporations to step into the breach. In contrast to the success of voluntary good works, Reagan said on January 14, "too often those meant to benefit most from government-imposed solutions paid the highest price and bore the deepest scars when they failed." But the superiority of voluntarism is not just a matter of results; it is a matter of principle. That principle, Reagan said, is freedom: "This can be an era of losing freedom or one of reclaiming it." He went on to compare a summer job program sponsored by New York corporations (private sector initiative) with the Soviet crackdown in Poland (Big Government). Reagan prefers the private sector initiative.

Of all of Reagan's reasons for cutting back on government help for citizens in distress—the need for tax cuts to stimulate productivity, bureaucratic waste and fraud, the harm welfare does to its own beneficiaries, and so on—this notion of substituting private philanthropy is surely the most fatuous. Consider, for example, the problem of rescuing people who are drowning in the Potomac as the result of a plane crash. One approach—the Reagan approach, apparently—is to rely on the private sector initiative of people like Lenny Skutnik. The other approach—the Big Government approach—is to send National Park Service helicopters to lift people out of the water. At this early stage in the Reagan revolution, the Park Service still has helicopters, and four lives were saved on January 13 through an atavistic exercise of burdensome government interference. Big Government, 4; Private Sector Initiative, 1.

But perhaps it's not that simple. Conservatives argue that the existence of massive government welfare services has numbed the charitable impulse in individuals. When the government cuts back on social welfare (cutting people's taxes in the process), the charitable instinct will flower. Perhaps, in other words, if those gawkers along the Potomac knew for sure that the government would not be sending in helicopters (and ice-cutting boats and ambulances and other paraphernalia of the welfare state), more of them might be willing to dive in themselves. Government shouldn't be discouraging such noble instincts. So cancel those helicopters. Right?

In this context the argument sounds absurd, as it's intended to.

That's because nobody, not even Reagan, maybe not even libertarian philosopher Robert Nozick, treasures his freedom so much that he would rather drown than see the coercive powers of the state used to finance his rescue. Voluntarism is fine, but drowning people shouldn't have to rely on it.

But this absurd example clarifies exactly what the Reagan people wish to muddle with their talk of replacing government programs with private initiative. Labeling the matter "rights" is a red flag, so let's just say it's a question of what help people ought to get. The call for "voluntarism" is a way of denying people government help while still claiming to believe that they ought to be helped. I think there are a lot of poor, sick, uneducated, jobless people who—given the resources of our society—ought to be helped. President Reagan claims to think so too, yet he would leave them to be helped by "private sector initiative." He can't mean it. In truth, he must be willing to let them drown.

The argument for private enterprise and the argument for private philanthropy are very different. It is one thing to say that free-market capitalism, by channeling selfishness into socially productive activity, can do more to lift people out of poverty than any number of well-meaning government programs. President Reagan says this, and he's right. It's quite another matter to concede that the invisible hand cannot do everything that needs to be done—that certain legitimate national goals must depend on selfless, social instincts—but to insist that the government, as society's proxy, should not do these things.

The Reagan administration has slashed federal housing subsidies. Meanwhile, though, it trumpets the virtues of an organization called Habitat for Humanity, which uses private donations to build subsidized housing for the poor. This group recently opened a development in Plains, Georgia, of all places. The first tenant was a black farm worker named Johnny Murphy, who earns ten dollars a day. Now, does a just society supply subsidized housing to a person like him or not? One might well say that a healthy adult male ought to support himself. That would be principled conservatism. What the Reagan administration seems to be saying is, yes, he ought to get subsidized housing, but no, society is not going to supply it. He'll just have to wait for some Lenny Skutnik to come along.

Here is another example, from a Reagan speech to the National

Alliance of Businessmen in October. José Salcido, a Los Angeles
man with thirteen children, lost his wife to cancer. Then he was
crushed to death in a freak accident involving his own truck. Let the
President pick up the story: "But [the children] were not orphaned by
their neighbors or even complete strangers, who immediately began
collecting contributions. . . . They also discovered how kind the
people of this land can be."

Very nice. But many children are orphaned in ways that do not
involve freakish accidents, which get media attention. Are they any
less dependent on the kindness of strangers? Why is it an act of
generosity to send a small check in a well-publicized case and an act
of oppression to support a government program that will help all
such people, publicized or not?

Libertarian purists like Professor Nozick would say that the
difference is coercion. A government program forces all taxpayers to
be generous, even those who don't feel like it. There is no answer to
such purists, except to point out that their logic would have
consigned four more people to an icy death on January 13. Many
freedom-loving nonpurists are satisfied with the thought that in a
democracy, government-imposed generosity cannot for long exceed
the will of the majority. You can call government-style generosity
"coercion," or you can call it "collective action." For every Lenny
Skutnik, there are ten of us who aren't prepared to risk everything but
are willing to make a more modest sacrifice, *if others do the same*, so
that together we can maintain a certain level of generosity in our
society. This process of saying, "I will if you will," is called voting.

Reagan and company may believe that by 1980 the government
had exceeded the generous instincts of the majority, and they may be
right. But they must have doubts about how deep the New Stinginess
runs, or they wouldn't be salving people's consciences with a lot of
malarkey about private initiative.

The logic of collective generosity, which Reagan rejects in the case
of government, is precisely the gimmick of United Way, which he
celebrates as a model of private initiative. United Way collects
money from people in relatively painless amounts and aggregates it
for greater effect, at the same time saving them the nuisance of
weighing various worthy causes or coming into contact with the

beneficiaries of their largesse, which tend to be the most traditional and uncontroversial sorts of charities, like the Boy Scouts. The more you think about United Way, in fact, the harder it is to keep in mind the difference between the coercive, bureaucratic, impersonal, stultified social welfare of the federal government and the voluntary, personal, creative, life-enhancing nature of so-called private giving. United Way lacks the consummate coercive power of the government, but it does have ways of making you pledge, most of them involving solicitation by your boss. Stories like TELLER DISMISSED FROM JOB FOR OPPOSING CHARITY DRIVE (*New York Times*, November 29, 1981), about a bank teller fired after he refused to cough up for United Way, are never long absent from the news columns.

A recent American Enterprise Institute study compared the efficiency of government welfare and United Way in terms of how many cents of each dollar make it to the intended beneficiaries. The method of investigation was not to go and find out but, in the modern style, to take a poll. Fifteen hundred people across the country were asked, and the median answer was that fifty cents of each United Way dollar gets where it's headed, compared with only twenty-five cents of each federal dollar. A handsome chart with two circles illustrates that fifty cents is twice as much as twenty-five cents. President Reagan actually cited this poll in his January 14 speech as a reason to prefer private over public welfare services. Pardon me for challenging the consensus of 1,501 ignorant people, 1,500 of them scientifically selected, but my own little poll of two people—public information officers at United Way and the Department of Health and Human Services—concludes that the government claims an efficiency of 99.5 cents on the dollar (for Aid to Families with Dependent Children), and United Way 90 cents on the dollar. As the following chart demonstrates, 99.5 is larger than 90:

The main thrust of the President's Task Force on Private Sector Initiative is to increase philanthropic activity, not by individuals, but by corporations. "I plan to speak out in favor of an offensive response by business every chance that I get," is the curious way C. William Verity, Jr., chairman of Armco Corporation and head of the President's task force, put it in a recent speech. There is something a bit confused about cutting social welfare in order to give business more money to invest, then expecting business to divert money back into social welfare. And there is something very confused indeed about supposing that philanthropy by large business corporations is "voluntary" on the part of those who are really paying.

Talk about being generous with other people's money (a favorite conservative taunt about government bureaucrats)—consider Chairman Verity's suggestion of a "statewide governor's honor roll" for companies that give away more than 2 percent of their stockholders' earnings every year. "You know an annual 'Night at the Governor's Mansion' will attract a lot of attention. And for five percenters, they can stay for the weekend." We all want to encourage voluntarism, but the Governor of Ohio, where Armco is located, may have second thoughts when more than 100,000 shareholders of this publicly traded corporation descend on his house for the weekend. Or perhaps what Chairman Verity has in mind is that only he—along with other top executives—should be invited to weekend with the governor, on behalf of his shareholders.

In theory, shareholders can vote out the management if they think it's being too generous, but so can taxpayers. Plunging further into theory, a miserly minority shareholder can sell his stock and get out, which a miserly citizen cannot. In practice, there is far less democratic control over philanthropy by corporations than by government. Most corporate stock today is held in trust for pensioners and insurance beneficiaries. These people have no say whatever in how much of their money is given away, or to whom. "Voluntarism is an essential part of our plan to give the government back to the people," Reagan told business executives in October. In fact, by cutting social spending and encouraging corporations to step into the breach (and by doubling the amount of philanthropy they may deduct from their taxes), Reagan is taking social decisions *away* from the people and giving them to an unelected group of corporate officers.

*   *   *

According to one of many reports from the Heritage Foundation, "The growth of the voluntary sector is . . . viewed by the Administration as necessary to the effective rebuilding of notions of social obligation . . . that have been eroded by the growth of government." It would be more accurate to say that Reagan's cutbacks of government aid reflect an abandonment of notions of social obligation, if the words "social" and "obligation" have any nuance at all. Reagan himself goes further, telling his task force, "What we're asking you to do is to help rediscover America—not the America bound by the Potomac River but the America beyond the Potomac River." He liked the line so much he repeated it in his January 14 speech. The next time he helicopters by, he might consider the America *in* the Potomac River, and think again.

"Penumbras," Anyone?

WALL STREET JOURNAL, *August 8, 1985*

The Justice Department laments wittily, in a brief filed last month urging the Supreme Court to overturn its notorious *Roe v. Wade* abortion decision, that constitutional law is becoming "a picnic to which the framers bring the words and the judges (bring) the meaning." This is the familiar conservative complaint against "activist" judges who impose their own views on the nation in blithe disregard for democracy and the Constitution. The grousing began with Chief Justice Earl Warren, intensified with Justice William O. Douglas's 1965 discovery of birth control in the "penumbras . . . formed by emanations" from the Bill of Rights, and reached a crescendo with Roe in 1973.

The Reagan people want to appoint judges who think differently. Short of poisoning the soup in the Supreme Court cafeteria, that is their right. But there are different ways of thinking differently. A Reagan Supreme Court could take seriously the decades of conservative sermonizing about strict constructionism and judicial constraint. Or it could launch a new era of right-wing judicial activism. I suspect the latter. There are no strict constructionists in the ideological foxholes.

Attorney General Ed Meese said in January 1985 that a key goal of the second Reagan term would be "to institutionalize the Reagan revolution so it can't be set aside no matter what happens in future presidential elections." Not much respect for democracy in that ambition. And the surest way to fulfill it would be to appoint lifetime judges who will read Reaganite values into the Constitution. The 1984 GOP platform contains the usual boilerplate demanding judges "who are our commitment to judicial restraint." But in the next breath the platform asks for judges who "support . . . the sanctity of innocent human life." This refers to abortion, and can only mean judges who would rule abortion unconstitutional, even if states wished to legalize it. Nothing restrained about that.

A year ago, the Supreme Court upheld a Hawaii land-reform statute in language that was a strict constructionist's dream. "Subject to specific constitutional limitations," the court declared, "when the legislature has spoken, the public interest has been declared in terms well-nigh conclusive." Who should object to this but the *Wall Street Journal*. "The court is trying to abdicate its responsibility," the editors of this paper scolded. State and local governments "will have close to carte blanche."

Heavens! Can't have that.

The *Journal*'s editors frequently interrupt their flow of tributes to federalism, and denunciations of meddlesome jurists, to demand that the Supreme Court stomp on some duly elected state or city legislature that has had the temerity to pass a law they disapprove of. Last year, when the Supreme Court took a case involving rent control, the *Journal* advised the justices to ignore all the technical arguments and simply "declare the law unconstitutional on its face." Nor is national legislation safe. Recently the *Journal* has demanded "final burial" by the court of the Federal Election Campaign Act, and has objected bitterly to a court ruling that federal labor laws can be applied to state and local governments. This latter editorial invoked the holy spirit of "federalism," of course. But only three weeks ago the *Journal* was back at it, upbraiding the justices for not crushing a state trucking regulation and a city sewer requirement.

This last editorial, entitled "Economic Civil Rights," argued generally that courts should consider "the public's vital interest in the free market" in their decisions. Now the free market is a fine thing (and rent control is idiotic), but where is this in the Constitution? Oh, well, "The Constitution explicitly protects economic rights, in clauses dealing with eminent domain, due process, equal protection and freedom of speech." The leap from these specific protections to "the free market" is every bit as bold as Justice Douglas's leap from the Bill of Rights to birth control. "Penumbras," anyone? And the *Journal* is not alone in making the leap. A cadre of conservative legal scholars is already busy supplying the footnotes for as-yet-unwritten Supreme Court decisions that would make *Wall Street Journal* editorials unnecessary by imposing free-market ideology on the country without the bother of persuading the citizenry of its merits.

There's no mystery about where this could lead; we've been there before. For three decades starting in 1905, the Supreme Court routinely threw out child labor laws, health and safety laws, and so on, under the rubric of "freedom of contract." President Roosevelt complained in 1937, in words that could be President Reagan's today, "The court has been acting not as a judicial body but as a policy-making body . . . reading into the Constitution words and implications which are not there." Perhaps a future Supreme Court would be wise enough to distinguish between stupid economic regulations and wise ones. But it's precisely the point conservatives have been making for thirty years that these policy decisions shouldn't be up to unelected judges. Will they forget all that now that they're feeling their oats?

Of course, conservatives will argue, rightly, that "strict construc-tionism" and "judicial restraint" are not necessarily the same thing. Sometimes a more literal reading of the Constitution can lead to a more activist approach, as with the First Amendment protection of free speech. Some conservative activists argue that this should be read to proscribe all government regulation of truth in advertising. Furthermore, "judicial restraint" can't be absolute, or the courts would have no function at all. But honestly believing that your own

policy agenda really is part of the Constitution is not good enough if
you want to keep your "strict constructionist" merit badge. After all,
no one in the history of constitutional analysis has ever claimed to be
a "loose constructionist."

Dining on Red Herrings

WALL STREET JOURNAL, May 9, 1985

When I heard that conservative intellectuals were
assembling last week from all over the world for a conference about
"moral equivalence" at a fancy Washington hotel, funded in part by
a $45,000 grant from the State Department, I naturally assumed the
subject was President Reagan's recent observation that the contras in
Nicaragua are the moral equivalent of our Founding Fathers. The
concept certainly could use some fleshing out. I anticipated stimu-
lating discussions of rebel atrocities at Bunker Hill, and so on.

Imagine my disappointment to read in the *Washington Times*
that, according to the director of something called the Shavano
Institute, which sponsored this gabfest, "We're going to spend two
days trying to establish that there is a moral distinction between U.S.
and Soviet behavior." This takes two days? According to this same
gentleman, John K. Andrews, "Moral equivalence is patently
absurd." Most of the leading neoconservatives who attended the
conference made the same point. Midge Decter, for instance: "Such
a view of the world is—need one say it?—perfect nonsense."

And yet, these prominent intellectuals are under the impression
that they are battling an enormously powerful myth. Their basic text
was a speech given last year by Jeane Kirkpatrick. She asserted:
"Many, perhaps most, of the most influential treatments of East–
West differences during the last decade or so propose tacitly, and

sometimes explicitly, that the differences are not that great after all."
They do? I don't know *anyone* who believes that the United States
and the Soviet Union are "morally equivalent." I missed the
conference. But having read and listened to excerpts, I fear these
neocons are suffering from several small confusions and one grand
delusion.

One confusion involves the rhetoric of the antinuclear movement,
which often posits a seeming symmetry between the superpowers—
"two scorpions in a bottle," and so forth. But metaphors like this
were popularized by the early nuclear strategists, who were far from
left-wing. They concern the nature of the nuclear stalemate and
have nothing to do with moral judgments about the players.

A second confusion involves the intellectual's task. Norman
Podhoretz stated that intellectuals are "overwhelmingly hostile to the
kind of society we live in." No doubt a word count would reveal that
Western intellectuals spend far more time criticizing the societies
they live in than they do criticizing communism. So what? It is the
nature of intellectuals—their duty, too, I'd say—to carp. Norman
Podhoretz may have changed political stripes, but he, too, generates
more bile over what he sees as complacency about communism in
the West than he does about communism itself. It shouldn't be
necessary for every criticism of one's own society to come with an
SEC-style disclosure statement, "Caution: Nothing herein is meant
to imply that communism isn't worse."

The conference organizers included in the program, as an
example of "moral equivalency" thinking, a statement by Tom
Wicker: "There are too many instances where we have abandoned
what I think are sacred American standards of behavior and acted too
much as if we did not claim moral and political superiority." Thus
a third confusion: that there is something morally bankrupt about
holding America to a higher standard of international behavior. The
neoconservatives themselves, more than anyone else, have promoted
the idea that in a dangerous world we cannot always afford the luxury
of, for example, obeying international law or promoting human
rights. This may be right or wrong, but it's patently unfair to accuse
those who disagree of morally equating the United States and the
Soviet Union.

Indeed, the conference participants had some difficulty finding hard-core examples of "moral equivalency" thinking. A museum in New York has on display a computerized composite photograph of Ronald Reagan and Konstantin Chernenko. Sidney Hook told the gathering that several years ago on National Public Radio he heard someone named Dr. Foner comparing Mr. Reagan's bust of the PATCO strike with the Soviet crushing of Solidarity. Others brought up such central figures in our culture as William Sloane Coffin and William Kunstler.

What is it about the neoconservative mentality that enables these people to sit in the Madison Hotel, surrounded by journalists, enjoying honoraria of up to $4,000 paid for partly by the taxpayers and partly by the growing network of right-wing foundations, congratulating one another on their latest high government appointments, and yet complaining of (as *Time* magazine put it) "an intellectual double standard that inhibits discussions of communism and criticism of the Soviet Union." What are they talking about?

It is time for the neoconservatives to grow up and admit they've won. Even Tom Wolfe, the formerly acute social observer, seems to have missed this development. "I want to congratulate you all on the courage you've shown in coming here," he told the conference participants at a banquet, as if they were partisans gathered by flashlight in Rock Creek Park.

"Ideas can become articles of fashion which are adopted with no more foundation than styles in clothing," Mr. Wolfe has written. Yet he doesn't seem to realize that he and his friends are dressed to the nines in this year's fashion. If you were a young intellectual-on-the-make, with no ideological predispositions but an enormous hunger for the ego rewards described in Podhoretz's 1960s classic *Making It*, can there be any doubt that today you would choose to become a neoconservative?

A cornerstone of neoconservative thinking is the concept of the "new class." In the American context, this refers to intellectual leeches on the capitalist system who float on a sea of grants and honoraria, holding conferences and issuing studies and writing op-ed pieces to affect the direction of society and government policy. There is now a whole "new class" of conservative intellectuals who spend their lives and make their livings complaining about the "new class" of liberal intellectuals. For a list of their names, get the Shavano conference program.

The media, government, and the academy, asserted Irving Kristol, are now full of people "who sometimes write discussions of practical policy as if they were citizens of another planet." The neocons pride themselves, above all, on being realists. Yet in some ways they are spectacularly unworldly. They see "socialism" everywhere. They think left-wing intellectuals dominate our culture. (They are *The Nation's* most devoted readers.) Why? In part because their own sense of self-importance depends upon it.

Tom Wolfe told the conference that the (alleged) widespread appeal of Marxism could be explained by its "secret promise . . . of rule by intellectuals." The new class, he said, dreamed of being "handed the reins of power in the name of the proletariat, without having touched the proletariat in any way." He's got the dream right, but not the dreamers.

Blaming America First

THE NEW REPUBLIC, *July 29, 1985*

One oddity of the current triumphant conservative mood in America is a subtle undercurrent of contempt for American values. This strain of thinking has been especially noticeable in the reaction of conservative commentators and intellectuals to the Walker spy case and the TWA hijacking. Democracy, liberty, even capitalism are presented as debilitating self-indulgences in the fight against the forces of evil in the world.

Some conservatives speak almost wistfully of the advantages enjoyed by ruthless totalitarians on the one hand and medieval religious zealots on the other, compared to the fluttery, distracted, secular, civilized societies of the West. We are caught, it seems, at a tragically vulnerable stage in political evolution, at the mercy of both the precivilized passions of Islamic fundamentalism and the postcivilized machinations of the Soviet Union. "Democracy," writes Jean-François Revel in his oft-cited recent book, *How Democracies Perish*, ". . . is not basically structured to defend itself against outside enemies."

There are five counts in the indictment. First, liberal democratic societies weaken themselves through constant internal criticism. At a recent conservative conference, the philosopher Sidney Hook mourned about "how fragile a self-governing democratic society is. . . . For its very own rationale encourages a constant critical approach that its enemies can exploit to weaken it." Revel, in his book, complains that "democracy faces an internal enemy whose right to exist is written into the law itself."

Second, liberal democracies are fickle. We don't know what we want, or we think we know and then change our minds. We start a defense buildup and then lose interest halfway through. We lack the single-minded concentration on destroying our enemies that fundamentalism breeds from below and communism imposes from above.

Third, nations like America are too decent and humanitarian for our own damn good. Midge Decter, head of the Committee for the Free World, complained at another recent conservative conference that such scruples had "hamstrung" the Reagan administration about using American military might. Many conservatives argue that a naive fastidiousness about human life, even innocent American human life, stupidly prevented us from giving the Beirut terrorists a taste of their own medicine.

Fourth, the openness of American society makes us too easy a target for espionage and subversion. Secretary of State George Shultz observed at (yes) yet another conservative conference that "the very qualities that make democracies so hateful to the terrorists also make them so vulnerable. Precisely because we maintain the most open societies, terrorists have unparalleled opportunity to strike against us." In the wake of the Walker case, many have made the same point about spies.

Fifth, and most ironic, capitalist affluence itself turns a society flabby and distracts it from the urgent task of survival. Obsessed with consumption, we refuse the necessary sacrifices, financial and personal, to protect ourselves.

And uniting all these complaints is a thorough exasperation with

America's free press, which amplifies dissent, undermines consensus, thwarts realpolitik by sentimentalizing every situation, publishes government secrets, and stimulates consumer appetites.

Is it really so grim? In the true spirit of patriotism, why not reflect on some of the obvious advantages a liberal democracy like America enjoys over the world's uncivilized forces, even by the most practical and unsentimental calculation. Consider just four.

First, capitalist prosperity means we don't face any genuinely painful trade-off between a strong defense and satisfying our private appetites. The July 6 *Economist* argues that Mikhail Gorbachev will soon have to choose between "a crash defence build-up" and "rescuing the Soviet economy." Our leaders can't mobilize the entire economy for military production, but they don't need to either.

Second, an open society has practical advantages. The July 8 *Fortune* reports on the primitive state of the Soviet computer industry. The Soviets desperately need computers for both economic and military reasons, but dare not let computers develop out of a realistic fear that the arrival of PCs will undermine state thought control. Closed societies waste vast resources on internal security and lose a lot of competitive edge in the process.

Third, freedom and Western culture are priceless assets in the espionage, propaganda, and terror wars. While conservative intellectuals of the West fret about a few left-wing highbrows who aren't sufficiently critical of the Soviet Union, Communist bloc leaders must live with the knowledge that millions of their subjects go to bed dreaming of America. Unlike us, the Soviets have to worry that every diplomat they send abroad may decide to defect at any time. When recruiting spies, the Soviets must find an eccentric adventure-seeker like John Walker. We can approach any number of people who might reasonably long for escape. According to the *New York Times*, even several of the jihad-crazed terrorists of Beirut told the TWA hostages that they'd like their children to live in the United States.

Fourth, even though democratic governments must put up with a lot of carping, they know that the vast majority of their citizens—including the carpers—fundamentally support them. Oppressive regimes can jail the carpers but are stuck with the silent dissenters. This limits their options. If the Soviets invaded Poland, could they trust their own troops to fight and Polish troops not to rebel? It may be harder for a democracy to start a war—as it should be—but it's easier for a democracy to fight one.

I wish the putative defenders of American liberty and democracy would show a bit more enthusiasm for these fine things. Instead, they criticize America's openness, its idealism, its raucous dissent as unsuitable to this cold world. They present its eighteenth-century values as disadvantages in battling the forces of the twentieth-century and the twelfth. But then, they always blame America first.

Back to Nature

THE NEW REPUBLIC, May 7, 1984

*I*nternational law. It's sort of a goofy notion, isn't it? I mean, how can you have law without cops? The enemies of freedom do whatever their interests dictate and their power permits. Third World buffoons have turned the United Nations into a joke. So if the United States thinks it serves the cause of freedom to run a little war against the nasty Sandinistas in Nicaragua, why shouldn't we? In this hard world, aren't the Marquess of Queensberry rules just for saps?

Actually, no. There are good, hard-nosed reasons for even superpower America to take international law seriously.

International law is a living example of that poli-sci conceit, social contract theory. The nations of the world start in a state of nature, mutually suspicious and alone. Their only hope for avoiding perpetual chaos and war is to agree on some rules. There is no central authority to enforce those rules, and—despite the hopes of some woolly-minded idealists—there never will be. What's amazing, though, is how many rules there are and how often they're obeyed even so. Why? Because each state, in deciding whether to obey a particular rule, must consider its vested interest in the rule of law generally. The thicker the web of rules, the stronger each rule becomes.

International law has been most successful in relatively technical areas such as rights at sea. It has enjoyed modest success in regulating the conduct of war. Its record is poorest in actually preventing recourse to war. Nevertheless, even the Soviet Union pays at least lip service to Article 2 of the 1945 United Nations Charter, which forbids "the threat or use of force against the territorial integrity or political independence of any state," and the United States—until now—has come rather close (for a superpower) to actually obeying it.

In a self-defeating attempt to deny the Nicaraguans a "propaganda victory," the Reagan administration has told the World Court we won't recognize its authority for the next two years in any cases involving the United States and Central America. Submitting to the World Court is strictly voluntary, but at its founding in 1946 we ostentatiously submitted to "compulsory jurisdiction" on most matters. We promised to give six months' notice before withdrawing. That solemn gesture is a joke if we can slice off new exceptions every time we smell a case coming along that we don't like.

What's appalling about the administration's preemptive maneuver is not that the World Court won't get to decide this case—it has never yet settled a real war issue—but the implicit acknowledgment that this country is acting illegally. Obviously there would be no "propaganda victory" for Nicaragua if we were to win the case, and the case could include our own countercharges against the Sandinistas. The World Court has *not* turned into a kangaroo court like other organs of the U.N. It is a serious judicial body. We ourselves bring cases to it. We're ducking this one because we know it's a loser.

The administration says that our war against Nicaragua is a legal exercise of "collective self-defense" against "an armed attack" under Article 51 of the U.N. Charter. There are three defects in this argument. First, our campaign against Nicaragua comes closer to being "an armed attack" than Nicaragua's troublemaking for its neighbors. Second, where's the "collective"? We're acting without the participation, or even the clear support, of the threatened countries. Third, the U.N. Charter requires that exercises of self-defense "shall be immediately reported to the Security Council."

The American government won't even officially acknowledge this enterprise to its own citizens.

Defenders of the administration can't understand why senators and others who went along with funding for the contra guerrillas should burst into moral outrage over the mining of Nicaragua's harbors. The reason is that the mining clarifies the nature of the exercise. This isn't covert aid. This is war. Americans are running this show. The CIA designed the mining operation, supplied the mines, and supervised their installation. And mining a harbor is economic warfare. The target is not the army or even the government, but the Nicaraguan people themselves. Incidental victims include neutral ships. The evident goal is not merely to stop the Sandinistas from harassing their neighbors, but to bring that government down. If this constitutes "collective self-defense" under international law, then the concept has been bent to the breaking point.

Does it matter? What do we lose by abandoning the idea that international law should constrain our behavior as a superpower? Will we lose the fight for freedom if we don't abandon it?

International law is not an impossible ideal, even in a world where others don't obey it. Specifically, it does not require the United States to stand by helpless while Communist countries subvert their neighbors. But international law requires certain public procedural steps. And it requires that military actions be clearly related and proportionate to legal ends.

These formalistic restraints may seem petty, but Nicaragua is a good example of why they're not. It is obvious to the Reagan administration and its supporters that our goals in Central America are admirable. This is not obvious to many Central Americans—and not just Sandinistas—who remember our forty years of support for the Somoza tyranny. Thanks to Jeane Kirkpatrick, a whole subspecialty of political science is now devoted to the question of the proper level of cordiality with unattractive foreign governments. But no special expertise is needed to wonder whether the successive regimes in Nicaragua warrant the extremes of total embrace followed by total hostility. One function of an unenforceable set of rules like international law is to clarify an inherently muddled situation like this one, and to neutralize distrust, by obviating the question of motive. It matters less what we're up to as long as we're obeying the law.

In our invasion of Grenada, the legal situation was dubious but the moral situation was unusually clear. If every foreign policy decision involved a relatively certain cost, a clear and immediate result, and a sharp moral calculus, we could play Superpower like a video game. Most foreign policy decisions are messy, with results that are factually unpredictable and often morally indeterminate. That is why it's useful to us to be known for upholding neutral rules of international behavior.

What's more, we believe in these rules, don't we? What do we mean when we accuse others of "state-sponsored terrorism"? Do we actually object only to their goals, not to their methods? In the cause of democracy and freedom, will we break any rule our enemies break?

In fact, we won't. Unlike the Soviets, we suffer from "a decent respect to the opinions of mankind." The closer the world is to a Hobbesian state of nature, the more of a disadvantage this becomes. International law is a shaky edifice in need of constant shoring up. The United States will always bear a disproportionate share of that burden. But we get a disproportionate share of the benefit, too.

Manila, Managua, Pretoria

THE NEW REPUBLIC, *March 24, 1986, and United Media Syndicate,*
July 1986

> We stood for democracy in the Philippines. We have to stand for democracy in Nicaragua.
> —*President Reagan*

The analogy is preposterous. In Haiti and the Philippines we withdrew our support—at last—from dictatorships we'd embraced for decades. In Nicaragua Reagan wants us to finance a guerrilla war against the government. To subsume these two exercises under the general rubric of "intervention" (or "assist[ing] in the transition to democracy," as a *New Republic* editorial delicately puts it) is to abandon all capacity for making distinctions. Yet this is the lesson that defenders of aid to the contras—and of a generally belligerent foreign policy—want us to draw from the events of the past few weeks.

The United States never "intervened" against Ferdinand Marcos when he still had a grip on power. Far from it. Less than a year ago, the administration was asking for a 150 percent increase in military aid to his regime (using arguments similar to the ones now made for aid to the contras). It's said now that Marcos was completely out of touch with reality by the end. But who can blame him for thinking that Washington wouldn't begrudge him a little stolen election? Who can suppose that the United States would have given him the push if the Filipinos themselves hadn't forced our hand? As for Nicaragua, if all Reagan proposed was offering Daniel Ortega a free plane ride out and a safe haven for his collection of designer sunglasses, few would object.

Ironically, even as they draw a fatuous parallel between the Philippines and Nicaragua, conservative distinction-makers are working overtime to explain why the lessons of the Philippines *don't* apply to more obvious places like South Korea and South Africa, where we continue to maintain friendly relations with oppressive regimes, hoping that "quiet diplomacy" and "constructive engagement" will do the trick.

"The primary victims . . . would be the very people we seek to help. . . .We do not believe the way to help the people . . . is to cripple the economy upon which they and their families depend for survival." That's Reagan making the case that economic sanctions against South Africa would be "immoral and utterly repugnant."

But where is this exquisite moral sensitivity when it comes to Nicaragua? After all, the issue in South Africa is only withdrawing economic cooperation. In Nicaragua, where we did that long ago, the issue is fomenting war. The only way such a war can be won— or even can succeed enough to force negotiations—is by worsening conditions in the country. That is, by hurting "the very people we seek to help."

This obvious point has been obscured by the talk about contra "human rights abuses." In his pro-contra speech June 24 [1986], Reagan conceded that such abuses have occurred and said they are "intolerable." He promised that our boys will be cured of nasty habits like raping and murdering civilians. That would be nice. But what does Miss Manners say about blowing up roads and power lines, burning crops and storage facilities, and causing economic havoc generally? These are not unfortunate by-products of a guerrilla war. They are its purpose. You can't attack "Sandinismo" in the abstract. You go after the government by attacking the country, and people suffer. There's no other way. Reagan likes to tell a story about some contras refusing to blow up a power plant because "this would hurt the people of Nicaragua." If the story is true, we are wasting our money.

A key goal of guerrilla warfare is to generate discontent by goading the government into a crackdown. In his South Africa speech, Reagan all but blamed the African National Congress for the Pretoria regime's suppression of freedom. "The mining of roads, the bombings of public places," he said, are "designed to bring about further repression [and] the imposition of martial law." But what exactly is similar behavior by American-funded contras "designed to bring about"?

Elliott Abrams, assistant secretary of state for Latin America, says that the payoff would be "if the press is free, if people can speak out or hold rallies," and so on. Sure. Meanwhile, though, his deputy for Central America, William Walker, said it would also be progress "if the Sandinistas have to turn the screws down to silence the opposition" and "more people" become "refugees." Lenin called it "heightening the contradictions."

Secretary of State Shultz says that sanctions against South Africa would backfire by giving whites a scapegoat for the economic deterioration that is occurring anyway. Sanctions, he argued, allow people to say, "These foreigners are responsible." Without them, whites will have to blame apartheid itself for "this shamble we have on our hands." In Nicaragua, Daniel Ortega has been using just this "blame America first" technique to explain his country's economic collapse. But the Reagan administration doesn't trust Marxism to ruin the country on its own, and certainly does not see the propaganda angle as any reason to avoid making trouble.

Sanctions, says Reagan, "would destroy America's flexibility, discard our diplomatic leverage and deepen the crisis." But on the subject of Nicaragua, flexibility and diplomatic leverage are for naifs.

"Without power," he lectures, "diplomacy will be without leverage."
And, "The only way to get the Sandinistas to negotiate seriously . . .
is to give them no other alternative." Meanwhile South Africa,
according to Shultz, "is not a country that can be bossed around by
the United States. There are no such countries." An economic
boycott apparently constitutes an attempt to "boss around," but
running a guerrilla war does not.

The one theme that runs through Reagan's pronouncements on
both Nicaragua and South Africa is the metaphor of abandonment.
South Africa: "Many Americans understandably ask . . . why not
wash our hands and walk away from that . . . bleeding country?"
Nicaragua: "Too often . . . the United States failed to identify with
the aspirations of the people of Central America. . . . So we took the
path of least resistance and did nothing."

The metaphor is preposterously inverted in both cases. It is a
fatuous misrepresentation of the case for an economic boycott to
suggest that anyone supports it out of indifference (let alone
"understandable" indifference) to South Africa. The Nicaragua
passage—heralded by supporters as a handsome acknowledgment of
past United States misbehavior—is an Orwellian summary of America's role. Far from "doing nothing," we installed the regime Reagan
belatedly congratulates the Nicaraguans for overthrowing.

President Reagan is legendary for the beauty of his rhetoric. But is
a little logical consistency too much to ask as well?

Still Chosen

THE NEW REPUBLIC, December 3, 1984

Jews live like WASPs, the saying goes, and vote like
Puerto Ricans. A nice surprise of the election was that this remains
true. Walter Mondale got over two-thirds of the Jewish vote. That's

more than among any other identifiable group except blacks and the unemployed.

In fact, more Jews voted for Mondale this year than for Jimmy Carter and John Anderson combined in 1980. President Reagan, who scored 8 percent better than last time among the general population, scored 7 percent worse among Jews. A conservative trend beginning in 1972 was reversed. To the frustration of the Republican Party, and of some self-consciously tough-minded Jewish intellectuals, the most affluent ethnic group in America continues to vote its values instead of its interests.

The Reagan people spent $2 million chasing after Jewish votes. They hired professional telephone salespeople (most, it seems, black or Hispanic) to call Jews, identify themselves as "Harry Goodman" or "Betty Goodman," and urge support for Reagan. They sent the candidate into the heart of Jewish Long Island wearing a red, white, and blue yarmulke. In the election's silliest cat-and-mouse game, they plotted to photograph Mondale embracing Jesse Jackson, while Mondale plotted to avoid being caught *in flagrante delicto*. All to no avail.

What is it with Jews, anyway? It's several things. Like other late-arriving ethnics, American Jews got their Democratic politics early on, in the slums and sweatshops. But unlike other ethnics, Jews rarely change their politics with their economic status. That's because (and I generalize grossly—but I'm entitled) Jews are slower to forget. Every Passover, Jews remind themselves, "We were slaves to Pharaoh in Egypt." The Nazi Holocaust is still a living memory for many. So Jews get regular inoculations against complacency about their own present good fortune and frequent opportunities for empathy with others who don't share it. Jews also, based on religious belief and historical experience, take it as both a moral duty and a sensible precaution to hold themselves to a higher standard. Although it annoys Jewish hard-liners and anti-Semites alike, mainstream American Jews traditionally have felt they can't behave like any other selfish interest group. They must be like Caesar's wife.

The one subject on which Jewish voters are unabashedly selfish is Israel. Democrats have a longer and more glorious history of supporting the Zionist cause, but some people feel Israel is better served by the greater Republican passion for military strength. Two years ago Reagan was in trouble with supporters of Israel because of

his sale of AWAC planes to Saudi Arabia, his stupid attempt to make
pals with Syria, and what some saw as an unjustified lack of
enthusiasm for the invasion of Lebanon. But the administration
spent a busy two years making amends on the Middle East front. The
experts think that in terms of Jewish votes in the election, the Israel
issue was a wash.

But the Republicans had great hopes on other fronts. A mass
conversion of the Jews seemed imminent. You could detect four
styles of apostasy. First, *assimilationist*: affluent Jews who, two or
three generations off the boat, finally started thinking and voting like
other Americans of their class. Second, *intellectual*: the predominantly Jewish neoconservative movement. Neoconservatives have
challenged the liberal orthodoxy on a variety of matters, but are
especially vehement about affirmative action, which threatens Jewish
opportunities for places in medical school, tenured university slots,
and so on.

Third, *traditional*: lower-class, urban, nonassimilated Jews react-
ing to changing neighborhoods and rising crime rates. And fourth,
libertarian: the heavy representation of Jewish students, dizzy with
Friedman and Hayek, in campus conservative groups. Libertarian-
ism has a natural appeal for computer jocks, lab mice, and other
brainy and self-sufficient Jewish kids.

Yet these rivulets of reaction never rolled into a torrent. Two men
made the difference: Walter Mondale and Jerry Falwell. The pollster
William Schneider points out that Mondale, compared to George
McGovern and Jimmy Carter, is "the exact kind of Democrat Jews
feel comfortable with."

Mondale's operatives prevented a resolution against anti-Semitism
from coming to a vote at the Democratic Convention, for fear that
Jesse Jackson's black supporters would be offended. This was
Mondale at his worst, pandering wildly and sacrificing his principles
to the petty machinations of his staff. But Jewish voters saw through
this to Mondale at his best, the heir to Hubert Humphrey, a *mensch*,
which Ronald Reagan is not.

By contrast, the world of the Dallas Republican Convention—a
world of "greedheads, Barbie dolls, and fundamentalist Ayatollahs,"
as a *New Republic* editorial nicely put it—did not look inviting. Jews
peered into the abyss and pulled back.

Writing in *Commentary* a few months before the election, Irving Kristol, the neoconservative guru, deplored this kind of sentimental thinking. Jews, he argued, must get pragmatic. Gritty realism is where it's at, my boys. "This real world is rife with conflict and savagery. It is a world in which liberalism is very much on the defensive, in which public opinion runs in the grooves established by power, in which people back winners not losers." This advice he applied both to America's dealings in the world and to Jews' dealings in the American political system. Interests matter more than values. Idealism is childish. Stop acting like some kind of chosen people.

In particular, Kristol said, it was time for Jews to cut a deal with Falwell and friends. What does it matter, he asked, what else Falwell may believe, "as against the mundane fact that this same preacher is vigorously pro-Israel?" But in the end, Jewish voters decided that the specter of Jerry Falwell, and the vision of a Christian America that the Republicans seemed to endorse, frightened them more than the specter of Jesse Jackson.

Was this naive? I don't think so. What ought to disturb Jews about the culture and platform of Reaganism is not just the religion issue but the general celebration of conformity, complacency, and social intolerance.

Jews hold no special brief for homosexuality and abortion. They have no anointed responsibility for blacks and the poor. But at barely 2 percent of the population and shrinking, with a history of victimization by prejudice, smart Jews know they are not likely to thrive in a society where power relationships are all that matter. Just as you can't let America abandon its commitments to the rest of the world and still expect it to defend Israel (a favorite neoconservative point), you can't allow intolerance of other nonconforming groups to flower in American society and expect tolerance of Jews to survive.

It's a similar mystery to me why some American Jews should want our country to adopt a purely pragmatic, interests-over-values approach to the world at large. Sure, a case can be made for Israel as a vital link in America's self-defense. But that case is complicated. What isn't complicated is the case for Israel as a unique exemplar of the American values of democracy and freedom in a region dominated by tyrannies of various sorts. Any Jew who's discussed the subject with gentiles knows that this is the real wellspring of American support for Israel.

And what about Soviet Jews? They are no more than a side issue in the superpower conflict. America's interests are not engaged. Once again, just as you can't reasonably ask for a defense policy just strong enough to protect Israel, you can't ask for a human rights policy just strong enough to help Soviet Jews.

Would-be Republican Jewish power brokers are bitterly disappointed that 1984 was not the breakthrough year. They argue, unconvincingly, that the pollsters are wrong and that close to half the Jewish vote went for Reagan after all. Naturally they're upset. A fine Moses you make if you can't deliver your people. And what was that we kept hearing about liberal Jews being out of touch?

In the continuing war among Jewish intellectuals, neoconservatives reasonably object to being dismissed as lacking "compassion," as if that were the end of the argument. It's time they stopped brandishing accusations of naiveté with the same definitive flourish. Most American Jews, it turns out, still see their values and their interests as one and the same.

No White Feather, Please

THE NEW REPUBLIC, *June 16, 1986*

As an American male who might have served in Vietnam but didn't (like 92 percent of my male age cohort), my attitude toward Vietnam veterans is a mixture of respect, sympathy for those who suffered, and a sneaking envy. Envy of the moral credential, and also of the "classic male experience," as William Broyles sardonically labels it in his new book, *Brothers in Arms:* "Gentlemen in England, now a-bed, shall think themselves accurs'd they were not here" (*Henry V*). Well, I wouldn't go that far. But I certainly don't begrudge Vietnam vets their belated glory.

On the other hand, should I actually feel ashamed for not having served in a war I didn't support? That is the drift of a lot of recent commentary on Vietnam. I never dodged the draft. In fact, I was clear in my own mind that opposition to the war couldn't justify evading military service, though I left open the possibility of cowardice. Fortunately, thanks to a high lottery number, I was never put to that test. But I could have enlisted, I suppose—an idea that certainly never crossed my mind.

My friend James Fallows wrote a seminal article eleven years ago observing that the burden of the Vietnam War fell mainly on lower-class kids without the wit or connections to avoid the draft. If the sons of the decision-making class had been fighting and dying— or going to jail in protest—the war would have ended a lot sooner, he argued.

Fallows's point was that his Harvard classmates were morally culpable for not having made greater sacrifices to *stop* the war. Yet his theme has been taken up and twisted over the past decade by people with the opposite agenda. The most recent example is President Reagan, who said at Arlington Cemetery on Memorial Day, "It was the unpampered boys of the working class who picked up the rifles and went on the march." The "boys of Vietnam," Reagan said, "fought a terrible and vicious war without enough support from home. . . . They chose to reject the fashionable skepticism of their time; they chose to believe and answer the call of duty."

Broyles's book, like every other Vietnam memoir I've read, makes vividly clear that there was no lack of skepticism, and no great belief in the larger goals of the war, among those who did the fighting. But this characteristic Reagan flight of fancy is just part of a larger moral inversion. The burden of remarks like Reagan's is that it was somehow the antiwar movement, rather than the prosecutors of the war, who sent American boys off to fight and die in a dubious cause.

The notion that people who opposed the war were indifferent or even hostile to the fate of American soldiers does not accord with my memory. This is what the protests were mostly about. And who can doubt that if it weren't for the protests, many more would have fought and died? In fact, a common radical critique of the main-

stream antiwar movement was that it was too concerned about the
American body count, ignoring the cost of the war to the Vietnam-
ese. It's this radical critique that rings somewhat hollow today, given
what happened to Vietnam after we gave up. But the focus of most
opponents of the war—ultimately, a majority of Americans—was
that the cost of what we were trying to achieve was simply too high.
It was clear at the time who was bearing the cost.

Public sympathy toward Vietnam veterans has been wrongly
enlisted in a campaign to undo this historical judgment and its
implications for the present foreign policy debate. The campaign has
involved an interesting reversal of postures. The standard neoconservative "new class" analysis of liberal causes accuses liberals of
ideological self-aggrandizement in the guise of compassion. Liberals,
the argument goes, instill a sense of grievance and victimization
among groups such as blacks and the poor in order to justify
government programs that create work for cadres of professional
liberals (the "new class") and promote the liberal agenda.

If ever there was a group persuaded by ideologues that it could
blame its problems on society, it is Vietnam veterans. Only this time
it is conservative ideologues who have joined with the usual legions
of media hypesters and "caring professionals" to encourage brooding
self-pity. Most Vietnam vets actually "had a good war," as the British
say. Ninety-one percent in a 1980 poll said they're glad they went.
As a group, Vietnam vets have higher education levels and incomes
than men of their age group who didn't serve. Of the small fraction
who have had readjustment problems, there's no question that many
are genuine victims of the war.

But thousands of vets are wasting their lives hanging out at
storefront "vet centers." Sixty or so were reported recently to be living
like wild men in the Florida jungle because, according to one of
them, "Vietnam vets are square pegs in round holes." The defense
of "post-traumatic stress disorder" (PTSD) has been invoked to beat
raps from chronic absenteeism to murder. The flashy vet suicide is
a newspaper staple. Yet you don't hear conservatives suggesting that
"liberal guilt" has created a "vet culture" of dependency and
irresponsibility, because this culture serves their ideological purpose.
The vets' grievance (nobody appreciates them) bolsters the conservative grievance (nobody appreciates the war).

Obviously there's no logical connection. It's possible to appreciate the veterans' sacrifice without approving of the last war—let alone the next one—or feeling guilty about not having served. Those who insist that nothing less than full retroactive support for the war is a dishonor to the veterans are the ones denying them their full due.

In England during World War I, as thousands were dying pointlessly in the trenches, pretty girls went around handing white feathers—a symbol of cowardice—to men who weren't in uniform. The one group currently being handed white feathers who may deserve them are the so-called war wimps or chicken hawks— prominent Americans helping to spread war fever today who avoided service during Vietnam, like Sylvester Stallone (who was teaching at a girls' school in Switzerland) and various Washington hard-liners. As for those of us who opposed that war and didn't serve, it's true we'll never know for sure in our hearts whether we'd have the courage to answer the call if our nation really needed us. But so far, at least, we've gotten it right.

A *"Public Choice"* Analysis of *"Public Choice"* Analysis

WALL STREET JOURNAL, *October 30, 1986*

I had no idea it was so easy to win a Nobel Prize. Professor James Buchanan of George Mason University in northern Virginia, this year's Nobel laureate in economics, is said to have discovered the principle that politicians find it easier to spend money than to raise taxes, and government deficits are the result. Is it really possible that this fact was never observed by Tocqueville or Lord Bryce or one of those guys? Maybe so. But in that case I feel like quite a chump for failing to point it out myself. Big bags of kronor and a free trip to Sweden were just sitting there for the asking, and someone else grabbed them.

Or does this do Professor Buchanan an injustice? The newspapers, in their attempt to simplify for the layperson, often make important scientific breakthroughs sound trivial, a matter of peering into the microscope and discovering "a new kind of particle that is vital to our understanding of how waffles are formed." Professor Buchanan has actually founded an entire economic discipline called public choice. According to the New York Times,

> Some of Dr. Buchanan's early insights, once regarded skeptical-ly, have now become widely accepted. For example, policy theory previously held that government authorities strove to achieve certain social and economic goals for the general welfare. . . . Yet Dr. Buchanan and others in the public choice school . . . did not accept this simplfied view; instead, they sought explanations for the political behavior of officials and voters that was [sic] more in the self-seeking mold. . . . For example, politicians may ignore the general welfare and take actions more likely to secure positions or power, while special interest groups seek to receive large budget allocations.

The Washington Post quotes another economist, identified only as a well-known member of a rival school, as saying of Buchanan's prize, "I'm amazed. The choice just baffles me." This man is clearly a Keynesian, mired in old-fashioned modes of analysis. The Nobel committee's decision to confer this honor on an obscure right-wing eccentric becomes less baffling if we apply the insights of the burgeoning "prize choice" school of Nobel scholarship.

The theory of the Nobel Prizes previously held that Nobel selection committees strove to select scholars of maximum distinc-tion who have made the most important intellectual breakthroughs and done the most to improve the condition of mankind. Yet the "prize choice" school does not accept this simplified view. Instead, it seeks explanations for the selection committees' sometimes bizarre choices that are more in the self-seeking mold. For example, the selectors may choose to ignore true scholarly distinction and make choices more in keeping with the fashions that sweep world politics, while the Swedish Central Bank, which chooses the selectors, may prefer selectors who will award prizes that earn plaudits from the international finance community.

The praise for the Buchanan selection in some conservative newspapers can be explained by the increasingly influential "editorial choice" school of thought. Journalistic theory previously held that editorial writers strove to endorse views on issues that they honestly thought were right, in order to serve their readers' need for understanding and the general cause of truth and justice. Yet the "editorial choice" school does not accept this simplified view. Instead, it seeks explanations for the behavior of editorialists that are more in the self-seeking mold. Newspaper owners tend to be rich and to have rich friends. Rational editorial writers will maximize their career possibilities by writing editorials that are likely to appeal to rich businessmen.

And how did Professor Buchanan come by his theories about the nefarious role of government? Newspaper accounts have emphasized his youth as a Southern farm boy and his decades of scholarly spadework. But a more sophisticated answer might make use of the analytical tools of the increasingly influential "academic choice" school of thought. Scholarship theory previously held that academics strove to discover the truth about human affairs in order to add to our understanding of the world, and possibly to improve it.

Yet the "academic choice" school does not accept this simplified view. Instead, it seeks explanations that are more in the self-seeking mode. For example, a professor may decide that there's no prosperity in being just another Keynesian, let alone a Marxist. Instead, by coming up with a lot of fancy theories to justify the self-interested desires of the business community—for lower taxes, less regulation, etc.—he may find himself earning a six-figure salary (one-third subsidized by corporations) as the head of his own center, and winning all sorts of awards to boot. Take a prejudice, give it a name ("public choice"), call it a school or a discipline, *et voila!*

Of course, it's only a theory.

The Case for Glee

THE NEW REPUBLIC, *December 22, 1986*

The only irritating aspect of the otherwise delightful collapse of the Reagan administration is the widespread insistence that we must all be poker-faced about it. The *Washington Post*, second-to-none in moral dudgeon over the Reaganites' misdeeds, nevertheless declares that anyone who enjoys or is entertained by the spectacle is "reprehensible," no less. The approved attitude is to don the mask of tragedy: Oh, woe is us, another failed administration, policy-making in disarray, etc.

And, of course, what must The Allies be thinking?

The President's critics are required to appear even gloomier than his supporters—*de rigueur*, it seems, if you're going to go around invoking democracy and the Constitution. The columnist William Raspberry, having admitted that he cares nothing at all for Ronald Reagan and less than nothing for Reagan's record as President, writes that "only a partisan fool could find pleasure" in Reagan's downfall.

Dear me. Am I really the only one here who's having a great time? Would I like to share the joke with the rest of the class? Or should any right-thinking person succumb without regret to the fever of solemnity sweeping the nation? No, upon tortured reflection, I've concluded that the case for glee remains compelling.

First of all, simple honesty requires any Washington type to admit that this is the kind of episode we all live for. The adrenaline is flowing like Perrier. Everyone—Reagan supporters no less than his opponents—is wandering around in a happy buzz induced by those oft-denounced but rarely eschewed twin intoxicants, "gossip and speculation." C'mon, everybody, admit it. We're high.

Second, "disarray" is the essence of farce, and pratfalls are just as funny when committed by the National Security Council as when committed by the Three Stooges. The Iran episode has not lacked for pies in faces, missing pants, stubbed toes, confused identities, mistaken embraces, role reversals, strange noises, and other classic elements of lowbrow comedy. It's only human to laugh.

Third, it's a healthy democratic instinct to enjoy seeing the mighty fall, whether the mighty deserve it or not. No one was acting mightier, especially since the 1984 election, than the Reagan administration. Children generally find the story of Humpty Dumpty more amusing than tragic. When, as in this case, the mighty do deserve their tumble, it would be evidence of political decadence *not* to relish the sight.

Democrats and liberals, beaten down after six years of Reaganism, have every right to whistle a happy tune as they throw off their chains of timidity and go on the offensive. Politics is not just a game, but it *is* a game. The voices urging a weighty solemnity are the same sort who deplore the apathy of the electorate. But if people are going to be scolded for cheering whenever their side scores or the other side fumbles, they will quite rightly turn their attention back to professional sports.

There are subtler pleasures to be had as well. It's nothing short of delicious that contempt for democracy should have done Reagan in. For six years, democracy has been the biggest frustration of the President's opponents.

It seemed to us, the carping critics, that this man was not terribly bright, not terribly thoughtful or well informed, not terribly honest, and in most other ways not up to the most important job in the world. But a large majority of people seemed not to mind. And so a gradual consensus grew that if he lacked conventional mental and moral assets, he had some kind of special magic.

Even Reagan's critics became deeply superstitious about this alleged magic. They became afraid to say—or even forgot they think—that he's just an old movie actor. They themselves came to believe that to criticize Reagan personally was to cut yourself off from the democratic life force and condemn your soul to that circle of hell "inside the Beltway." Like knocking on wood or whistling past the graveyard, superstitious critics would preface any dissent from Reagan's policies with expressions of respect for him personally. One reason the President's political opponents nervously refrain from chuckling over his present predicament is a superstitious fear that the magic monster is only asleep, not dead, and the sound of laughter will reawaken him.

Democracy used to be Reagan's opponent's problem. Now it's his problem. As his poll results plummet, he waves his magic wand in bewilderment, puzzled that the magic doesn't seem to work. "This is a Beltway bloodletting," said Reagan in his appalling interview with *Time* magazine. What this pathetic remark revealed is that it is Reagan who is now trapped "inside the Beltway," isolated in a cocoon of advisers, cut off from the democratic life force. And in fact the contra war has always been an inside-the-Beltway enthusiasm, which is what led to Reagan's difficulties in the first place.

Democracy is a terrible inconvenience. "The Salvadoran guerrillas or the Sandinistas don't have to worry about all this when they deal with the Cubans and the Russians," a contra leader complained to James LeMoyne of the *New York Times*. "All this" refers to Congress, public opinion, the press, the law, and the other impedimenta of the American way. The Reagan administration, on whom democracy had lavished its greatest blessings, couldn't be bothered with democracy's inconveniences either.

So there's no need for gloom. Liberals and others who feared for their own faith in democracy can breathe easy. Reagan's comeuppance is democracy's salvation. It turns out that you can't fool all the people all of the time after all. Dry those tears and repeat after me: Ha. Ha. Ha.

THE PRESS

INTRODUCTION

The parody of the weekly TV show "Agronsky and Company" that opens this section is one of the oldest pieces in the book (1981), and out of date in several respects. George Will has gone on to greater things. He also seems to have developed some self-restraint about the use of quotations—long his most noticeable literary tic. This reform may be in response to published mockery. Or it may derive from a sense (certainly justified) that a man of George Will's stature is licensed to coin his own aphorisms.

The art of televised journalistic gasbaggery also has evolved, although many would say the evolution has been back toward the monkeys rather than forward to higher forms of civilized life. I'm not exactly blameless here, having appeared several times on Agronsky's rival, "The McLaughlin Group," and done my best to help lower the tone. On the evolutionary scale, "McLaughlin" falls about halfway between "Agronsky" and the primordial ooze.

Even worse, I've served as a summer replacement on the Cable News Network show "Crossfire," which makes "McLaughlin" look like tea with Nancy Reagan. On "Crossfire," two journalist "hosts" snarl and scream inhospitably at two bewildered "guests" and each other for half an hour every weeknight. It took a while to get the hang of this. My first show, while I was desperately trying to remember the name of the congressman I was supposed to be harassing, my head suddenly exploded with the voice of the producer, coming through that little thing they put in your ear, shrieking, "Get mad! GET MAD!!" By the end of my two-week stint I was a trained killer, unfit for human society and in need of plastic surgery to remove the permanent sneer from my face.

"William Shawn and the Temple of Facts" and "How Time Flies," about controversies involving the New Yorker and Time, both concern the role of facts in journalism. In brief, I think they're overrated (facts, that is). The cult of the New Yorker is a mystery to me. Sometimes I think I should leave the magazine business when half a dozen people tell me some New Yorker article is fascinating and I find it unreadable. Since my job involves reviewing a lot of manuscripts, I also see the malign influence of the New Yorker on aspiring writers. Everyone wants to write like John McPhee or Ann Beattie. The only hope for American letters is that Robert Gottlieb, the new editor appointed by owner Si Newhouse after the involuntary retirement of "Mr." Shawn, will ruin the magazine as many aficionados predict.

General Sharon lost his libel case against Time. The jury concluded—as it had to—that Time had gotten its facts wrong but that Sharon, as a public figure, was not entitled to recover damages. To complete the circle, Sharon's lawsuit later became the subject of one of those interminable and mysteriously influential New Yorker articles.

"Yes, We Have No Bananas" and "Cockburn the Barbarian" concern journalistic ethical controversies in which I was personally involved. "You stand for two things in the public mind," says a friend [sic]: "writing about people's sex lives and going on junkets." As recently as the fall of 1986, more than four years after the notorious event, a letter to the editor of the Wall Street Journal from a tobacco company spokesman, responding to a column of mine, said, in effect: "Who's Kinsley to accuse us of murdering millions of people? He once went on a free trip to Israel." There are few things more tedious than being the center of an ethical controversy. So you can be sure that it took a lot of vanity to want to preserve these histories between hard covers.

The "banana convention" of not writing honestly about politicians' sex lives did not collapse in 1980, as I predicted, but is collapsing in 1987. As I write, Gary Hart has just ended his presidential campaign after disclosures about his extramarital liasons, and the press is enjoying an orgy of agonized self-scrutiny about whether it has Gone Too Far. I think not. In fact, I suspect it will turn out that politicians and their journalistic protectors have been needlessly snobbish in assuming that the voters can't be trusted with certain information about their elected leaders. Representative Gerry Studds has been reelected repeatedly in a heavily working-class district in Massachusetts since admitting that he's a homosexual. Bob Kerry, the divorced former governor of Nebraska, shot up in the polls every time the actress Deborah Winger came to spend the night in the governor's mansion.

The worst violation of journalistic ethics I routinely commit is letting Charlie Peters, editor of the *Washington Monthly*, put his words in my mouth. Part of the fun of writing for the *Monthly* is finding out what you think about a subject by reading your own article in print. Rereading the piece on Alexander Cockburn's ethical problems, I see that Charlie has me half-endorsing the notion that one should avoid "even the appearance of impropriety." Actually, that's a formulation that especially annoys me—a cowardly substitute for clear-headed analysis. If the appearance is incorrect, why truckle to it? It's the journalist's job to bring perceptions in line with reality, not to bring reality in line with perceptions. It's true that I've turned down junkets during the past five years, just to avoid trouble. But I'm ashamed of myself for every one I didn't go on.

And I wish I had a dollar for every junket a friend or colleague has taken without a hint of controversy. Beyond a certain point, in fact— I'd say somewhere between two weeks and a month—a "junket" mutates into a "fellowship" and actually becomes something one can put on one's résumé.

The arbitrariness of what is and is not considered news is one point of "What the Helga??"—about Andrew Wyeth's allegedly secret cache of love paintings, which made the covers of both *Newsweek* and *Time* even though every key element of the story was either already known or transparently false. The same art-world stunt men perpetrated the idiotic Mona-Lisa-as-Leonardo-in-drag brouhaha a few months later.

Thanks to "Worthwhile Canadian Initiative," I now receive boring headlines from all over the country and exchange them regularly with my friends over on the *Washington Post* editorial page. Just the other day, I clipped "A Sound Compromise on U.N. Budgeting" from the *New York Times* op-ed page and was about to send it over with a note observing that you needed the byline ("By

Elliot L. Richardson") for the full-bore effect. The phone rang and it was Ken Ikenberry from the *Post:* "I've got one for you, but the byline really makes it."

Some other good ones in the months following that column: "Hyattsville Building Still Closed" (*Post*); "Pan Am Jumbo Jet Lands Safely" (*Post*); "Library Group Confers on Vexing Issues" (*Times*); "Tribal Fighting in Papua New Guinea Nothing To Worry About, Officials Say" (*Baltimore Sun*); "Panel on Ethics Urges Cuomo To Form Commission" (*Times*); and "Privatization Is Samoa's Answer to U.S. Budget Constraints" (*Wall Street Journal*). The *Times* continued its tradition of inscrutable hortatory editorial titles with, "No Reason To Flip-Flop on Lumber," while the *Journal* editorial page warned ominously but elusively that, "Coordination Could Be Washed Out." For vacuous high-mindedness, "Global Growth: A Task for All" (*Times*) rivals "Worthwhile Canadian Initiative" itself.

"How Many Thoughtful Observers Does It Take To Answer a Vital Question?" was the first of what I hope will be an annual column having fun with Nexis, the computerized media data base. Anthony Lewis commemorates the Christmas bombing of Hanoi every year; I play with my computer.

The final item in this section, "Reston for President," is a small hostage to fortune: a case study, written before I entered the fray, about what happens when a columnist becomes complacent.

Jerkofsky & Company

THE NEW REPUBLIC, *September 9, 1981*

MARTIAL MUSIC (*Love Theme From Jerkofsky & Company*). *Under the Great Seal of Jerkofsky & Company, Washington's leading savants gather to perform group exegesis on the events of*

the past week. We hear a low, rumbling noise, which is the voice of
. . .

MARVIN JERKOFSKY: The President urges support for his policies, but leading opposition spokesmen express objections. Negotiations proceed in major trouble spots, amidst increasing criticism of the current approach. Concern mounts in Washington about any number of things. Life on earth continues, but doubts arise about its purpose or justification. Hugh, how do you like my new tie?

HUGH SIDEWALL: You know, Marvin, we sit here in Washington pretending that we have some kind of special insight into the world, and really we don't know much more than anyone else. As for all the issues you raise, they're important issues, and they'll all have to be studied with care, with very great care indeed, and in fact, if anything is clear at all—which I doubt—it is that these very troubling questions are being deeply considered by some of the finest minds in town, who agree—to a man, I might say, or a woman, Elizabeth—that these are all very, very difficult challenges for the nation. But as for what comes next, we just can't say, Marvin. It's too early to tell.

JERKOFSKY: I see. Well, tell me this, Hugh. If, as you seem to suggest, you know nothing about anything, why do I pay you to drone on week after week on my show?

SIDEWALL: Well, you know, Marvin, that's a very good question, and it's one I've heard being asked at the very highest reaches of government in my major lunches around Washington and in traveling across the entire country. But there are no conclusions at this point, and we'll just have to wait and see. It's hard to say. No one knows for sure. Any guess would be premature.

JERKOFSKY: Hugh, do you have any brains left at all?

SIDEWALL: I don't know, Marvin. We just can't say.

JERKOFSKY: George?

GEORGE III: On the subject of Hugh's brain, Marvin, I'm reminded of Samuel Johnson's remark that the prospect of a hanging concentrates the mind wonderfully. Foolish consistency, Marvin, is the hobgoblin of small minds, as Emerson so aptly put it. And I believe it was Pope who said, " 'Tis education forms the common mind: Just as the twig is bent, the tree's inclined." But the Bible says, "A fool uttereth all his mind." And "what fools these mortals be," as Shakespeare so wisely observed.

JERKOFSKY: Thank you, George. Haynes?

HAYNES UNDERWEAR: Marvin, I was interested in Hugh's remark about traveling across the entire country, because frankly, Hugh, I think that's my turf, if you don't mind. I'm just back from Out There, as a matter of fact, taking the pulse of the nation, speaking to millions of ordinary Americans, be they shopkeepers, or baseball fans, or Presbyterians, and all of them agree with remarkable unanimity that this is a very crucial time for our nation. In fact, Marvin, in my entire career as a Pulitzer Prize-winning reporter, this is one of the most fascinating periods we have ever passed through as a country. Americans are nervous, yet they remain calm. They have lost faith, yet they retain, I think, an underlying confidence. They are certain, yet somehow unsure. It's hard to define, Marvin, but it's definitely there. I know, because I've talked to every single one of them. For me to pass among the American people at this fleeting yet crucial moment in history, touching an outstretched hand here, accepting a gentle kiss on the foot there, was as stirring and moving for me as a journalist as it was for them as the American people.

JERKOFKSY: I'm sure you're right, Haynes. Elizabeth?

MS. SHREW: I think we have to be very careful in defining our terms here, Marvin. By "people," does Haynes mean "human beings making up a group or assembly or linked by a common interest"? Or does he mean "the mass of a community as distinguished from a special class"? In talking with people—and I use that term advisedly—up on the Hill this week, I've discovered a sharp divergence of views and not a little confusion on this point.

JERKOFSKY: An important distinction, Elizabeth. Congratulations. Carl, what do you think about Elizabeth's distinction?

CARL ROLYPOLY: Welllllllll,   Marrrrrrvinnnnnn,   lllllllet mmmmmmmmme jussssst say one llllllit-tulllllll thaaaaaaaaang.

You knowwwwwwww, it's allllll jussssst fine and dannnnnnnn-deeeeeeeeee for Haynes and Eeeeeeelizzzzz-uh-beth to sit heeeeere and talk abouuuuuut . . . the peeeeeeeee-pulllllll. But what I would like to knowwwwww is thisssssssss.

JERKOFSKY: Yes? What is it?

ROLYPOLY: What it isssssss, Marrrrrvinnnnnnn, is jussssssst one simmmmmmpulllllllll quesssssssssschunnnnnnnn.

ALL: Yes? Yes?

ROLYPOLY: Myyyy quessssschunnnnnn issssss thissssssss. Hhhhhhhwat abouuuuuut blaaaaaack peeeeeeee-pulllllll?

JERKOFSKY: A good question, Carl. Thank you. Jack?

JACK CURMUDGEON: Harrumph. Balderdash. Poppycock. Horse-feathers. Et cetera.

JERKOFSKY: That's the last word, Jack. Thank you, Elizabeth, gentlemen.

ALL (waving): Goodbye, boys and girls! See you next week!

William Shawn and the Temple of Facts

THE NEW REPUBLIC, *July 16, 1984*

A dyspeptic friend, who earnestly dislikes the *New Yorker* for its smug insularity, its tiny dada conceits passing as wit, its whimsy presented as serious politics, and its deadpan narratives masquerading as serious journalism, writes:

I have had my suspicions about the vaunted *New Yorker* fact-checking department ever since I met a *New Yorker* fact checker at a dinner party several years ago. This fellow—a real individual, not a composite—regaled the gathering with tales of chartering airplanes to measure the distance between obscure Asian capitals, sending battalions of Sarah Lawrence girls to count the grains of sand on a particular beach referred to in an Ann Beattie story, and suchlike tales of heroic valor in the pursuit of perfect accuracy. After several hours of this (actually, one hour, seventeen minutes, and fifty-three seconds), he turned to me with a polite smile and said, "Tell us about your fact-checking system at *The New Republic*."

I was editor of *The New Republic* at the time. I replied, "You're looking at it."

He turned pale. Actually, he didn't turn pale. I embroider. But he did say, "That's odd, because if I'm checking a story in the *New Yorker* and find the fact I need in *The New Republic*, I consider it checked."

So I was less shocked than many people, though probably more pleased than most, at the recent revelation that a *New Yorker* writer named Alastair Reid has been fabricating the details in his reports for the magazine over more than two decades. A bar in a Spanish town was invented and populated with chatty locals; a son at Yale was turned into a more colorful grandniece; that weariest of all journalistic devices, an opinionated taxi driver, was conjured up; and so on.

The *Wall Street Journal*, which uncovered this story, has known sorrow itself recently. When one of its reporters was caught trading in the stocks he was touting in the paper, the *Journal* investigated and published a brutally frank report on its own front page. That is not the *New Yorker*'s style. This is a publication that doesn't even run letters to the editor, and will only publish a correction once in a blue moon under the genteel heading, "Department of Amplification." The initial response to the *Journal*'s story from William Shawn, the *New Yorker*'s legendary editor, was in keeping with this self-satisfied tradition. Though the revelation had come from Reid himself, Shawn simply refused to acknowledge it. He stonewalled. "I've worked with Mr. Reid for many, many years, I trust him completely. . . . He's a man of utter integrity, and that's all I have to know." Case closed. The world's best fact-checking department is very nice, but please don't confuse Mr. Shawn with the facts about his own operation.

*   *   *

Within a day, stonewall segued into cover-up (though, to pursue the
Watergate imagery, never into anything so unrefined as a modified
limited hangout). Shawn told the *Washington Post* that Reid had
changed the details of his Franco-era reports from Spain in order to
protect his sources from reprisal. This was a concern Reid had failed
to mention in his several homilies, quoted in the *Journal*, about the
difference between facts and truth. It also fails to explain why Reid
made up anecdotes like the touching little number about meeting
the poet Czeslaw Milosz and telling him that they were born in the
same year ("He lighted up at once . . . ."), when in fact Reid is fifteen
years younger. Nor does it explain where those fact checkers were
when Reid was spinning his petty fantasies.

Shawn also took an ugly swipe at the young reporter who'd written
the story for the *Wall Street Journal.* "This was a very subtle matter
and this young woman who did the piece is not a subtle writer," he
huffed to the *Post.* There was no suggestion that she'd gotten her
facts wrong. But it appears that William Shawn regards "not subtle"
as a more damning indictment of a journalist than "not accurate."

Actually, there's something to this point of view. Alastair Reid is
right to protest that the fundamental truth of his articles shouldn't be
judged on the basis of a few phony flourishes. The ornamental
details he faked have about as much to do with the soundness of his
reports as the broken pediment on top of the AT&T Building reveals
about the structure underneath. Bars, taxis, sunsets . . . it's just
decoration. But where does this leave the *New Yorker,* a weekly
monument to the proposition that journalism consists of the endless
accretion of tiny details?

> *Shortly after noon on Monday, January 24, 1983, the principal
> members of Governor Mario M. Cuomo's staff assembled in the
> Governor's office, on the second floor of the State Capitol, in
> Albany.*

So begins part two of a recent profile, majestically entitled, "Governor." This piece (by a good journalist in other contexts) goes on to
describe every other person at the meeting; what Cuomo was
wearing—"a white shirt, a red striped tie, and a three-piece gray
suit"; and where he sat—"at a glass-topped table." You're probably

wondering what was on the table. Well, "it was bare except for a telephone console and a black loose-leaf binder." If you're also wondering what all this has to do with anything, where the article is going, or why the author has written it, you're out of luck. To pique the reader's interest with a clever title or a snappy lead or—God forbid—a line or two at the top summarizing what the article has to say would be vulgar salesmanship.

Indeed, the very notion of an article having something to say offends William Shawn, who told the *Wall Street Journal* that his magazine "is as close to being scientific in its objectivity as reporting can be," with "no advocacy, . . . no prejudices." Just the facts, and plenty of 'em. Of course this pretense is as phony as Alastair Reid's grandniece. The Cuomo profile, for example, radiates admiration for the governor. This admiration undoubtedly is justified. But the pretense that no argument is being made saves the *New Yorker* writer from having to present and defend the argument he or she is, in fact, making. The reader's critical facility is benumbed right there in the opening paragraph with the information that the New York State Capitol is in Albany and the governor's office is on the second floor.

Not long after meeting the *New Yorker* fact checker, I found myself in a job interview with the legendary Mr. Shawn himself, which foundered on this very question of "the facts." The interview wasn't going too well anyway, as it took the form of a vicious duel of competitive gentility, and I was at a hopeless disadvantage against an old master. Mr. Shawn's posture was that I was a terribly busy and important man who, motivated by purest charity, had taken the time out of a hectic schedule to spend a few moments brightening the life of an aged and forgotten invalid. "Oh, Mr. Kinsley," he cooed. "Thank you so very, very much for coming to see me. It's so awfully kind of you," and so on and so forth. Thoroughly disoriented, since this was a meeting any young journalist would kill for, and since only moments earlier I had been ushered into his office as if to a shrine, I could only mumur, "Not at all, not at all."

The discussion eventually turned from the topic of my condescension in agreeing to meet with the editor of the *New Yorker* to the *New Yorker* itself. What, as an editor, did I think of it? Well, I said as tentatively as possible, I thought that some of the articles tended perhaps to go on just a bit, and that occasionally it was hard to follow (I refrained from saying "detect") the thread of the writer's thinking. One function of an editor, I recklessly opined, is to ask while reading a manuscript: "What's the point?"

"Oh, Mr. Kinsley," said Mr. Shawn piteously. He looked deeply wounded, as if I'd taken this thing called "the point" and run him through with it. Okay, so he didn't. I exaggerate. A bit. He did say with a sigh, as if describing a treasured family custom which an outsider couldn't possibly be expected to understand, "Here at the *New Yorker*, Mr. Kinsley, we believe in letting the facts speak for themselves." Soon he was waltzing me toward the elevator, thanking me deliriously for visiting him, and clutching my pile of writing samples to his bosom like a gift of flowers.

The June 18 *New Yorker* has an article about corn. It's the first in what appears to be a series, no less, discussing the major grains. What about corn? Who knows? Only the *New Yorker* would have the lofty disdain for its readers to expect them to plow through 22,000 words about corn (warning: only an estimate; the *TNR* fact checkers are still counting) without giving them the slightest hint why. Here is how it starts (after a short introductory poem):

> When the New England farmer and botanist Edward Sturtevant retired, in 1887, as head of the New York Agricultural Experiment Station, in Geneva, he left behind a bulky manuscript that was published in 1919, twenty-one years after his death, as "Sturtevant's Notes on Edible Plants." Dr. Sturtevant, who was also a graduate of the Harvard Medical School but never practiced medicine, had scoured the world's botanical literature for mentions of all the plants that human beings were known to have eaten (he did not count tree bark, which in times of famine was often one of them), and had come up with, among more than three hundred thousand known plant species, two thousand eight hundred and ninety-seven edibles. (Latter-day scientists believe he may have missed as many more.) But, of all these, only a hundred and fifty or so have ever been widely enough consumed to figure in commerce, and of those a mere handful have been of any real consequence.

Now, there are some facts for you. No doubt every single one of them has been checked. You stand in awe as they tumble toward you, magnificently irrelevant, surrounded by mighty commas, mere numbers swollen into giant phrases ("two thousand eight hundred and ninety-seven"), all finally crashing over you with the bravura announcement that nothing you have just read is "of any real consequence." How true this is! From the end of the paragraph, you gaze back on receding vistas of inconsequence, as far as the eye can see. Even supposing we would like a bit more information about corn, and even supposing we might be relieved to know how many other plants, edible and otherwise, are *not* going to be discussed in this article, why are we being told about a man whose count apparently was off by half? Even supposing we need to know about Dr. Sturtevant's book, when it was published, and when the good doctor died, why do we need to know when he retired? Even—stretching it—supposing that we need to know that this gentleman "was also a graduate of the Harvard Medical School," why, oh why, do we have to learn that he "never practiced medicine"? As for the business about tree bark, that has just got to be conscious self-parody.

Meanwhile, in the "Talk of the Town" section of the same issue, the anonymous voice of Eustace Tilly is opining about Central America. It is in favor of freedom and against repression. A sound position. Offered in defense of it, however, is this dubious proposition: "Moreover, quite apart from ethical considerations, we find that repression abroad is eventually inimical to liberty at home. In the long run, either the repression abroad or the liberty at home must give way."

That is a typical piece of *New Yorker* political analysis: sweet, but not terribly acute. It's the kind of thinking you get when you're committed to the pretense that you're not thinking. The world would have a pleasing symmetry if support for repression abroad inevitably produced repression at home, but there is no such pleasing symmetry in the world outside 25 West 43d Street. The British Empire, for example, had a good long run, during which Britain itself became more democratic, not less, and which ultimately broke down for reasons having nothing to do with concern about repression at home. How did this one get past the fact checkers? Simple. It's not a "fact" of the checkable sort. The *New Yorker* has no sense checkers. Indeed, because of its pretense that all that matters are "the facts," its hermetic editorial process, and its refusal to submit what it publishes to a reality test such as letters to the editor, there is less of a check on nonsense there at the *New Yorker* than at any other major publication.

"I venture to say that the *New Yorker* is the most accurate publication not only in this country, but in the entire world," Mr. Shawn ventures to say. This would be an unimpressive boast, even if it were true.

How Time Flies

THE NEW REPUBLIC, *January 21, 1985*

The current issue of *Time* magazine lists 274 word journalists on the masthead, and contains about 28,000 words of copy. That works out to slightly over 100 words a week per journalist. This does not mean that newsmagazine journalists are slackers. Quite the contrary. Each member of *Time*'s complex hierarchy of correspondents, researcher-reporters, writers, and editors generates reams of copy, almost none of which ever sees print. It is a system of literary creation like nothing else on earth, except *Newsweek*. Advocates might compare it to distilling a thimbleful of perfume from several tons of rose petals. Skeptics might describe it as more like chartering a fleet of trucks to carry your briefcase home from work.

This system is now on trial in the libel case of *Ariel Sharon v. Time Inc.* General Sharon directed the Israeli invasion of Lebanon in 1982. An Israeli government commission blamed Sharon indirectly for the massacre by Lebanese Phalangist soldiers of Palestinians in the Sabra and Shatila refugee camps. *Time*'s story on the commission report went further. *"Time* has learned," it said, that a secret appendix dealt with Sharon's visit to the family of the assassinated

Phalangist President of Lebanon, Bashir Gemayal, shortly before the massacre. According to this appendix, *Time* said, Sharon and the Gemayels discussed taking revenge for Bashir's death.

Any reasonable person studying the documents in this case would have to conclude that *Time* has no evidence that Sharon discussed revenge with the Gemayels and that the secret appendix almost surely doesn't mention this matter at all.* This doesn't settle the libel issue, but it does raise the question of how *Time* flies.

The notion that Sharon had talked revenge with the Gemayels first surfaced in something grandly called a "World Wide Memo," a sort of in-house international gossip sheet with tidbits supplied by *Time* correspondents around the world. It was a few weeks later, though, when the commission issued its report, that *Time*'s D-Day level maneuvers began. A writer was appointed. Two reporter-researchers were assigned. "Queries" were sent to foreign correspondents (on a form called an "Editorial Query Sheet"). The Jerusalem correspondent supplied information to the Jerusalem bureau chief, who incorporated it in a "file" sent to New York, where some twenty people got copies via something called the "news traffic desk."

The writer digested the "files," and the "World Wide Memo," and the products of the researcher-reporters, and produced a story, which went to the senior editor, and thence to the managing editor ("You're getting closer to the final version," explained the World Section Chief of Reporters and Researchers in a deposition, "but by no means are you there yet"), and thence back to the researcher-reporters for "fact checking" and back to the correspondents and bureau chiefs for review, known as the "Playback," and ultimately into a computer-printout version called "the Yellow" (not to be confused with the "World Wide Memo," which is "kind of an ugly orange-yellow") and very ultimately into *Time* magazine as we know it.

This elephantine procedure is supposed to provide depth and accuracy. In practice, it seems to function more like that party game of "rumors," where "Uncle John has a limp, pass it on," becomes "Uncle John is a pimp, pass it on." Who knows what the Jerusalem correspondent's "highly reliable source" actually told him. What he

---

* Lawyers ultimately got access to the secret appendix, and, sure enough, there was nothing in it about Sharon meeting the Gemayels.

wrote in the "World Wide Memo" was that at Sharon's meeting with the Gemayels, Sharon "gave them the feeling . . . that he understood their need to take revenge." This smells strongly of overinterpretation, and the correspondent has since suggested that this "feeling" was communicated nonverbally, which is even fishier. The writer of the story turned this into, "Sharon also reportedly discussed with the Gemayels the need for the Phalangists to take revenge." A Time, Inc., PR man then wrote a press release with the headline, SHARON SAID TO HAVE URGED LEBANESE TO SEND PHALANGISTS INTO CAMPS. Finally, the *New York Times* picked up the release and reported that, according to *Time*, Sharon had met with the Gemayels "and urged them to take revenge."

There is a natural human tendency to stretch the facts a bit. Even journalists are not immune! The facts can survive one stretching, but not several. Furthermore, the ordinary pressures that discourage a journalist from stretching are badly weakened in a system where the journalist's work product is dropped into a meat grinder with everybody else's and turned into unidentifiable bits of a larger corporate sausage. Then, too, the very corporate voice with which *Time* and *Newsweek* speak encourages (shall we say) bold interpretation of events.

But what of *Time*'s elaborate fact-checking system? According to a *Time* official, fact checkers are supposed to "mark each word [of a story] with a dot or a line [to indicate] that they have verified that particular word as being true and accurate." *Each word! Time*'s guide for researchers says that there should be one other source besides a correspondent's file before a fact is considered verified. So how did the apparent error about Sharon sneak through? Well, it seems there is an exception. If the correspondent reports something that can't be independently confirmed, the checker is supposed to trust the correspondent's judgment.

This rather large loophole has been cause for some mockery. It seems to me, though, that the basic standard is what is ridiculous. If everything a *Time* journalist sends in must be independently verified, *Time*'s own correspondents are barely more than checkers for what has appeared in the *New York Times*.

Twenty years ago Otto Friedrich (now, as it happens, a senior writer at *Time*) published a wonderful essay about the role of facts in newsmagazines called, "There are oo Trees in Russia." The title referred

to the newsmagazine practice of writing a story with ostensibly significant facts missing, then getting the researchers to fill in the blanks.
Friedrich's point was: How significant can a fact be if the writer doesn't
even know what it is? Friedrich said that having lots of "facts" actually
serves two purposes for newsmagazines: first, to give the impression
"that knowledge of lesser facts implies knowledge of major facts"; and
second, "to dramatize the basic thesis" of the story.

The Sharon story is a perfect case in point. The "fact" in dispute
hardly matters. Even if Sharon did "discuss the need for revenge" with
the Gemayels, this hardly proves he authorized the slaughter of
hundreds of innocent noncombatants. Yet even if that particular
discussion never took place, Sharon worked intimately with the Phalangists, knew exactly what they were capable of, and invited them into
the camps anyway. The *published* part of the Kahan Report said,
"From the Defense Minister [Sharon] himself we know that this
consideration [the risk of atrocities] did not concern him in the least."

But mere monstrous negligence was not dramatic enough for
Time. They wanted a smoking gun and chose to imply they had it by
embroidering the report of an inconsequential meeting. As a result,
one of the world's most odious characters has been given the
opportunity for a propaganda vindication and political resurrection.
As another result, other bullies will be encouraged to bring libel suits
against publications less well-padded than *Time*.

Yes, We Have No Bananas

THE NEW REPUBLIC, November 24, 1979

A few relatives may have noticed the absence of my
name from this journal's masthead for a couple of weeks recently,
but probably only I noticed the decline in editorial quality: unin-
tended rhymes in the book reviews; misspellings of words like

"antideluvian"; subtle anti-Zionism of the sort that can creep into even the most seemingly unrelated article without constant editorial vigilance. My departure was caused by one of those disputes people assure me are endemic to small magazines: my employer killed an article I felt very strongly attached to. This action, which he saw as an assertion of principle, I saw as a bad case of the stuffies. So I quit, which I saw as an assertion of principle and most people around me saw as a misunderstanding about the nature of capitalism. Upon reflection, I have come around to their point of view, and it does feel good—deflating, but remunerative.

The article in question, by Suzannah Lessard, will appear in the December issue of the *Washington Monthly**. Interested readers can study it there and can decide for themselves whether it violates responsible standards of taste or ethics. Thrill seekers will be disappointed. It is my experience that readers like to express their strong feelings about the content of magazines by canceling their subscriptions. Some do so several times a year. We editors are resigned to such childish gestures. Correspondents to this journal merely are asked, in fairness, to indicate whether they are upset because the article was censored or because the perpetrator was reemployed.

I would have liked to resign over the cancellation of an article urging compassion for the boat people, but such was not my good fortune. Instead, the dispute arose over a less ennobling subject. The article was a feminist argument that a certain matter should be of serious political concern to women. The particular example was the presidential candidacy of Senator Kennedy. The editor-in-chief and publisher of this journal, as I understand his position, did not necessarily disagree with the author's argument. The problem arose from her forthright definition of the matter she was concerned about. It is difficult to discuss the issues raised in our little dispute (as the editor-in-chief says I may) without committing the same transgression. Alfred Kahn, President Carter's court jester for inflation, faced a similar dilemma last winter when he was reprimanded for publicly using the word "recession." He solved the problem by substituting the word "banana."

---

* "Kennedy's Woman Problem, Women's Kennedy Problem," *Washington Monthly* (December 1979).

The editor-in-chief's scruples about discussing the bananas of public figures are widely shared in the world of journalism, but the convention is a complex one. It is permissible, for example, to write (as the New York Times did the day Kennedy announced for President): "The scene, as played out today, will not dispel all the gossip and speculation about the Senator's private life." Responsible journals of opinion may comment: "Finally, among those who are dissatisfied with Kennedy's past record are some feminist leaders, whose unhappiness arises not from Kennedy's position on the issues, but from uneasiness about his personal life." (The New Republic, November 10). "Personal life"? "Private life"? I suspect these writers are not talking about the time Kennedy spends with his wife, his children, or his widowed mother. What could they be referring to if not to banana? The reference is permissible, though, because it is encoded; and because it refers only to "gossip and speculation about" and "uneasiness about" rather than to the banana itself, thereby avoiding any direct suggestion that the writer believes the banana exists.

A second important subtlety in the banana convention is that what is impermissible in an article about the banana itself may be perfectly acceptable in an article about the controversy around the banana. The New Republic has performed a great service to other publications in this regard by creating such a controversy and thus liberating them to report and comment on banana-related matters. The Washington Post, for example, was offered the original article about Kennedy's banana after The New Republic turned it down. But the Post also declined to publish the article, on the grounds that its serious political arguments were based on assumptions that violate the convention. Nevertheless, the Post was happy to run several paragraphs containing the article's raciest passages (not very racy, I'm afraid) in its gossip column, in a story about the fuss over at The New Republic. (This was followed by an item bringing us up to date on the relationship between Arnold Schwarzenegger, the body-builder, and Maria Shriver, the Kennedy niece. They are "still seeing.")

What purpose does this elaborate convention serve? There are several, I am told. First, it is unfair to publish potentially harmful statements about someone without "proof." This standard, appeal-

ingly enough in the abstract, would be easier to take seriously if the
convention did not contain so many escape clauses. The convention
doesn't really force journalists to prove what they write about a
politician's extracurricular activities; it simply forces them to encode
it (like so). Whatever this may do for the journalist's sense of
propriety, it is hardly fairer to the subject if the "extracurricular
activity," or "private life," or "controversial life style" does not exist.

When the *Post*'s gossip columnist, Maxine Chesire, called me to
confirm her hot tip about wild goings-on at *The New Republic*, I
asked her why the newspapers don't prove or disprove the "gossip and
speculation" about Senator Kennedy once and for all. She said: "It's
easier to prove Watergate than the fact that two people are [you know
what]. Two people can check into the Madison [Hotel] every night
of the week, but they may be just plotting the overthrow of the
government." In fact, it is not beyond the investigative talents of a
newspaper like the *Washington Post* to pin down a story like this.
The real problem is that such an effort is thought to be beneath it.
The standard-bearers who insist on "proof" are the same people who
recoil, for other reasons, from rooting out and printing the details
that such proof would consist of.

The oddest thing about this insistence on "proof" is that it comes
from people who have no doubt about the accuracy of the few very
general statements about Kennedy's [   ] contained in the article so
many of them would not publish. Believe me, those of you who live
outside of Washington and Massachusetts, these are not wispy and
elusive rumors we're talking about. The air is thick with anecdotes,
many of them emitted by the same journalists who take offense at the
suggestion that (as Lessard's article put it) the matter is "widely
known." Such people are caught in an epistemological quagmire:
they may believe something to be true from the observations of their
own eyes, or from the repeated accounts of friends and acquaintances; but they refuse to admit that they "know" it until it has
appeared in the *New York Times*. Before the *Times* or some other
official organ has proclaimed its existence, such information, however widespread, remains mere "gossip and speculation." As such, it
may be passed around, but it may not be discussed seriously.

The second pillar of the banana convention is "privacy." People
ought to be able to live their lives without suffering what is called

"the glare of publicity." How to balance the legitimate desire for privacy against competing considerations is a serious question. But a politician's privacy is a very odd fish. No politician that I know of ever has objected to public revelations, however intimate and detailed, about his regular family life. If a man running for office ever declined the campaign services of his wife, if he refused to let photographers near his kids and household pets, if he told reporters that his church volunteer activities were none of their business, I could listen without snickering to pleas that any interest in his relations with other women was an unfair invasion of his privacy. But of course this never happens. Instead, great effort goes into arranging, or even fabricating, elaborate family tableaux for the benefit of the press and the public. The day Senator Kennedy announced his presidential bid produced a classic staging of such a tableau, as only the Kennedys can do it. The day also produced a new wrinkle: Kennedy's press secretary informed reporters that afternoon that the senator had spent the previous night in his wife's apartment. The reporters duly published this information. Nobody asked where he had spent the previous 364 nights: that would be an invasion of privacy.

From the politicians' point of view, then, what the press is protecting by its enormous and uncharacteristic self-restraint on the banana issue is not privacy, but rather . . . hypocrisy? deception? Well, let's just call it a pleasant illusion of regularity that the voters seem attached to. Still, it is not like journalists to be so accommodating where falsehood is involved. There must be something else. I think we can hear the official view making itself heard through my friend Mort Kondracke in last week's *New Republic* "Diarist" column: "This country has rather more urgent things to debate in 1980 than our candidates' marital or extramarital activities." (Beautiful codework in that "marital or," by the way.) To discuss such things is "trivial, gossip-minded, leering, and pandering to a low grade of public taste." Well! Rather! In other words the press, by its restraint, is preserving the integrity of the political process and the dignity of the journalistic profession from "low-grade" attempts to drag both into the slime.

One of the things that attracted me to journalism was its lack of dignity, so it's always alarming to see journalists trying to act dignified. To their credit, the performance is rarely convincing. In this case, the alleged indignity attaches only to sharing banana stories with readers, not to acquiring them and swapping them among colleagues. Nor is it clear to me what's so dignified about participating, or at least acquiescing, in the deception of one's readers.

What looks to Mort like a dignified effort to keep the political debate on a high plane looks to me like a conspiracy between politicians and journalists to deny voters information they may not be sophisticated enough to handle properly. People in Washington may believe that banana, or apple, or papaya, or other personal habits are irrelevant to a politician's qualifications for high office, but this is not why they don't want these matters written about. Their true concern is almost exactly the opposite: that many people outside Washington—enough to make a difference—will think such matters *are* relevant.

Thus I offer a handy guide to those who agonize over the question, Where do you draw the line? You draw the line between information you truly believe average citizens will not find useful in assessing their political leaders and information you're afraid they'll find all too useful. This doesn't mean you have to pursue and pass on, in an undignified fashion, every juicy tidbit about VIPs that readers might find titillating. Not all of us can achieve the Olympian lack of curiosity of an Arthur Schlesinger, Jr., who told the *Washington Post* he truly was not interested whether Eleanor Roosevelt was a lesbian. But reporters have no moral obligation to feed such curiosity. Nor need they report how often a politician cuts his toenails, just because some crackpot somewhere wishes to vote on that basis. But if a reporter suspects that many readers would find some information politically relevant, it's not for him or her to decide that it's none of their business.

It's the hypocrisy that gripes me. If a politician ever truly attempted to keep his private life private, or, alternatively, if he announced to the world that he and his wife had decided the nuclear family is an outmoded social form, I would not be concerned about most of what is generally hidden behind the veil of "privacy." (Of course, this is not to claim I would not be interested.) Suzannah Lessard makes a more sophisticated argument in her article. She argues that certain types of banana-related conduct reflect an attitude toward women in particular and people in general, and a level of maturity and wisdom, that are important—not conclusive, but important—in judging a man's fitness for higher office. In short, she argues that character is important and cannot be judged exclusively from positions on issues. This is not a novel view. An insightful political observer, for example, wrote about Kennedy fourteen months ago:

> Of course, there remains the question: Does he have character? . . . Kennedy's character could affect the course of American history if he became president. Johnson's did. Nixon's did. We survived them both, and maybe Kennedy's flaws, whatever they are, should be discounted against his considerable merits. Fortunately, it's not something we have to decide today. (Morton Kondracke, The New Republic, September 23, 1978)

Now we do have to decide, yet now this same observer maintains that all personal matters are of no concern unless they "involved criminality or reckless conduct, or if they subjected him to blackmail." I don't think Mort, and other intelligent Washington journalists, really believe this. I think it's squeamishness at best, and an odd mixture of servility (toward politicians) and arrogance (toward readers) at worst.

Cancel my subscription.

Cockburn the Barbarian

THE WASHINGTON MONTHLY, April 1984

The *schadenfreude* flowed like champagne the day Alexander Cockburn got caught with his hand in the cookie jar. Cockburn (rhymes with "slow burn"), best known for his columns of press criticism and political commentary in New York's *Village*

Voice, was described accurately enough by David Denby in *The New Republic* as "a talented, despicable writer who enjoys vicious teasing as a kind of journalistic blood sport." (Even more accurately, Denby called Cockburn "irresistibly readable.") Cockburn is a hard leftist, even something of a Soviet apologist, and virulently anti-Israel.

Cockburn's views and his acid wit assured him lots of enemies, all of whom were thrilled when the *Boston Phoenix* revealed that he had received a $10,000 grant from something called the Institute of Arab Studies. The grant was to write a book about the Israeli invasion of Lebanon, which he never wrote. He also never told his editor or his readers about the grant. Shortly after this revelation, Cockburn was "suspended indefinitely" by the *Voice*, and will have to fulminate for at least a while in the smaller, less remunerative, and marginally less fashionable *Nation* magazine.

I, too, was happy to see Cockburn embroiled in controversy, though for a different reason. In 1982, when I was editor of *Harper's* magazine, I accepted an invitation from the Israeli government to visit Israel and Lebanon at its expense. Right or wrong, this is an extremely common practice. Our own government, through the USIA, brings over about 150 foreign journalists a year. American journalists from publications as respectable or otherwise as *Foreign Affairs* and the *Manchester Union-Leader* have gone on such government-sponsored trips before and since. But for reasons having to do with the internal politics of *Harper's*, this particular trip became a minor *cause célèbre*, and since then I have become a standard reference point in many discussions of journalists' ethics. I had begun to imagine that someday they'd find out that James Reston had been a paid Soviet agent for the past fifty years and the story would include a sentence to the effect, "This reminded many observers of the time Kinsley let the Israelis fly him to the Middle East." Now I'm off the hook. From now on, it will remind many observers of Alex Cockburn's grant from the Arabs.

Sometimes it's hard to know where ethics stops and insanity begins. Last fall, when the *Washington Monthly* held a conference on neoliberalism, the *Washington Post* refused to cover it. Why? Because the impresario, Charles Peters, had decided that journalists should pay the fee and help cover the cost of the conference like everyone else. Several editors at the *Post* grandly declared that this would be purchasing a news story, and thus unethical. So by the very highest ethical standards, you're damned if you pay and damned if you don't pay. Clearly the subject needs some rethinking.

Cockburn's crime, according to the editor of the *Voice*, David Schneiderman, was, first, "to receive money from a group with a special political interest," and second, "not to disclose it." This actually leaves out the fishiest part of the Cockburn story, which is that, a year and half after the grant, he had not yet begun the book that the $10,000 supposedly was meant to finance. Was the money just a payoff? Cockburn insists he honestly intended to produce the book, but never got around to it. Having done editorial business with Cockburn, I find this plausible. (Less plausible is his claim that he was just about to give the money back when the story broke.) But ripping off research grants is a different ethical question. For purposes of this discussion, we'll assume that the transaction was made in good faith all around.

But shouldn't Cockburn have told his readers about the grant? Simple answer: yes. Disclosure is important, because it helps the reader to assess what he or she is reading. Anyone who goes on a propaganda junket like mine to Israel should reveal the nature of the trip when writing about it. Cockburn's nonexistent book certainly should have indicated who paid for the research. He says it would have. But Cockburn could have taken an opportunity to mention the grant in one of his weekly columns, too.

Of course, there are limits. If some tortured souls of journalism had their way, newspaper and magazine articles could come to resemble a stock prospectus, in which half the space is taken up with warnings about why you shouldn't make this investment.

But disclosed or not, was it wrong for Cockburn to take the grant? The pristine view on this matter was nicely summarized by the chairman of *Harper's* at the time of my own troubles. "There are two rules that apply to *Harper's*," I was surprised to read in the *Washington Post* one morning. "First, *Harper's* does not solicit or accept money from people whom it plans to write about. And second, *Harper's* does not write about people whom it has accepted money from."

This formulation strikes a note of ringing clarity. It charmingly suggests that anyone who violates it has, in effect, taken a bribe. It also is absurd. *Harper's*, for example, had received $1.5 million grant from the ARCO corporation. Should it therefore have been foreclosed from writing about energy? All publications energetically solicit advertising. Should they stop? Or should they cease writing about anything related to their advertisers? This kind of ethical standard could turn into a nice protection racket: selling ads to organizations that wish to guarantee they won't be written about.

Obviously advertising does hold a potential for corruption. Most publications think they can rise above it. (One saving grace is that the ad itself constitutes disclosure of the potential conflict.) Ironically, though, it is the richest, most ad-clogged publications that can afford to take the prissiest attitude about the financial arrangements of their writers. On a NATO-sponsored junket to Europe for American editorial writers a while back, it was the *Los Angeles Times* that insisted on paying its employee's expenses. (Of course, he got precisely the same one-sided propaganda show as the leeches from poorer publications.) Such high-mindedness is financed by a daily flood of ad revenues that must touch in some way on every conceivable story the newspaper might write about. The *Los Angeles Times* trusts itself not to be corrupted by millions of dollars from tobacco companies, but doesn't trust its employees not to be corrupted by a plane ride from NATO.

And this brings up the silliest aspect of the anguished moral debate about things like press junkets and who picks up the tab when you lunch with a source. The insistence that journalists should "pay their own way" ignores an important financial reality: professional journalists rarely pay their own way. The company pays. As a rule, the sterner a journalist's moral outrage at the thought of accepting a freebie, the longer it's likely to have been since the last time he actually paid for his own lunch. It's not a very impressive display of personal integrity to decline as a gift something you're going to get for free, anyway.

Now $10,000 in cash is a touchier business. But even with cash the purist view is nonsense. *Foreign Affairs*, for example, could hardly forbid its authors to accept cash from the nations they write about, since it routinely publishes articles by heads of state. A *Washington Monthly* specialty is articles by present and former employees about their experiences working for government agencies. The purist view would exclude them, too, though the point of the *Washington Monthly* article most likely would be to criticize the very source of their paycheck. The question is, what was the quid pro quo? A Prime Minister's salary is not suspicious. A large grant to a professional journalist can be.

In this case, though, it's hard to work up much suspicion. Alexander Cockburn is not a head of state, but he might as well be the Sultan of Oman for all the doubt there is about where his head is at on the Middle East. Some writers are interesting precisely because of their prejudices. Any would-be corrupter of journalistic morals who spends $10,000 trying to bias Alexander Cockburn against Israel ought to be drummed out of the profession for rank incompetence. Why buy a cow when the milk is free?

Nevertheless, even if the purist approach is absurd, shouldn't there be some rules? Of course. But many of the distinctions that are made are quite silly. Cockburn himself, for example, thinks it makes a difference if the money comes from a government. He wrote in the *Voice*, "I sought and was given assurances that the Institute [for Arab Studies] was not financed by nations or organizations, but by individuals both within and without the United States." So what? I doubt Cockburn would find that much of a defense if he uncovered a network to bribe journalists financed by wealthy American Jews.

Cockburn's critics, on the other hand, think there's a difference between a grant from the provocatively named "Institute for Arab Studies," with its ill-concealed didactic agenda, and a grant from the Guggenheim Foundation or the Council on Foreign Relations. No one objects to journalists sucking on respectable tits like these. Yet surely it would be far more corrupting for a man with Cockburn's views to be taking money from one of these groups. The *Boston Phoenix* accused Cockburn of retrospective hypocrisy for a column criticizing the Pacifica radio network, a string of counterculture noncommercial stations, for pondering whether to take grants from corporations. Cockburn's point, though, was that such grants would create pressure for the stations to trim their sails and turn respectable. And surely the rewards of respectability, such as Guggenheim grants, comprise a much more dangerous temptation to American journalism than favors bestowed by shoestring groups like the Institute for Arab Studies.

The most ridiculous web of pointless distinctions I've come across in this field has been woven by the *Nation*, whose editor expressed disapproval of my junket, then hired Cockburn on rebound from the *Voice*. The *Nation* publishes freelance articles from a wide variety of interested parties, but ostensibly maintains strict curbs on staff freebies. A staff writer named Christopher Hitchens was offered a junket to Israel by an Arab-American group. On orders from the editor, he quit the staff, took the junket, rejoined the staff, and wrote the article. According to the latest formulation of its policy in a recent editorial, the *Nation* "prohibits editorial workers from accepting travel or other expenses from any source in return for a commitment to write an article for the magazine." This sonorous language promises more than it delivers. Read literally, it means you can take any freebie and write anything about it as long as you don't *promise* to write something. "We are constantly refining our guidelines on a case-by-case basis," the editorial reassures. You'll not be surprised to learn that the editor of the *Nation* is a lawyer.

Not all distinctions are ridiculous. It's reasonable, for example, to hold newspaper reporters to a more fastidious standard than writers who are presenting opinion labeled as such. It's not that reporters can actually achieve the pristine blankness of mind—called "objectivity"—that is the conceit of their calling. Rather, it's that reporters must obscure their biases, whereas opinion writers are paid to display them for public assessment.

A few rules about journalists' dealings with the outside world are perfectly reasonable. But the simple-minded obsession with airplane tickets and research grants is a grand exercise in missing the point.

The trump card of the stuffed-shirt element in discussions like this one is the proposition that journalists must avoid what is usually called *even the appearance of bias*. That is, he or she should avoid anything that might give rise to suspicion, however illogical or unwarranted. After some confusion about what his objection really was, *Village Voice* editor David Schneiderman ultimately settled on the appearance factor as his reason for suspending Cockburn.

However, what piddling rules and pompous ethical pronouncements prevent is not *even* the appearance of bias. It's *only* the appearance of bias. Take once again my visit to Israel and Lebanon at the height of the Israeli invasion. The truth is, it was very hard for me to perceive the situation there objectively. It would have been even harder to come back and write a vigorous denunciation of Israel, if that were my conclusion. Why? Any number of reasons. Like everybody else on the trip, including those whose companies paid their expenses, I was getting a more or less one-sided view of the story. Furthermore, I am Jewish, and a sentimental Zionist. My close friend (once and future boss) Martin Peretz, editor-in-chief of *The New Republic*, is one of the leading American defenders of Israel. Inevitably in the back of my mind as I wrote an article would have been the thought, "How will I face Marty?" Maybe I could rise above all these factors, maybe not. But of all the things that made it difficult for me to be clear-minded about the war in Lebanon, who was paying for my airline ticket loomed very small.

Likewise when Alexander Cockburn writes about the Middle East or any other subject. No doubt he brings a great deal of intelligence to bear. But he also brings personal baggage, and he operates in a milieu where anti-Zionist sentiment is the fashion. The Middle East is a particularly contentious issue, but any writer on any subject carries a similar burden.

Cockburn thinks the very notion of objectivity is a farce. In his farewell column in the *Village Voice*, he wrote that the *Voice* "is, and should be, a bundle of opinion and prejudice advertised as such. The *New York Times* is a bundle of opinion and prejudice masquerading as 'objective fact.' " This is silly. Even Alexander Cockburn wouldn't want to get all his information from a paper like the *Village Voice*. The *Times* aspires to a more neutral approach, and usually succeeds, though it's useful to have someone like Cockburn around to point out when it fails.

True, the cult of objectivity often produces conventional wisdom labeled as neutral reporting and obfuscation in the name of balance. That's why there's also room for opinion journalism of the sort you find in the *Voice* or the *Washington Monthly*. Cockburn's even right that most opinion journalism is too sodden with respectability to counteract the "objective" mush all around. But even opinion journalism can aspire to intellectual honesty rather than sinking complacently into a mudbath of "prejudice."

The heaviest baggage a writer carries to the word processor is his or her previous opinions, especially if they've been expressed in print. More than any financial arrangement, this is what prevents the journalist from seeing the subject fresh and discussing it with an open mind. Cockburn, for example, has been thinking nasty thoughts about Israel, and writing them down, for half his life. Even if those opinions derived long ago from the most disinterested weighing of the facts and the purest cogitation, they're now his. He's stuck with them, and whatever may happen in the Middle East, it's hard to imagine any mere new fact coming along to change them, even if it came wrapped in $10,000 from the Israelis.

Changing your mind is a tough mental exercise. Are we all up to it every time we sit down to write? As corrupters of clear thought and roadblocks to objectivity, the matters that ethics obsessives go on about seem petty in comparison.

What the Helga??

THE NEW REPUBLIC, *September 1, 1986*

W ould-be news managers in Washington should sit at the feet of Mrs. Betsy Wyeth and my friend Jeffrey Schaire, editor of *Art & Antiques* magazine, the two impresarios of the story of Andrew Wyeth's secret paintings. Rarely have so few caused so many to make so much fuss about so little. The lesson is that while it may be hard to con the media for very long, it's not so hard to trap them in a shared conspiracy of hype. Call it journalistic stone soup: a delicious news event concocted from nothing.

The story, as originally presented, had three elements. First, a secret cache of paintings and drawings by a leading painter, hidden even from his wife, and revealed only when he thought he was dying. Second, the subject of the pictures: a mystery woman named Helga, whose identity is also a deep secret. Third, the question of

Wyeth's relationship with the mystery woman. Every initial news story quoted Mrs. Wyeth's dramatic one-word explanation of her husband's motive in this project: "love."

Even taken at face value, it's hard to see that this is a major news story, if you accept the premise that news is something not already known and in some way surprising. A large addition to the Wyeth oeuvre may be important to the art world. But front pages across the country? Features on the evening TV news? The covers of both *Time* and *Newsweek?* Come on. It is not unusual for a living artist, especially a wealthy one, to have stacks of paintings he hasn't put on the market. Wyeth was well known, among people who cared before last week, for producing a lot but selling very little. Nor is it especially amazing for an artist to protect the identity of someone who modeled for him nude. As for the sex angle, well, "Artist Sleeps with Model" is surely a "Dog Bites Man" story if ever there was one.

But it's August, after all. The first wave of publicity is understandable. The real journalistic comedy began after the initial "revelation." Over the next week, you could watch the story building and unraveling at the same time. This process culminated with the two newsmagazine cover articles, which heralded Wyeth's "Stunning Secret" (*Time*) and "Secret Obsession" (*Newsweek*, the winner), even as they reported information that undermined the whole premise.

How secret were these pictures of Helga? Not very. One of them was reproduced a year ago in *Art & Antiques*, the magazine that now celebrates their existence as a scoop. Several others have been on display for years in the museum at Chadds Ford, Pennsylvania, Wyeth's hometown. Another was reproduced on a French poster several years ago, and yet another was published in an art magazine in 1979. Mrs. Wyeth, who is her husband's business manager (and a helluva good one), has actually sold three of the Helga portraits over the years.

It turns out that it was Mrs. Wyeth who gave the provocative name, "Lovers," to the painting that has stirred the most interest ("a striking blond nude . . . glancing across the room toward an unseen object or person, in apparent expectation," according to an excitable *New York Times* reporter). Far from hiding this picture from his wife, Andrew Wyeth gave it to her four years ago. Regarding the size of the cache, *Art & Antiques* itself quoted Wyeth a year ago saying,

"There's a whole vast amount of my work no one knows about."
Even the multimillion-dollar sale of these paintings was reported in
full, without fanfare, in the local *Delaware County Daily Times* last
April. The Wyeths now deny that the announcement and sale had
anything to do with thoughts of dying.

And the mystery woman? A hilarious second-day story in the
Times portrayed a Twilight Zone atmosphere in Chadds Ford, with
all the locals intent—"fiercely," of course— on protecting the town's
dark secret from the inquiring outsider. "Down the street at the
Sunoco station . . . the reply was terse: 'No, I'm sorry, I can't help
you.' " Art-world promoter Thomas Hoving piped up in this
dispatch to say that Helga had "gone back to Germany." (Hoving was
playing catch-up ball. His own magazine, *Connoisseur*, reports the
Wyeth cache in its current issue, just like *Art & Antiques*, but no
one is paying any attention.)

Unfortunately, the mystery quickly dissolved. Within a day, more
voluble, or possibly better informed, sources than the Sunoco station
attendant identified the model as one Helga Testorf. She has not fled
to Germany. According to *Time*, she "lives with her husband in a
secluded home across town from the Wyeths." That adjective
"secluded" is a desperate touch, since it develops that Mrs. Testorf
has worked all along as a cook and cleaning lady for Andrew Wyeth's
sister, Carolyn. Betsy Wyeth insisted to *Time* that she never saw
Helga because she "never visits her sister-in-law." It's possible, I
suppose. On the other hand, *TNR* contributing artist Vint Lawrence
recalls attending a dinner in Wyeth's honor some years ago at the
Chadds Ford museum, where several Helga paintings were on
display and Helga herself was in attendance.

Which brings us to "love." After six days of publicity, Mrs. Wyeth
granted a telephone interview to the *Times* (published under the
wonderful headline "Betsy Wyeth Talks of Helga, Art and the
Meaning of 'Love' "), in which she explained that the love in
question was "the love for hills, the love for breathing, the love for
storms and snows." The obviously disappointed reporter got her to
"acknowledg[e] the possibility of sexual feelings in the model-artist
relationship," adding with hopeful caution that she "said she
believed such feelings were never consummated."

Meanwhile, though, Andrew Wyeth told another local paper that he has a deep love for anything he paints, whether it be "a tree, a model, a house or a hill," and, "No, that doesn't mean sexual, of course." Oh, well. Artist Doesn't Sleep with Model. Man Bites Dog?

But by now, for the press, there was no turning back. *Time*, thrashing wildly and sinking fast, decided on a strategic sacrifice of the "love" angle in order to build up the "fiercely protective neighbors" motif. One neighbor is quoted as saying, "This whole thing could be a ploy." That's "fiercely protective"? Sure. Explains *Time*: "So protective are they [the neighbors] of any charge of infidelity that they are willing to entertain . . . the possibility of a Wyeth scam."

Possibility, did you say?

Worthwhile Canadian Initiative

THE NEW REPUBLIC, *June 2, 1986*

Readers of TNR have responded generously to our request for examples of boring headlines. The entire staff is comatose with appreciation. In the late 1920s the British writer Claud Cockburn* won a contest among editors of the *Times* of London to see who could get the most boring headline into the paper. Cockburn's entry, which has become a legend in British journalism, was: "Small Earthquake in Chile/Not Many Dead." This is pathetic, another example of Britain's long decline as a civilization. In just the past month or so, without even trying, our American headline writers have produced any number of headlines far more boring than this ostensible classic.

*Father of the subject of "Cockburn the Barbarian," page 114.

The occasion for *TNR's* survey was an April 10 headline over Flora Lewis's column on the *New York Times* op-ed page: "Worthwhile Canadian Initiative." We posed the question whether this might actually be "the most boring headline ever written." *Le tout* Canada soon erupted in outrage at the suggestion that there is something intrinsically boring about matters Canadian. The *Toronto Star* treated the libel as front-page news, which some might say proves the point. Dear Canada: there are worse national images to have than that of being thought boring. Look at Libya.

But references to Canada are not essential to a boring headline. Merely helpful. Almost as boring as "Worthwhile Canadian Initiative" was the headline on a column by *Times* economic correspondent Leonard Silk: "U.S. Leadership Needed." (There, now, Canada. Feel better?) The editors at the *Times* op-ed page, in fact, are geniuses at coming up with headlines that refer to virtually nothing. I was impressed by "Trade, a Two-Way Street" (April 26, over an essay by Governor Richard Celeste of Ohio), and positively bowled over by "Beyond the News, Larger Issues" (subhead on a James Reston column, May 4). "Thoughts at Graduation Time" (subhead for some Robert Coles ruminations, May 11) wasn't bad, either.

When *Times* headline writers do get excited, they start issuing orders. "End Textile Quotas," they might command, or (May 10) "Continue Manned Flight in Space." Who, me? Well, okay, I'll get right to it. But what on earth were we readers supposed to do April 21, when the headline over a *Times* editorial demanded: "Make Foreign Flights More Familiar"? I read the editorial, and I still don't know.

My favorite genre of boring headline is the one gravely informing you that a development you weren't aware of and don't care about has reversed itself, ideally in some distant part of the globe. "Nepal Premier Won't Resign" is a golden-oldie example, but there was a masterpiece in the *Times* as recently as April 26: "Chill Falls on Warming Relations Between Australia and Indonesia." Closer to home but almost as choice was "University of Rochester Decides To Keep Name" (*Times*, April 18). A close cousin of the reversed-insignificant-development headline is the nothing-happened-at-all headline. An outstanding recent example in that category was "Dramatic Changes Fail To Materialize on Hill" (*Washington Post*, April 23). Then there's the nothing-is-going-to-happen headline.

The judges found "Surprises Unlikely in Indiana" (*Chicago Tribune,* April 29) almost poignant.

Of course the largest category of boring headline falls under the general rubric of dog-bites-man. In the subcategory of stating-the-obvious, it would be difficult to top "CIA Analysis Sees Soviet Economy in Need of Changes" (*San Diego Union,* May 31, 1983). But "Prevent Burglary by Locking House, Detectives Urge" (*Boston Globe,* April 21) is pretty good, and I like the wacky specificity of "Methodists Oppose Use of Nuclear Arms" (*Times,* April 30). And maybe an honorable mention in this category should go to "Sorry, the Deficit Is a Big Problem" (over a recent column by—whoops—me).

April and May brought a magnificent spring flowering of hardy perennials. These are headlines that reappear regularly. Generally it is the news itself, rather than the headliner's art, that deserves the credit here. The events these headlines chronicle can be subdivided wearily into things that always happen ("B-1B Bomber Cost Expected to Rise," *Times,* May 4) and things that never happen ("Newark Hopes for Rebound," *Times* [front page!], May 5). Other recent hardy-perennial blossoms: "Teamster Chief May Face Renewed Federal Charges" (*Post,* April 24); "Bush Seeks New Hampshire Support" (*Times,* April 18); and "E. Germans Open Party Congress" (*Post,* April 18).

A reader in Milwaukee rather viciously sent in "Economist Dies," from the *Wisconsin State Journal,* April 20. Every day, it seems, the economics profession develops new evidence to support Lord Keynes's famous proposition that "in the long run, we are all dead."

For its brilliant counterpoint of overexcited adjective with mundane and obscure subject matter, I was tempted to award first prize in this competition (one copy of *A Time to Heal* by Gerald Ford) to the lead headline on the "Washington Talk" page of the *Times,* May 13: "Turbulent Days for Donald D. Engen." That middle initial is an especially bravura touch, I think. It fills the reader with an urgent desire not to know who Donald Engen is and with disbelief that his days could be all that turbulent.* But in the end, the judges chose

*He's the head of the Federal Aviation Administration.

a months-old subhead from the *Times* science section: "Debate Goes on Over the Nature of Reality." Further examples are welcome, but somehow, I don't think that one will ever be topped.

How Many Thoughtful Observers Does It Take to Answer a Vital Question?

THE NEW REPUBLIC, *February 3, 1986*

Nineteen eighty-five was a busy year, as always, for thoughtful observers. Their opinion was sought on issues ranging from whether "Mr. Reagan used his first term to start a process of change" (*New York Times*) to "the limits inherent in even the most precise expressions of unaided human reason" (*Christian Science Monitor*).

I get this information, not from the National League of Thoughtful Observers, but from Nexis, the computerized data base maintained by Mead Data Central of Dayton, Ohio. Nexis files away the words published in the *Times*, the *Monitor*, the *Washington Post*, *Time*, *Newsweek*, and so on, along with such exotica as the BBC Summary of World Broadcasts. For a fee, you can look up any word or group of words and see how they were used. Thoughtful observers have piped up (and I see them with pipes—don't you?) sixty-seven times since Nexis got started in 1977.

Not surprisingly, the publication with the best contacts among thoughtful observers is the *Times*, which has surveyed them on nineteen different subjects. The *Monitor* is a distant second with twelve citations. More surprising, and disappointing, is that thoughtful observers spend as much of their time as everyone else chattering about professional sports. True, they're concerned about "the alienation and withdrawal of young people" in Namibia. But more often, they're pondering whom the Dallas Cowboys will draft or the commercialization of tennis or "whether the forces of destruction in baseball can be dispelled."

Thoughtful observers are a dyspeptic lot. They're always rejecting "simplistic arguments," demanding "careful thinking on the part of policy makers," declaring "it is time for a reassessment," and warning of "a major shakeout" or even "a vast, but still avoidable, tragedy" if "the numerous negative strands in the present situation continue to concatenate." And wouldn't you know that, "Some thoughtful observers believe we have reached the stage where we must accept the harsh truth"—I forget about what.

In Zimbabwe (though it could be anywhere), thoughtful observers see "the danger that everything . . . could quickly unravel." When joy is in the air, "thoughtful observers can't help but think that disenchantment will naturally follow." Only when ordinary mortals are gloomy and pessimistic do "more thoughtful observers" become "delighted."

If there's anything that animates a thoughtful observer, it's a vital question. In 1985 alone, there were fifty-five vital questions, according to Nexis. Most of them, I'm sorry to report, were raised by foreigners. Communists seem to have a special enthusiasm for vital questions.

A Hungarian official quoted by the BBC in April declared that the fate of socialism and the future of mankind "are still vital questions," even though they are "questions which Lenin addressed himself to and solved." In an article entitled, "What Should Literary Heroes Be Like?" a Soviet literary critic announced his preference for "reflective heroes" over "stereotyped ideal heroes" because the former are "searching for the answer to vital questions."

In America, we have only Bill Moyers, who (says a reviewer) "doesn't hesitate to deal with all of the vital questions which arise." But can Moyers carry the ball alone? Americans not only raise fewer vital questions; they also apply the label recklessly to questions of dubious vitality. To East German boss Erich Honecker, a vital question is the future of mankind. To the *Financial Times* of London, a vital question is "the role of the family in Swedish society." To *MacLean's* magazine of Canada, it's the cause of earthquakes. To the *New York Times*, "Whether 26 cards fit well together is a vital question in [bridge] bidding strategy." And to the

Washington Post, "Elvis switching to electric guitar [is] a vital question at this juncture in Presley's career."

If there is a shortage of high-quality vital questions, there is a virtual famine of easy answers. "The people are looking for an easy answer," declared Bernhard Goetz (one of "the twenty-five most intriguing people of 1985") in *People* magazine December 30. Yet on no fewer than eighty-eight subjects in 1985, according to Nexis, there were "no easy answers" at all.

The *Washington Post* won the bewilderment stakes with no easy answers to a whopping twenty-three questions, thus trouncing the *New York Times* at fifteen and the *Christian Science Monitor* at thirteen. Among the highlights, there were no easy answers regarding: "the best way to link computers," the "Afghanistan Question," how to kick a football into a headwind, the proper way to sing "bel canto," peace in the Middle East, "how to pick a long-distance phone service," how astronauts go to the bathroom (honest—"no easy answer," *Washington Post*, June 12), "where, and under what circumstances, American power should be employed," the use of sulfites in salad bars, "the contradictions and paradoxes of Judaism," "Western Europe: Center or Periphery," and, of course, abortion.

An economist wrote in *American Banker* that President Reagan "faces a five-part economic policy dilemma." Not only are there "no easy answers," but "inflationary monetary policy . . . is not one of them." The same *New York Times* bridge columnist who thought that bidding strategy raised vital questions tortured himself further by noting, "If one had to select the best card-player of all time, there would be no easy answer."

Even more disturbing, perhaps, than the lack of easy answers is the volume of things that remain to be seen. Over 2,500 of them, in fact, since Nexis began, and 1,223 in 1985 alone.

This is an ominous trend. Even the most thoughtful observer can't see as many things in the course of the day as are being added to the list of things that remain to be seen. On the other hand, in the first ten days of 1986, only fourteen new items remained to be seen. These include the future of communism (*Christian Science Monitor*), whether Mayor Harold Washington of Chicago will eat some cheese steaks given to him by Mayor Ed Koch of New York (*New York Times*), whether Star Wars will work, whether new rules

will benefit the cosmetics industry, whether machines can be taught
to think, and "how those in power [in Nigeria] will conduct
themselves" (BBC). No one can gainsay that these are vital questions.
But so far they're piling up at a nonseasonally adjusted annual rate
of only 511—less than half of last year's torrid pace.

Is this the beginning of a turnaround? Well, there are . . . no, I
just can't say it. Let's just say that only time will tell.

Reston for President

THE NEW REPUBLIC, November 15, 1980

Occasionally I've thought about trying to write a
Washington novel featuring a distinguished columnist who produces
all his columns long before the events they purport to analyze, but
who operates at such a lofty level of generality that nobody ever
notices. Naturally, such a person is completely a creation of my own
and bears no relation to etc., etc., living or dead. So I was indignant
to find James Reston, the distinguished columnist for the *New York
Times*, of all people, living or dead, putting my idea into practice.

Reston's technique can be observed by comparing his column in
the city edition of the November 5 *Times* with the same column in
the late city edition. The early edition quite evidently was written
without the benefit of any election results, the later one after
Reagan's landslide was known. Comparing the differences is amusing
enough, but what's really impressive is how little Reston had to
change. The first version is called, daringly, "The Morning After,"
and begins as follows:

WASHINGTON, Nov. 4—*After the celebrations come the
hangovers. It would be pleasant to think that everybody would*

now close ranks and get on with the nation's business. The sad thing about this election, however, is that it has not clarified the nation's problems but deepened them; not unified the people but divided them.

At the Presidential level, it was too personal and negative. Despite the long months of fierce campaigning, it has not produced any general agreement about the policies that should guide the American people through the early 1980s.

Instead, it has left the winners with no clear mandate, and the losers without much public regret. And it has left our allies and adversaries with profound doubts about the future of American leadership.

The revised version is called "Reagan's Startling Victory," and a few quick brush strokes are all it takes to suggest that Reston's brooding was precipitated by the news of Reagan's triumph. "After the celebrations over Ronald Reagan's spectacular victory, come the hangovers. It would be pleasant . . ." and so on. The disappointing failure of everyone to agree amiably about everything now comes despite not only "long months of fierce campaigning," but also "Governor Reagan's sweep of the major states." The landslide result might have embarrassed a lesser pundit out of his assertion that the winner has "no clear mandate," but Reston easily fixes this by amending it to read that Reagan "has no clear policy mandate." The loser, now specified as Jimmy Carter, still is reported to be "without much public regret."

The *sans*-information version contains the cunning observation that, "We will in any case now have a one-term president, without fear that he will try for another." In Round II, Reston happily fills in the specifics: "We will have a one-term President, without fear that Reagan, at his age, will try for a second term."* Both the pre-result and post-result versions see the result as mandating "a reappraisal of American political life." Both report "considerable anxiety" about "the loss of national purpose." Reston says impishly in the prefab version, "It will take some time even to think about all this," and he even more impishly retains it in the rewrite.

* Whoops.

The pre-facts version states: "One thing is clear and has been dramatized in the election campaign." In the rewrite, that one thing is only "fairly clear," even though by then it "has been dramatized by the Reagan victory." And what is that one increasingly blurry thing? It is: "None of these problems can be resolved in ideological, personal, or partisan terms." Animal, vegetable, or mineral terms? What terms will Reston accept? The early version is more expansive here, arguing that "the nation is in trouble" and suggesting creatively that "something must be done about it now that the election is over." Reston predicts that "the victory of one man or one party," unspecified, will not solve everything, and recommends instead:

> . . . a philosophy of cooperation rather than confrontation between the contending forces at home and abroad, and a change in the attitudes of the people toward the irresistible transformations brought about by science, machinery and the turbulent shifts of population in the industrial world and the rise in power of the oil-producing nations.

By coming to this incisive cure-all more directly, the Revised Version finds room near the end for the timely observation that, "Obviously there has been a conservative sweep of opinion in the nation." "But it does not follow," Reston warns, that any conservative policy will get through Congress. This oddly specific, and probably wrong, statement is necessary to bring the amended column back to its crowning generality, which is that "the winners" (#1) or "Mr. Reagan and his supporters" (#2) "may well be looking around for some way to bring the White House, the Congress and the other separate principalities of the nation into some kind of an agreement on how to cooperate in the national interest in the coming years."

Who but James Reston could have guessed, before the returns were even in, that the winner might want everyone to help serve the national interest? The man's a genius.

BUSINESS

INTRODUCTION

One of the minor ridiculous figures of the early 1980s was J. Peter Grace, the man with the mission of bringing the efficiency of the business world to government. (Grace's company, W. R. Grace, did its bit for government efficiency by paying no federal taxes for much of this period, while buying TV commercials decrying the federal deficit.) The unifying theme of the following nine pieces, if any, is that there is just as much bullshit in corporate America as there is in Washington. Capitalism is a fine thing: a mighty engine of prosperity, and even freedom. But President Reagan, Peter Grace, and other glorifiers usually fail to distinguish between capitalism itself and business as actually practiced in America, especially at the top.

The further adventures of Mary Cunningham, following her escapades at Bendix described here ("Love in the Boardroom"), illustrate the great American theme of upward failure. Workers' lives can be ruined by executives' ineptitude, but, above a certain level, ineptitude seems to be largely risk free for the executives themselves. Or perhaps what the Cunningham saga illustrates is the great American theme of naked celebrity as a marketable asset. In any event, after leaving Bendix, Cunningham went to work as a highly paid "strategic planner" for Seagram, the liquor company, where she spent two years coming up with a recommendation for a major expansion of Seagram's wine business. In late 1983 Seagram bought the wine subsidiary of Coca-Cola. Cunningham declared this was the culmination of her "plan." In December 1986, Seagram announced it was getting out of the wine business, which had become a terrible drain on its profits.

After my review of Letitia Baldrige's business etiquette book ("The Right Thing") appeared, with its disparaging remarks about her disparaging remarks about ankle socks, she was kind enough to send me a pair of dress knee socks. Needless to say, I wrote a thank you note. Tom Peters was also quite polite, when I met him a few months later, about my criticisms in *Fortune* of his "Excellence" cottage industry ("Excellence by the Hour"). And why not? In Liberace's immortal words, he's crying all the way to the bank.

The national infatuation with business heroes like Lee Iacocca and Peter Ueberroth ("Strongmen") does seem to have faded, as I suggested it might. Ueberroth's book did not sell nearly as well as Iacocca's, and later efforts by Victor Kiam (the "shaves-as-close-as-a-blade" man) and An Wang, among others, were outright failures. Talk of Iacocca or Ueberroth for president has died out as the time comes to get serious and as the Democrats start to climb out of the deep pit of desperation they had dug for themselves.

The decline of Michael Jackson ("The Prisoner of Commerce") has been even more extreme: he's practically disappeared from the screen. I hope he can do something with the shards of his life. In contrast to Jackson, his successor as rock gigastar, Bruce Springsteen, seems to be so normal and mentally healthy that both political parties are fighting to claim his iconography.

At last report, the egregious Dr. Armand Hammer was still alive and traveling. The lust for "executive porn" may have peaked with the Ivan Boesky affair, but it's too soon to tell.

Give me some points, please, for including "The Myth of Books" (arguing that nobody reads them) in this book. I hope we can all agree that for any reviewer to make the obvious rhetorical use of this item would be a cheap shot. And don't go looking in this book for hidden slips of paper offering five dollars to anyone who discovers them, because I'm not that dumb either.

The energy price collapse (discussed in "Let 'Em Rot in the Sun") will be seen, I think, as Ronald Reagan's last lucky break. Yet as I write OPEC is regrouping and the administration is doing nothing about it. There are reports that the White House actually wants OPEC to succeed in raising prices again, to reduce pressure from the oil states for an import tax. An import tax is a bad idea. Nevertheless, it is surely the ultimate insanity of the Reaganites' antitax obsession that they would rather see money go into government treasuries in Riyadh, Tehran, and Tripoli than into the government treasury in Washington.

Love In the Boardroom

FORTUNE, *June 25, 1984*

"What you need now is to be mentored," said William Agee to Mary Cunningham. Then he lifted her gently in his strong, pinstriped arms, carried her to his executive desk, and mentored her till dawn.

No, no, not at all, says Cunningham in *Powerplay: What Really Happened at Bendix.* According to Cunningham, Agee did indeed utter the preposterous phrase, "What you need now is to be mentored." But this was the beginning of a *business* relationship. Only later did it bubble into love in the caldron of shared victimization by journalists and business rivals. Her story, written with Fran Schumer, is as follows:

She was a naive twenty-eight-year-old Catholic girl when she arrived at Bendix in June 1979 fresh from Harvard Business School. "What I knew about the world and people I'd learned from reading Plato and Thomas Aquinas." Her only ambition was to do good. "I viewed myself as a latter-day Joan of Arc." Her saintly impulse had inclined her toward a career in investment banking. But then she met William Agee, the brilliant young chairman of Bendix. Agee enticed her to be his special assistant by appealing to her "missionary zeal." "He needs my help," she realized. After just one interview her stigmata were bleeding: "In the taxi on the way back to my hotel I was already shouldering the burdens of Bendix and getting a headache because of it."

Nevertheless, she wavered. Should it be investment banking after all? Nonsense, Agee said. "Just think of how it'll slow down your learning curve." Cunningham confesses: "That was the real killer. I was a sucker for steep learning curves." Soon they were making beautiful business together. " 'So what's your opinion on this one, Cunningham?' he'd challenge me. 'Oh, I think it's full of prunes, Agee,' I'd say, and we'd both crack up."

Within a year she was promoted to vice president for corporate and public affairs, "the youngest female corporate vice president of a Fortune 500 company in America," as she tells us. She didn't really want the job, but Agee insisted. " 'If I can't appeal to you on the basis that I truly need you here (he knew he always could), let me appeal to you as your mentor,' he said."

But this bliss was short-lived. People began spreading rumors that there was Something Going On between Agee and herself, both then married to others. " 'How dare they,' I said, my voice rising, the anger welling up inside me." (Elsewhere she complains about journalists presenting "my life as soap opera.") She began suffering chest pains. The rumors continued. She told Agee that she couldn't take it anymore and—although "I'm not trying to downgrade the importance of my learning curve"—she wanted to quit. He dissuaded her. In fact, he promoted her to vice president for strategic planning.

Soon afterward their relationship came up at a meeting of Bendix employees, with reporters in attendance. Agee declared that Cunningham was "a very close friend of my family" but that her rapid rise was solely "because she's . . . a very talented individual." Mary burst into tears and was comforted by one of Agee's secretaries (in the Zasu Pitts role): " 'Don't let it get to you. They're just jealous. . . . You're so young. So pretty. So bright. They're just being mean.' I thanked her and eventually ventured out the side door to the waiting limousine." But the rumors turned into newspaper headlines, and after a few more days of agony, on October 8, 1980, the Bendix board gave her $120,000 and forced her to resign. She felt like an aborted fetus. "Their solution: 'Get rid of the problem. Nice and clean.' "

She was desperate: she considered lobotomy, suicide, a visiting professorship at Harvard Business School. According to *Powerplay*, she had no contact with Agee during this period, until they were reconciled several weeks later with the help of a psychiatrist. But phone records obtained by Allan Sloan, author of *Three Plus One Equals Billions*, another Bendix book, show several long calls to Agee's office, home, and New York hotel suite.

As Thanksgiving approached, she felt she couldn't go home (although she had just been there) because "I had put my mother through so much grief, given her such cause for worry, that I couldn't bear the idea of bringing any more of my problems home." By coincidence Agee called soon after she reached this odd decision. Would she please come out to his retreat in Idaho to help nurse him through a case of mononucleosis? Naturally she was concerned about how this would look. But she was even more concerned that "this whole experience was starting to change me from a compassionate human being to a kind of unfeeling pragmatist." So she went to Idaho, where she stayed in Agee's guest room. (Agee told Allan Sloan that she'd stayed with friends.) They had long talks. Agee said he might quit Bendix, but she warned him—this was late November—of "what I'd learned about unemployment since October 8th." (By her own account, she'd spent most of the period at the La Costa resort in California and at the Waldorf in New York sorting through "more than 200 job queries.")

Back in New York she tried dating other men, but "I felt so removed from them all. I was laden with history." One day Agee showed up unexpectedly to help her move to a new apartment. They packed a few boxes, went out to dinner, and then—it's page 216— they kissed for the first time. "How natural and good it felt." Nevertheless, showing more patience than many readers will be able to muster, Agee slept in the den.

In June 1982 Mary Cunningham and William Agee were married in San Francisco. Visiting the church the day before, they discovered that Mother Teresa was about to speak. "I quickly turned to Bill. I couldn't believe she was speaking here exactly twenty-four hours before we were to be married at that very altar. The coincidence was too much. How many times had my life almost taken her path."

Is there a more audacious phony around than Mary Cunningham? Oh, who knows when she and Agee started canoodling. All we can say for sure is that since, by her own account, she was openly dating the guy by the spring of 1981, she might have the goodness to stop whining about how outrageous it was to suspect they were romantically linked the previous fall. Likewise, having sought publicity at every opportunity—from the Couples page of *People* magazine to this book—she might stop posing as St. Mary, Martyr of the Media. ("Which of the saints, I wondered, had ever lived through a mass-media event?") Cunningham seems to believe that all the job offers and speech invitations she brags about are due to her prowess at strategic planning.

Everything about Cunningham's story rings false. Taken at face value, though, as an accurate portrayal of two top executives in action at a major American corporation, her book is even more appalling.

For one thing, is American business actually this gullible? Cunningham describes recruiting dinners while at business school ("I was usually placed in the most desirable seat right next to the managing partner") at which she "delved into issues": "Do you feel investment bankers spend enough time thinking about their responsibilities to society at large?" She reports smugly, "This approach . . . gave me a significant edge," resulting in many job offers. She attempts to gull her readers the same way. "I was ambitious for wordly success," she deadpans, "but only as a means to influence constructive change." Could anyone who meant this put it in such a stilted way?

For all the Mother Teresa talk, this book contains not a single selfless word or deed. Quite the reverse: Cunningham comes off as an almost clinical egomaniac. Every other page contains a reference to her "excellent grades," praise from superiors (usually Agee), adoration from fans ("my speech was interrupted twelve times with applause"). Every facet of her life is canonization material. Even before business school, "I was already making a name for myself at Kass Goodkind Wechsler & Gerstein"—where she worked as a paralegal specializing in debt collection—because "I felt it was my special mission to help these people" pay their bills. Even the annulment of her first marriage, we learn, "was granted in almost record time." What a gal! The Church recognized immediately that it was "my orientation toward helping people" that had misled her into wedlock.

Powerplay, however, contains no examples of Cunningham "helping people," other than Agee and herself. Indeed her attitude toward others is distinctly uncharitable. Almost everyone at Bendix except for Agee is a boob, sycophant, sexist, and/or racist. The first Mrs. Agee is a scheming bitch. Cunningham's idea of a compliment is to say of her first husband, a black graduate of Exeter, Harvard College, and Harvard Business School: "He's a street fighter."

There is nothing in *Powerplay* to support Cunningham's contention that she is a business genius. Her chatter about learning curves and other B-school buzzwords seems infantile. What little discussion there is of actual business consists mainly of genuflecting in front of a deity called The Strategy. The Strategy is what Mary and Bill were up to when nasty-minded people thought they were up to something else. Near as I can tell, it consisted of getting Bendix out of a lot of fuddy-duddy old-fashioned products and into glitzy high tech. What makes this a terribly ingenious idea, let alone a good one, she docs not say. But she became very attached to it. "How's The Strategy going?" she asked Agee the first time they met after her departure from Bendix. And at the book's emotional climax, as Agee realizes he's going to lose control of Bendix to Allied Corp., he says: " 'Of course, you know what this means? . . . The Strategy that we've worked on so hard'—and here he nodded at me—'won't be in our hands.' " And they cry.

Cunningham's breathless description of Agee's business skill calls her own into question. "For a long time," she writes at one point, "Agee had suspected that the company was losing its market share to foreign competition and even some U.S. companies in the manufacture of brakes." Suspected? How much brilliance does it take for a chairman to know his own company's market share? Elsewhere: "His sense of timing, as usual, was impeccable. Just at the time Bendix was buying, stock prices were going down and interest rates were going up. It was a perfect time to move out of cash and into stocks." It was? Well, what do I know about Strategy?

We don't really need to know about Cunningham's business acumen, or her sex life, to conclude that her rise in just one year from business school to, in essence, the No. 2 spot in a major industrial corporation was absurd. It cannot be explained (as she tries to explain it) as the inexorable result of "merit." Whether or not she was his lover, Cunningham was Agee's pet. As Cunningham describes it, gross favoritism is absolutely standard operating procedure in the business world. American capitalism is a veritable orgy of "mentoring." Agee himself had been "mentored" not once, but twice, and one of his mentors, Michael Blumenthal, also had a mentor, George Ball. And so on, I guess, back to Adam.

And talk about waste, fraud, and abuse! Where's Peter Grace when we need him? Unintentionally, Cunningham paints a picture of the corporate world as the Department of Energy with expense accounts. At Bendix under Agee, it appears, teams of executives spent days in preparation whenever the chairman had to give a speech, even a five-minute introduction. Official parties also sucked up huge chunks of executive energy, not to mention office politics. One of the most vital activities—assigned to Corporate V.P. Mary, natch—was opening the chairman's mail. (According to Allan Sloan's book, a corporate jet used to fly from Michigan to Idaho with Agee's mail during the long stretches when he was in residence there.) Meanwhile, you'd be hard put to learn from this book what exactly it is Bendix makes. Cunningham's offhand references to limousines and hotel suites (not to mention golden parachutes) make clear that millions were melting away in the care and feeding of the top birds. (Not that it turned her head, of course. In fact, toward the end at the Waldorf, "Just the sight of the silver cart sent me into the bathroom, retching.")

At their first meeting, Cunningham says, Agee listened to her for a while and then said, "Even I wasn't that sharp at your age." Today Agee and Cunningham are "doing strategy" together in their very own consulting and venture capital firm. They deserve each other.

The Right Thing

FORTUNE, December 9, 1985

W e live in perilous times, but I never realized how perilous until I read Letitia Baldrige's *Complete Guide to Executive Manners*. Like every business author of recent years, Ms. Baldrige describes her book as being "about . . . excellence." What it's really about is the hundreds of ways you can humiliate yourself on the job. Fortunately, Ms. Baldrige is here with detailed instructions about proper etiquette, a subject she characterizes, rather coldly, as "warm, human, and cost-efficient."

She says at the start that manners are important, "whether in the coal mines or in a mahogany-paneled boardroom." In fact, there is little here of use to a miner. Is coal passed up the shaft to the left or the right? We'll never know. Yet Ms. Baldrige is pretty encyclopedic, with strictures ranging from the obvious (wash your neck every day) to the puzzling (don't ask to use the phone when visiting someone else's office).

There have been etiquette books before, of course, including Ms. Baldrige's own classic 1978 update of *Amy Vanderbilt*. But this book is the first detailed offering of rules for the business world. We learn about proper behavior in an elevator, about "door protocol," about "corporate jet etiquette." ("When you land, always thank the crew and compliment them on a 'beautiful flight.'") Whereas Ms. Baldrige's 1978 book listed the appropriate gifts for wedding anniversaries—silverware for the fifth, diamonds for the tenth, and so on—she is now specifying the appropriate levels of publicity for a corporate anniversary: a "special press release" for the fifth, "an entire press kit" for the tenth, and a "full-scale publicity launch and media treatment" for the twenty-fifth. Rituals for marking births and deaths are well established, but what is the proper way to observe a merger or acquisition? According to Ms. Baldrige, the CEO of the acquiring company should give a present to the CEO of the company being acquired. Now you know.

She argues that instructions in manners are especially needed at this moment in business history. The lower executive ranks are being filled with post-sixties children who, however great their current dedication to capitalism, grew up without much training in establishment formalities. Meanwhile, the business establishment also must mend its ways to accommodate new social realities. So here are instructions for dealing with people who don't eat meat and for leaving a message on an answering machine. (No jokes: they waste time and tape.)

The biggest new social reality in the business world is the changed role of women. Among the book's fascinating recommendations for dealing with this reality: if a traveling woman executive must hold a meeting in her hotel room, she should group chairs around the bed and use it as a conference table, in order to make it "a very nonsexual object." I wonder if this works.

In general, Ms. Baldrige is scrupulously, even strenuously, nonsexist. She takes a hard line on "Ms.," asserting that "a woman may call herself what she pleases in her personal life" but must be "Ms. Jones" in business correspondence. The only sexual archaism I detected was the instruction that a host shouldn't light up a cigar "without offering one to his male guests." Why only males? (But then the author makes clear her general distaste for cigars.)

Ms. Baldrige's modernism is a touching combination of stuffiness and sang-froid. A section on "The Unmarried Executive Mother" discusses, without a hint of disapproval, the proper management response if a single woman in your office appears to be pregnant. (Be supportive.) By contrast, she is sternly disapproving of "men or women who wear running shoes to parties after work" and positively vicious about people who switch seating cards at parties ("despicable"). And don't get Ms. Baldrige going on the subject of ankle-length socks!

Private behavior is up to you, seems to be her attitude, but public behavior is up to her. Some of her declarations strike me as a bit arbitrary. I'm not sure I share her horror of ankle socks. On the other hand, I very much approve of her emphasis on inviting journalists when you're having a nice dinner party.

In dealing with foreigners, Ms. Baldrige is strictly nonjudgmental. Don't talk about "your lousy socialism" in socialist countries, she advises. Other tips: "Don't embrace, hug, kiss, or pat a Chinese." Also, "Refrain from making the okay sign . . . in Greece," where it's an obscene gesture. And (my favorite) "Never give an Argentinian a set of knives." Words to live by.

Is it really worth devoting half a page, though, to explaining "the classic way of folding a piece of paper and inserting it into a horizontal envelope"? (It's just what you think.) And can any executive who needs, and uses, Ms. Baldrige's detailed instructions on making small talk expect to have much of a career? Her brother

Malcolm, the secretary of commerce, will be glad to hear that it's apparently considered rude to disagree with anyone who "makes a strong positive statement about the economy." Just say, "I certainly hope you're right," Sister Letitia advises.

In fact, better to avoid controversial subjects altogether. Ms. Baldrige provides a list of approved small-talk topics. She urges that you practice a few in advance and "be ready to draw" on them as the occasion demands. Among her suggestions: landscape gardening, Princess Diana, "women astronauts having babies in space," "helicopter safety," "nutritional treatment of arthritis," and different kinds of teas. (Is there extra credit for twofers such as Princess Diana having a baby in space?) Ms. Baldrige prescribes exactly how much of this must be endured before business may be discussed in a variety of social situations. (Half an hour before dinner.) Come to think of it, maybe I don't want to be invited after all.

The essence of etiquette is artifice. Devotees argue with some passion and much justice that there's nothing wrong with this. Artificial rules of behavior and insincere words of flattery make life with other people bearable by padding the sharp edges of human selfishness. The suppression of true feelings and natural habits is essential to civilization. Fair enough. But what of etiquette in the service of business? Isn't this doubly artificial? Ms. Baldrige asserts flatly that "good manners . . . play a major role in generating profit." Such an attitude complicates the case for etiquette. The artifice and even hypocrisy that are a necessary part of "good manners" lose a bit of their justification when the purpose they serve changes from the suppression to the fulfillment of our crass motives.

Questions of motive and purpose arise most forcefully when Ms. Baldrige offers her elaborate instructions for business entertainment. (Sample suggestion: throw a party in an empty swimming pool.) She observes in passing that overly opulent entertaining can be in dubious taste "during poor economic times." Not, of course, that you should contradict anyone who denies that times are poor.

But what is the reason for lavish business entertainment in the first place? The most extravagant partying in America these days is sponsored by corporations, presumably to augment their profits. A growing industry, of which Ms. Baldrige is a member, helps companies to plan and execute their costly fêtes. Such gestures of hospitality can seem especially empty since neither the guests nor the hosts are paying for them. The stockholders aren't invited, nor are the taxpayers who pay indirectly because it's all tax deductible.

Ms. Baldrige urges corporations to stage charity benefits. Corporate charity, it seems to me, is almost an oxymoron. The imposition on the shareholders is justified on the ground that charity is good public relations. The P.R. derives from the impression that the company is being selfless. But if it really were selfless, the imposition on the shareholders wouldn't be justified.

Ms. Baldrige explains, with apparent approval, how a corporation can spend $75,000—including party and P.R. professionals—on a benefit that will generate $105,000 for charity. These aren't great odds. By the time you've figured in the lost federal taxes on that total of $180,000, the ratio of artifice to sincerity involved in this kind of generosity is more than even the legitimate claims of etiquette can bear.

Thank you so much for your kind attention.

Excellence by the Hour

FORTUNE, *December 10, 1984*

*L*ong after President Reagan has proved otherwise, people still cherish the belief that how busy you are is a measure of how important you are. This conceit is the basis of the booming market in fancy business-oriented desk calendars (often called "diaries," for a British flavour). Almost everyone with a desk needs a desk appointment calendar. In recent years, though, this mundane utilitarian object has undergone an apotheosis. It has become a status item. These leather-bound icons proclaim that their owner is a Very Busy Man. What's more, he's the kind of guy who needs to have at his fingertips the phone number of the Hotel Inter-Continental in Lagos, the average annual millimeters of rainfall in Sri Lanka, and his own hat size, among other "useful" information the leading versions provide or provide space for.

It all started with the Economist Diary, put out by the London newsweekly and promoted as "an indispensible statement of its possessor's importance in the business or professional world." This venture has proved so lucrative that the market is now crowded with imitators. Also variations: pocket calendars, wallet calendars, and— soon, no doubt—waterproof shower calendars on a rope. *Newsweek* puts out "the unique NW Collection," an awesome array of accessories that enable you to schedule a meeting and reek of leather in all conceivable situations.

Competition has led to some strenuous efforts at packaging and product differentiation in order to turn a pretty standard and pretty cheap item into something distinctive and expensive. *Newsweek's* personal information page has spaces for passport and credit card numbers, clothing sizes, blood group, driver's license, car registration, and key number. *Business Week's* has all these, plus "body serial number" (your car's, I guess, not your own), allergies (yours, not your car's), and the name of your attorney and stockbroker. *Fortune's* calendar has a calorie chart, but *The New Republic's* (pocket model) has a calorie chart and vintage tables for both California and European wines. One could spend hours browsing through all this fascinating information, except that one wouldn't have the calendar on one's desk if one weren't terribly busy, would one?

A new arrival is *A Year of Excellence 1985*, which emerges from the atelier of Thomas J. Peters and Robert H. Waterman, Jr., authors of the phenomenal bestseller, *In Search of Excellence: Lessons from America's Best-Run Companies*. That book was the Cabbage Patch doll of the managerial class—almost three million copies sold in two years—and, like that other fad, has turned into a minor industry. Spinoffs include *In Search of Excellence* tapes, lectures, sequels, and now this executive diary.

"This year," say the ads, "there's an appointment diary with a difference—and that difference is EXCELLENCE." In fact, *A Year of Excellence* contains a skimpy 11 pages of miscellaneous data, compared to 120 magisterial pages in the Economist Diary. But

Peters and Waterman claim to have come up with a "brand·new concept in appointment diaries" which "integrate[s] strategies for success right into the busy executive's daily schedule." This bold claim refers to two features. First, scattered throughout are anecdotes and aphorisms based on the principles of *In Search of Excellence*. (Week of April 8: "Have you scraped away any barnacles of bureaucracy lately?") Second, each page contains what the ads fancifully describe as "two-color MBWA appointment grids."

"MBWA" stands for "management by wandering around," one of the key notions of *In Search of Excellence*. Managers, say Peters and Waterman, should get out of their offices and make casual contact with employees and customers. The "new concept" in *A Year of Excellence* is to preassign certain hours every day for MBWA by shading them in gray. (The rest of the calendar is white. Thus, two colors.) So, for example, on Wednesday, January 30, the hour of 8 to 9 A.M. is to be spent wandering around, whereas on Friday, August 9, it's the two hours from 2 to 4 P.M.

Gray dapples the pages in no apparent pattern. Usually the assigned wandering-around hours are scattered, but during the week of May 6, all the MBWA is to be done between 11 A.M. and noon. Most days there is one hour assigned to MBWA, but some days are off, some are double-duty, and—holy moly!—drive carefully the afternoon of Thursday, September 5, because if Peters and Waterman have their way, millions of important business executives will be wandering around aimlessly for four solid hours, from 1 to 5 P.M.

Are Peters and Waterman serious? The basic idea behind MBWA is sound enough (though the acronym grates, like so much management-consultant jargon, by making it seem like a bigger insight than it really is). But let's not be absurd. Anyone who would let a random gray splotch on a desk calendar tell him that at precisely 4 P.M. on Wednesday, August 21, he should drop whatever he is doing and wander around is a nitwit who couldn't manage his way out of a paper bag. This is "excellence"?

There's no mystery why Peters and Waterman have attached their names to this novelty item. They struggle to explain why without mentioning the obvious reason. The ads assert that Peters and Waterman have "thought for years about the typical appointment diary and decided it didn't offer enough." In their four-paragraph introduction, Peters and Waterman assert that excellent managers invariably "tell us that the only real tool they have is their calendar." Well, perhaps. It's curious, though, that Peters and Waterman never once referred to the subject of appointment calendars in the 360 concept-chocked pages of *In Search of Excellence*. Maybe they just forgot. Comes from wandering around without a pocket diary.

Actually, the notion of a prestigious leather-bound appointment calendar is utterly at odds with the philosophy of *In Search of Excellence*, in two ways. First, in their book, the authors ridicule prestige hang-ups. They emphasize the value of unassigned parking places, informal attire, bosses who go by their first name. They praise a chairman for "bearhugging a colleague in the hall after lunch." It's hard to believe Peters and Waterman would have praised a manager who cared whether his desk calendar was bound in leather with gilded edges, and contained a list of official holidays in New Zealand, until they put out one of their own.

Second, the authors of *In Search of Excellence* did not give the impression they shared the mystical belief in the importance of a "busy schedule." They favored (another overcute term) "adhocracy." The ideal "communications system," they wrote, features unscheduled meetings. "Effective managers," they reported, "don't regularly block out large chunks of time. . . . Their time, on the contrary, is fragmented, the average interval devoted to any one issue being *nine minutes*." (The italics are theirs.) A *Year of Excellence* schedules time in minimum doses of *one hour*.

The bits of excellence "integrated" into the calendar are often a bit cryptic. "The first thing I worry about is the washroom," intones Britain's Lord Sieff, of Marks & Spencer, on Monday, June 24. Lord Sieff is right to worry, since we learned on April 29 that, according to "one good manager," "half our meetings are held in the hall, the other half in the washroom." Fair enough. But is this the sort of philosophy that can be implemented with the help of a desk calendar? Imagine . . .

> *Thursday, July 18:*
>   11 A.M. *Go out into hallway. Bearhug Drysdale.*
>   1 P.M. *Wander around loading docks.*
>   2:30 P.M. *Meet Jasperson and Blumberg in men's room.*

Especially when combined with the aroma of bonded leather, such a schedule might give your secretary the wrong idea.

A fancy desk calendar may be hard to square with the philosophy of *In Search of Excellence,* but in another sense—the marketing sense—the newer product is just the logical extension of the older one. (See *In Search of Excellence* Basic Principle Number Six: "Stick to the knitting.") Despite its generally sound advice and its seemingly egalitarian message—chairmen should go by their first name, good ideas can come from the guys on the line, and so on—the real appeal of *In Search of Excellence* is to vanity. You are in charge, it tells its millions of buyers, you can manipulate others, you are a big shot. And now you can be a big shot without having to plow through a 360-page book. The new product works its magic just sitting there, prestigiously, on your desk.

Strongmen

THE NEW REPUBLIC, *December 2, 1985*

A manly clenched fist fills the page. In the background, the American flag. Four words in block type: "THE PRIDE IS BACK." It's the front of a four-page foldout Chrysler ad now running in various magazines. Inside is a patriotic collage: the Statue of Liberty (of course), fireworks, a victorious runner in a "USA" T-shirt, another flag, and so on, plus a couple of cars and Chrysler's new slogan, "BORN IN AMERICA."

This should not be confused with the title of Peter Ueberroth's new book, *Made in America*—also, as it happens, what Chrysler chairman Lee Iacocca calls the first section of his own recent book. That book is titled simply *Iacocca.* Both books are examples of a genre best described as autohagiography. Iacocca's has sold more than 2 million hardcover copies. Ueberroth's publisher had 200,000 in print even before publication date. Iacocca and Ueberroth are exhibits A and B of that amazing recent development, the emergence of the businessman as hero and patriotic icon.

Both men get talked about for President. The talk usually is of one or the other riding to the rescue of the Democratic Party, although both are nominal Republicans. A recent poll shows Iacocca second only to President Reagan in eliciting positive feelings from the electorate, second only to Ted Kennedy as a favorite for the Democratic nomination, and triumphing over either George Bush or Jack Kemp in a general election.

Ueberroth shot to fame as head of the 1984 "private enterprise" Los Angeles Olympics. Now he is Commissioner of Baseball. Iacocca essentially purchased his national reputation at the expense of Chrysler shareholders and the taxpayers through years of television commercials starring himself as the feisty carmaker leading the charge to make America great again. Lately he has draped himself around the Statue of Liberty, as the well-publicized chairman of the corporate extravaganza raising money to refurbish the monument.

Ueberroth has not expressed many political views. His book doesn't get beyond patriotic boilerplate: "The United States of America is the greatest country in the world," and so forth. Iacocca, by contrast, has a clear political agenda. He stands for trade barriers and national economic planning through an alliance of business and government, beliefs he promotes in apocalyptic and xenophobic language. "America is losing its *ability* and maybe even its *will* to compete," he warns. While we look the other way, the Japanese are "taking over the backyard." He says, "When you're getting mugged . . . you should really look at who in the hell's mugging you." Iacocca favors quotas and taxes on imports, setting interest rates by law, and an industrial policy modeled on our present farm policy of price and production controls and subsidies. "Adam Smith went out of style decades ago," he declares.

Iacocca insists he doesn't want to be President. Indeed, he devotes an entire chapter of his book to insisting. But this is the usual stance of the businessman/hero: he does not seek challenges, they seek him out. He is at first reluctant . . . the challenge is beyond all human capability . . . but he succumbs to entreaties . . . he soon discovers it's even worse than he imagined . . . but in the end, with strong leadership, devoted followers, and a loving family. . . . *Iacocca* and *Made in America* both follow this leitmotiv. In any event, the interesting question isn't whether Iacocca and Ueberroth want to run for President. It's why so many other people want them to run.

The hunger for a leader who is "above politics" reminds some of the Eisenhower era. But Eisenhower's appeal was as a caretaker who wouldn't bother people much. People today look to Iacocca or Ueberroth as a savior who'll take bold action. It's the difference between a kindly uncle and a strong father. As political heroes, Iacocca and Ueberroth radiate a rather austere kind of charisma. It's not the personal warmth projected by successful modern American politicians from FDR through Ike to Ronald Reagan. It's more like the mystical ability to command that is the original meaning of "charisma."

As culture heroes, too, Iacocca and Ueberroth are a novelty. The American hero used to be a loner who rode off into the sunset. These corporate heroes sit atop large organizations and, in fact, are admired in part for their organizational skills. Even as business heroes, they are different from the entrepreneurs and inventors of the past, the Henry Fords and Thomas Edisons. They are salesmen, not engineers. Marketing, public relations, and lobbying are the keys to their success.

There used to be a name for the political philosophy of a strong charismatic leader, a Darwinian struggle among nations, and a privately owned but centrally planned economy, with a heavy emphasis on heroic images and pageantry. That name was fascism. Iacocca and Ueberroth are not fascists, of course, even in the clinical sense that Mussolini and Hitler made obsolete. But the flavor is definitely there. And it's a bit scary how appealing many find it.

Iacocca's vision of an economy managed by tripartite boards of government, business, and labor leaders is the classic corporate state of fascist ideology. It is capitalism without free enterprise, socialism without social justice, a deeply conservative and disastrous arrangement that would freeze the economy in place for the benefit of current property owners. His talk of Japanese "mugging" (which consists of selling people goods they wish to buy at prices they wish to pay) and of America's loss of "will" is straight out of fascist rhetoric about dynamic nations triumphing over complacent ones.

Ueberroth's Los Angeles Olympics were a tiny model of the corporate state. They may have been "private" in the sense that corporations financed and ran them, but almost nothing truly private or spontaneous was permitted to happen. Everything was planned and organized down to the tiniest detail. The mammoth security apparatus, the strict standardization of uniforms and decorations, the vast cheering crowds, the endless marching and singing in unison and standing at attention, demonstrated that even the world's freest city can be turned into an authoritarian fantasy world under the right kind of leadership.

Time made Ueberroth its "Man of the Year." The photos—gazing upward at him from a point about six inches off the ground, with some grandiose marble pile in the background—would have made Leni Riefenstahl proud. And America swooned. But the romance won't last. These guys aren't really our type.

The Prisoner of Commerce

THE NEW REPUBLIC, April 16, 1984

At age five, Michael J. was a healthy, normal child with a talent for music. Today, twenty years later, he lives in what observers describe as a "fantasy world," isolated physically behind tall gates and mentally in a Disney landscape, which he thinks is real. His favorite toy is an electric car modeled after Mr. Toad's Wild Ride at Disneyland. "He has had no adult life," writes one journalist who has studied his case. His closest friends are animals ("I think they're sweet," he explains), including a pet boa constrictor ("Snakes are very misunderstood"), and several life-size mannequins. ("I surround myself with people I want to be my friends. And I can do that with mannequins. I'll talk to them.")

Michael J. has developed weird androgynous looks and a high

falsetto voice. He favors an eccentric half-military, half-debutante style of dress. His keepers deny that he takes female sex hormones, but admit that he's had plastic surgery to give his face a softer look. Does he mind appearing schizophrenic? "I don't mind. I feel I'm Peter Pan as well as Methuselah, and a child."

Doctor, what has happened to Michael J? What's happened is that Michael Jackson has become the most successful musical performer ever, if success is measured in dollars (as of course it is). His album *Thriller* has sold 31 million copies. His next tour is expected to gross $100 million. He's bigger than Sinatra, Elvis, the Beatles, Jesus, Beethoven—all of them.

Michael Jackson's extreme abnormality is part of his act. Unless the media are perpetrating a gigantic hoax, it's also genuine. He's a freak. This total merging of person and performance is central to today's rock music, and, for all I know, it's art. But is it life? Of course artists throughout history have sacrificed their lives, even their minds, for art. But two features of Michael Jackson's sacrifice make it different.

First, he never really had much of a choice. As soon as Joe Jackson realized that his sons (who became the "Jackson 5") had musical talent, he began training them two to three hours a day. "They got a little upset at the beginning," he told *Time* magazine. Michael Jackson recalls in a paperback called *The Michael Jackson Story*, "When I was five, I was touring, singing, and dancing. Always gone, always out of school." In 1968, when Michael was ten, the Jacksons were discovered by Berry Gordy of Motown, who moved them to Los Angeles. Michael, already clearly the star, lived for a year and a half with Diana Ross instead of his family. Published Jacksonalia contain some vague references to school, but the Jackson office in Hollywood refuses to give a straight answer about what schooling Michael had and how far he got.

At first, Motown marketed the Jacksons as a wholesome Midwestern black family, and Michael as clean-cut and cute. During the 1970s, however, the image got funkier, especially after the family switched allegiances to a record division of CBS in 1976. During his teen-age years, when most children face an incentive structure that encourages them to act mature and rational, Michael Jackson was getting positive feedback for remaining childlike (voice and all) and turning weird. (Age nineteen, 1977: "I love rats, you know. . . . I really do feel like I'm talking to a friend when I play with them.")

This points up a second way Michael Jackson's sacrifice for art is different from, say, van Gogh's. Jackson's art is also big-time commerce. Corporations supervised his development, and even bigger corporations are making millions off him: CBS (which features Jackson on the cover of its 1983 Annual Report), Pepsico (which has $50 million riding on a Jackson ad campaign), Time Inc. (which sells magazines by putting him repeatedly on its covers), and others. Jackson's sacrifice has taken place in front of millions of paying customers.

What's happened to Michael Jackson isn't too different from what they used to do to young male singers in Europe a few centuries ago, to keep their voices sweet. In another way, it resembles the exploitation of child stars like Judy Garland in the heyday of the Hollywood studios. In fact, what American capitalism has done to Michael Jackson is even a bit like what the Soviets do to their women athletes.

A sickening cover story on Jackson in the March 19 *Time* takes as its theme that there is something wonderful about being an incompetent human being. "Jackson's world of fantasy is easier to dismiss with malicious gossip than understand with sympathy," *Time* scolds. It quotes Steven Spielberg: "He's like a fawn in a burning forest." Describing Jackson "chatting and swapping gestures with E.T.," Spielberg reflects, "I wish we could all spend some time in his world." Jane Fonda reports on a week ostensibly spent talking with Jackson about "acting, life, everything. Africa. Issues." Her conclusion? "His intelligence is instinctual and emotional, like a child's. If any artist loses that childlikeness, you lose a lot of creative juice. So Michael creates around himself a world that protects his creativity." *Time* notes with approval: "His friends [sic] . . . help him keep life at bay and illusion near at hand."

The only truly normal thing *Time* describes Jackson doing is listening to the soundtrack of *Oklahoma*. Of this, the magazine remarks defensively: "Jackson . . . can rise above embarrassment on such matters of taste."

Yes, I know, it's hard to feel sorry for Michael Jackson. Millions of dollars and zillions of adoring fans, a huge party in New York at which, says *Rolling Stone*, "a procession of CBS executives" rise to declare fealty. If he wants a duplicate of the Disneyland "Pirates of the Caribbean" ride built in his house (and he does), he can have it. But how many CBS executives or editors of *Time* would want their own child, at age twenty-five, to want such a thing, to be babbling about misunderstood snakes, to be "like a fawn in a burning forest"?

Michael Jackson supposedly is writing a book. Not an autobiography—"You know, he's not forty years old," his agent explains—but rather a "statement" involving "pictures and drawings and poetry, and then a substantial text." His editor is Jacqueline Onassis.

Write, hell. Can Michael Jackson read?

Incredible Dr. Hammer

THE NEW REPUBLIC, *January 20, 1986*

On March 4, 1976, Dr. Armand Hammer appeared in a Los Angeles federal courtroom to plead guilty on charges of making illegal secret contributions to the 1972 Nixon campaign. He arrived in a wheelchair, surrounded by cardiologists. Hammer, his lawyers said, was dying of heart disease. The case had been transferred from Washington because the seventy-seven-year-old chairman of Occidental Petroleum was said to be too weak to travel.

In light of Hammer's advanced age and poor health, the judge sentenced him to a year's probation and a $3,000 fine. (The employee who carried out Hammer's illegal payments got four months in jail.) One of Hammer's lawyers described him as "a sick old man [who] lives four blocks from the office, goes in late, goes home for lunch, and takes a nap in the afternoon."

That does not sound like very promising material for a coffee-table photo album entitled *The World of Armand Hammer*, one of the strangest publishing ventures of 1985. But "this incredible man"—as Walter Cronkite all too accurately describes Hammer in his sycophantic introduction—underwent a miraculous medical recovery when his legal troubles ended. In May 1976, just two months after his pathetic court appearance, Hammer stood at the podium at Occidental's annual meeting and, according to the *Los Angeles Times*, "displayed his characteristic forceful personality," parrying hecklers and dismissing his crimes as "insignificant." By October he was back in Moscow, scene of his first business triumphs. And now, at age eighty-seven, Hammer declares in this book, "I work fourteen hours a day, seven days a week. . . . I never feel my age."

Published by a company that specializes in lavish art books, *The World of Armand Hammer* consists of 225 oversized pages of color photographs of Hammer and the things and people he surrounds himself with. Although the photos and the minimal text are by one John Bryson, this clearly is an Armand Hammer production. Hammer commissioned it and was subsidizing it himself until the directors of Occidental generously voted to let the shareholders pick up the tab. (That information comes not from the book but from the *Wall Street Journal*.)

The vanity of this enterprise almost defies description. Along with chapters on Hammer's life story (highly selective), his company, his travels, and his good works, there are separate chapters on each of his three homes, on his airplane, and on his office (with, for example, a close-up of the clock on his desk). The general topic of Hammer's fondness for other VIPs, and theirs for him, is subdivided into chapters titled "Movers & Shakers," "The Royal Family," "The Beautiful People," and "Washington Elite."

Apart from one obvious customer, is there a market for this preposterous book? There may be. *The World of Armand Hammer* is the ultimate example of what might be called "executive porn." In this age of the glamorized businessman, serious business magazines like *Fortune* and glitzy upstarts like *Manhattan, inc.* regularly feed their readers' gray-flannel fantasies through salacious photos of high-powered executives posed with suggestive self-importance against a backdrop of corporate luxury. But this book breaks new ground in financial lasciviousness.

The World of Armand Hammer observes the somewhat contradictory conventions of executive porn. On the one hand, the important executive has overwhelming duties and works all the time. On the other hand, he socializes incessantly with famous people in fancy surroundings. On top of everything, he is constantly on the move.

Among its many riches, *The World of Armand Hammer* contains a foot-square blowup of Hammer's pocket calendar for March 1985. Busy, busy. A two-page photo spread shows Hammer in bed, simultaneously watching four TVs, eating breakfast, reading the paper, and "arranging by phone to have tea with the visiting Deputy Prime Minister of Bulgaria."

But all is not toil. "Hammer moves among the leaders of the world like no other individual in history." His taste in celebrities is catholic. We see Hammer unwinding with Merv Griffin, Barbara Walters, Frank Sinatra, Malcolm Forbes (who recently published a similar book about himself), "his good friend" the cellist Mstislav Rostropovich, "his friend Janos Kadar," party leader of Hungary, "his old friend Baron Hans Heinrich Thyssen-Bornemisza," "his friend Bruno Kreisky, former Chancellor of Austria," and many, many others. It's wonderful to have made all these friends. In a sentence that perhaps explains more than was intended, we learn that Hammer has "given some $14,000,000 to charities which Prince Charles holds dear and [has] become a close personal friend of Britain's future king."

The Armand Hammer legend, woven over decades, has badly frayed in parts due to revelations in recent years. This book does some delicate patchwork. Cronkite's introduction restates the fiction that Hammer is the "son of a Russian Jewish immigrant doctor, turned socialist and Unitarian." In fact, Julius Hammer was a founder of the American Communist Party and commercial attaché of the Soviet Union. The text mentions this in passing, but a large picture caption fatuously describes Julius as having "pursued the American dream."

The legend has it that Hammer became friends with Lenin in 1921 when, fresh out of medical school, he went to Russia to help famine victims and ended up with profitable business concessions. "His intentions were philanthropic," Cronkite writes. In fact, Hammer went as agent for his father's business and met with Lenin once for an hour. This book cautiously demotes Hammer from a close friend to "one of the few living acquaintances of Lenin," and yet asserts that this makes him "a folk hero in Russia." But then Lenin apparently had a genius for friendship. According to Hammer, "To talk with Lenin was like talking with a friend one knew and trusted, a friend who understood. His infectious smile. . .his intense human sympathy, his warm personal magnetism . . ." and so on.

As for Stalin, Hammer once described him as "unassuming," a remark that may hold the world record for bad judgment of character. In this book, the great mass murderer falls victim to Hammer's only unkind words for any famous person. "Stalin didn't understand the importance of business," he says.

Hammer left Russia in 1930. "Lenin had died, and I had lost my friend," he explains. (Lenin died in 1924.) He didn't return for thirty-one years. According to the official legend, restated by Hammer as recently as 1981, "my friendship with Jack Kennedy" led to a request that he visit Moscow and improve superpower relations. In fact, as Sovietologist Joseph Finder explained in his 1983 book, *Red Carpet*, Hammer planned the visit and then got a government endorsement, through a senator, from Commerce Secretary Luther Hodges. This book splits it down the middle: "President John F. Kennedy and Secretary of Commerce Luther Hodges sent him in 1961 to help improve relations."

Hammer retains a soft spot for Soviet leaders. We see him reading a eulogy at the funeral of "his friend . . . Leonid Brezhnev," and a few pages later "pay[ing] homage" at the funeral of Yuri Andropov. Hammer visited Konstantin Chernenko in December 1984 and, according to the *Washington Post*, found him "in fairly good health for his age: vigorous and alert." Naturally, Hammer was an honored guest at Chernenko's funeral three months later. This book features a large picture of Hammer and Mikhail Gorbachev on that occasion.

Armand Hammer is an extreme example of the sort of capitalist whose only measure of a government is whether it is willing to "do business"—the sort that his friend Lenin observed would sell the Soviets the rope they needed to hang him with.

Hammer's whole "world," in fact, is one of cynical mutual exploitation. He comes off in his book as a sad man, measuring his self-worth by the size of his airplane, attracted to people solely because they are rich or powerful or famous, and unaware or

indifferent that his so-called friends are attracted to him for the same
shallow reasons. Hammer's idea of heaven would be an extravagant
party, thrown by himself, at which dictators and duchesses, magnates
and movie stars came from around the globe to toast him, with his
own champagne, on his 150th birthday. Not incredible. Just
pathetic.

The Myth of Books

THE NEW REPUBLIC, *June 17, 1985*

Seventeen thousand book people are here in San
Francisco for the annual convention of the American Booksellers
Association, marching this year under the banner "Toward a
Reading Society." Fortunately for booksellers, though, their prosperity depends on people buying books, not on people actually
reading the bulky things. A report just published by the Book
Industry Study Group asserts that half the population reads books,
and that "the average book reader read 24.8 books over the six-month
period" preceding the survey. Oh, sure. Asking a self-defined "book
reader" how many books he's read lately is like asking a teen-age boy
how far he got on Saturday night.

"Contrary to popular misconceptions," scolds the Book Industry
Study Group, "book readers are not withdrawn and solitary, but are
involved in many different kinds of activities, including socializing,
spending time with the family, going to the theater, and participating
in various forms of recreation." Well, that's just the point, isn't it?
Where do these dynamos find time to read books? A hint to the
solution of this mystery may be found in a footnote to the study,
which reveals that "a respondent did not have to read the entire book
to consider it a book read."

How true. It has long been my suspicion that, especially in Washington, when people say they have "read" a book, they mean something other than turning every page and attempting to glean meaning from each sentence. I recently organized a small test of this hypothesis. At the beginning of January, my colleague David Bell visited several Washington-area bookstores and surreptitiously slipped a small note into each of about seventy books. The sample included a dozen copies of *Deadly Gambits* by Strobe Talbott, the book about arms control negotiations that Walter Mondale praised extravagantly in one of the presidential debates. *Deadly Gambits* is 352 pages long, 43 lines a page, about 13 words per line. Mondale ostensibly read it in the middle of his presidential campaign. Other books in the sample included a dozen each of *Double Vision* by Ze'ev Chafets, about how the American press covered the Israeli invasion of Lebanon; and Ben Wattenberg's latest valentine to America, *The Good News Is the Bad News Is Wrong*. These books were not chosen because they are especially boring or unreadable. They're not. They were selected to be representative of the kinds of books Washingtonians are most likely to claim to have read.

The notes were placed about three-quarters of the way through each book, hard against the spine. They could not be shaken out, or observed by flipping through, but they would be impossible to miss by anyone who actually opened the book to the page where they were placed. The notes said: "If you find this note before May 1, call David Bell at *The New Republic* and get a $5 reward," with our phone number. During five months, we didn't get a single response.

Now I don't claim much for this experiment. Conceivably the notes fell out; or the books, though near the top of the pile, were not sold; or people thought it was a joke. As a "control," David also slipped five notes into copies of the latest Len Deighton novel, *Berlin Game*, and we didn't hear from them either.

Still, unlike the Book Industry Study Group, I have backed up my survey with a few in-depth interviews of typical Washington "book readers." I asked a writer on defense issues, for example, "Have you read *Deadly Gambits*?" He said, "Of course."

I pressed further, "Have you really read the whole thing?" He frowned. "I wouldn't say I've read it cover to cover, but I've read large chunks of it." And what about Jean-Francois Revel's *How*

Democracies Perish? "I've written about that!" he said indignantly. "It's brilliant."

Yes, but have you *read* it—every word? "Well, I mean, it's not the kind of book you do that, is it?"

This typical respondent has stumbled on a central truth about a certain kind of book: the big nonfiction current events chronicle or policy tome or political memoir. These books don't exist to be read. They exist to be gazed at, browsed through, talked about. They exist, above all, to be reviewed. These aren't novels, written for the ages. These books are written for esteem, money, and policy influence. All those good things derive from the reviews far more than from the book itself.

A tree may fall in the forest and be turned into *The Blood of Abraham* by Jimmy Carter (number six on a recent *Washington Post* best-seller list), but a book like this "happens" as a consequence of the reviews. A review in even a small magazine like this one reaches more people than all but the most successful serious nonfiction book. (*TNR's* circulation is 95,000. *Deadly Gambits* sold 25,000.) Reviews (if favorable) are what feed the author's self-esteem and create sales. It's also overwhelmingly through reviews, not the book itself, that the author's revelations or ideas reach her intended audience—including most of those who actually buy the book.

Why do authors bother? As a magazine editor, I often beg journalists who contemplate spending a year or two writing a book on some worthwhile or even important subject to save themselves the agony, cut out the middleman, and just write the review.

The more you think about books, the more pointless they seem. Consider the memoirs of Carter's predecessor, Gerald Ford, which were the subject of a Supreme Court ruling last months. Harper & Row paid Ford some gargantuan sum and Ford dutifully produced 200,000 words, which Harper published as *A Time To Heal*. *Time* magazine bought the right to run a 7,500-word prepublication excerpt, but before it could do so the *Nation* obtained a copy of the manuscript and ran a summary of the best parts, such as they were. *Time* pulled out of the deal and Harper sued the *Nation*, arguing that the 2,250-word summary vitiated the value of *Time's* 7,500-word excerpt, to say nothing of the 200,000-word book. After years of litigation, the Supreme Court ruled for Harper, emphasizing the crucial importance of just 300 *words* of direct quotation.

Far be it from me to suggest that all the wisdom to be derived from Jeane Kirkpatrick's United Nations memoirs, for which Simon and Schuster recently paid a reported $900,000, could be summarized in just 300 words. But as for the memoirs of Geraldine Ferraro and James Watt, both due out this fall—well, I look forward to the reviews.

Let 'Em Rot in the Sun

THE NEW REPUBLIC, *April 21, 1986*

"Oil Recession Plunges Houston Into State of Mental Depression," says the *Wall Street Journal* headline. Good, say I. All the reports of economic catastrophe in America's oil regions fill me with unwholesome glee. The Germans (who else?) have a word for this feeling: *Schadenfreude*—meaning, roughly, joy in other people's suffering. It's not a very attractive emotion, and in due course perhaps I'll seek professional help. But first I'm going to enjoy it for a while.

The decline of oil prices has been a disaster for America's energy belt. Jobs are disappearing, businesses are going under, the real estate market has collapsed. The Texas state budget is $1.3 billion in the red, compared to a $1-billion surplus a few years ago. Only pawnshops are booming. Texas, says *Newsweek*, is "broke—and frightened."

It's sad. On the other hand, it's wonderful. After all, just a few years ago the *Schadenfreude* was on the other foot. In the early 1980s, when oil was thirty-six dollars a barrel and seemed to be going nowhere but up, there was little compassion down there for the agony of the Frostbelt. Texas cars sported bumper stickers reading, "Freeze a Yankee—Drive 75," or simply, "Let the Bastards Freeze in the Dark." Louisiana representative Henson Moore cited this sentiment with approval on the floor of Congress. Unemployed Michiganders who poured into Texas looking for work were derisively labeled "black tag people," because of the color of their license plates. Their desperation met with smug indifference or outright hostility. Today Texas's unemployment rate of 8.4 percent is approaching Michigan's 8.9 percent.

What often gets overlooked is that Texas's decade of prosperity was made possible by a classic illegal price-setting conspiracy. If the OPEC oil ministers weren't beyond the reach of American justice, they would all be in jail. But even though it was foreigners who staged this rip-off of American citizens and businesses, it was other Americans who raked in most of the profit. That's because, throughout the energy crisis, most of the oil America consumed was domestic, not imported. The oil states were, in effect, auxiliary members of OPEC.

Yet Texas, Louisiana, Colorado, Alaska, and the other energy states came down with a bad case of cognitive dissonance. They came to believe that their good fortune was actually the result of moral superiority: a rip-roaring capitalist spirit not shared by the rest of the country. They saw the traumas of the Northeast and the Midwest not as a cause for sympathy, but as an occasion for sanctimonious lectures about the virtues of free enterprise. "Houston lies largely at the mercy of forces beyond its control," the *Wall Street Journal* writes today. That was just as true during the glory days, but Houston didn't admit it.

With consummate gall, oil-state politicians now call for "stabilization" of oil prices through a tax on imports. Texas governor Mark White blames Texas's economic problems on "the Federal Government's lack of action to stabilize oil prices." Texas senator Lloyd Bentsen complains of "a flood of cheap foreign oil," and demands "an oil import fee to . . . stabilize this situation." Fred Hartley, chairman of Unocal, complains that the collapse of OPEC "leaves the world with no mechanism to restore the stability of oil prices."

Oil magnates and oil-state politicians sure weren't calling for federal intervention to "stabilize" the price of oil when that price was rocketing upward. Then, when OPEC ruled, they adamantly opposed any interference with the "free market." Today, when there really *is* something like a free market in oil, Senator Bentsen bawls that "what's happening to oil prices . . . has nothing to do with the free market. It has everything to do with a decision made in Riyadh." Fred Hartley whines about "predatory pricing," as if charging twelve dollars were more predatory than charging thirty-six dollars.

Speaking of taxes, remember the windfall profits tax? The idea was to use a small fraction of the OPEC-level profits being enjoyed by domestic oil producers to cushion the shock of high prices for oil consumers. Oil-state politicians were hysterical in their opposition. Meanwhile, during the late 1970s, both Texas and Louisiana enacted new taxes of their own on oil and gas shipped out of state, just to squeeze the last drop of blood from the rest of the country. Think of it as a "Yankee tax," a major Texas newspaper editorialized at the time. Now the rest of the country is being asked to cushion the shock to the oil states of OPEC's collapse. Well, forget it.

Even though only a third of the oil we consume is imported, an import tax would raise the price of domestic oil too. That's exactly the idea, of course. In effect, it would be a tax on all oil consumers, with two-thirds of the money going to domestic oil producers instead of to the government. Senator Bentsen and others would like the government to set a price "floor" of twenty-seven dollars a barrel. At the current market price of twelve dollars, that would require an import tax of fifteen dollars a barrel. (Or 125 percent!) Since Americans use nearly six billion barrels of oil every year, this would cost consumers almost $90 billion. The government would get $30 billion of that directly and a bit more indirectly through the windfall profits tax. But most of the $90 billion would go into the producers' pockets.

Some sort of new energy tax is actually a good idea right now. It would encourage conservation. And with prices falling, it would be a fairly painless way to raise some serious revenue. But any new tax should cover oil from all sources, foreign and domestic. An increased tax on gasoline and heating oil, for example, would raise billions without squandering most of the potential revenue in a subsidy to oil producers—hardly America's most deserving group.

Oil types insist that cheap oil will make us overly dependent on foreign supplies again. This is a danger, but only if such dependence leads to another price squeeze—exactly what, in their hearts, those expressing this alarm would dearly love to see. In any event, handing

$50 billion or so on a platter each year to domestic producers isn't a very sensible insurance policy. As insurance, it arguably makes more sense to use foreign oil now and keep our own stuff in the ground. In fact, for $50 billion—one year's insurance premium—we could buy a *two*-year supply of today's cheap foreign oil to sock away for a rainy day.

Cheap energy is the best thing that's happened to America's economy since the microchip. And Houston's anguish is no bad thing, either. The Sunbelt needed a good roughing up. It's the Frostbelt's turn to gloat. Let 'em rot in the sun. And don't let us catch any of your tatty Texas license plates loitering around our northern freeways, y'hear?

INFLUENCE
PEDDLERS

INTRODUCTION

A writer's nightmare. Right after finishing the bilious piece on Washington superlawyer Lloyd Cutler that opens this section, I went off on a week-long camping trip in the Rocky Mountains. Miles and days from the nearest dictionary, I was overcome by the conviction that I had misspelled the word "repellent" (as in, "Cutler is . . . repellent"). How humiliating: that is an adjective you want to release with a bang, not with a splat. After a week spent contemplating whether to adjourn permanently to the Colorado wilderness, I finished the hike, raced for Webster's, and discovered to my relief that the adjectival form is not spelled "repellant" after all.

The first five articles in this section trace the recent development of Washington influence peddling. "The Indulgence Seller," written eight years ago, is an authentic period piece. By the standards of the 1980s, my objections to Lloyd Cutler's dignified practice seem quaint (though still, I think, valid). The veil of "practicing law" has become utterly obsolete. And my argument that Democrats make better corporate lobbyists than Republicans, since they can claim more convincingly to share the larger goals of government, looks naive in retrospect. The deep cynicism about government of the Reagan era, shared by Republican lobbyists and Republican government officials, turns out to be an even more effective bond.

My friend Mickey Kaus captured the key change in the Washington lobbying scene in the title of his 1982 *Harper's* article, "There's No Shame Anymore." As I argue in "Curse of the Giant Muffins," a sense of stigma is what kept influence peddling in check, and the disappearance of that stigma helped create the influence-peddling explosion of the 1980s.

Fortunately, the "No Shame" era may be ending. We can even pinpoint the moment the tide shifted. It was in March 1986, when former White House aide Michael Deaver posed for the cover of *Time* magazine in his limousine, holding a telephone to his ear. *Time*'s brilliant headline: "Who Is This Man Calling?" That was too much. Deaver almost immediately sank into a morass of legal problems, where he was still stuck a year later. Clients abandoned him. Plans to sell his firm for $18 million to Saatchi and Saatchi, the British advertising moguls with close ties to Margaret Thatcher (which would have created the first trans-Atlantic influence-peddling conglomerate) collapsed.

Alejandro Orfila's liaison with superlobbyist Robert Gray ("Welcome to the Power House") also dissolved, in mutual recriminations of a legal and financial nature. Gray did manage to sell his firm to the P.R. giant Hill and Knowlton, but not for as much as he had hoped. Little has been heard from Robert Beckel ("Crabgrass Roots").

"Access My Foot" is about Deaver's troubles as an illustration of the absurd toothlessness of the Ethics in Government Act. As I write, there are *two* special prosecutors investigating possible illegal influence peddling by former Reagan White House aides: one on Deaver and another on Lynn Nofziger. But lobbying is an ideal illustration of TRB's Law of Scandal, which holds that the scandal isn't what's illegal; the scandal is what's legal. There will always be scofflaws; it's the behavior society chooses *not* to punish that tells you about prevailing ethical standards. In practical terms, the concentration on technical legal violations essentially legitimizes a whole range of sleazy behavior that isn't against the law.

By way of ironic contrast, this section closes with a short reflection on my former boss, Ralph Nader ("Saint Ralph"), who earned his influence the hard way and peddles it for the public interest. The piece was intended to be admiring, though Ralph (characteristically) took umbrage. For the record, he denies that he wants warning labels on French fries.

The Indulgence Seller

THE NEW REPUBLIC, *September 1, 1979*

*P*resident Carter hired Lloyd Cutler last week as his White House counsel for the same reason the Automobile Manufacturers Association hired Cutler in 1966 to help water down impending auto safety legislation, and for the same reason the Pharmaceutical Manufacturers Association has employed Cutler over the years to help explain away various pricing and safety infelicities, and for the same reason corporations pay Cutler's law firm millions of dollars every year to deal for them with the Congress, with regulatory agencies, and with the antitrust division of the Justice Department. Lloyd Cutler is one of the most respected men in Washington. Washington respectability is his stock-in-trade. Cutler is the very symbol of the unelected permanent government here, available for hire to special interests, which Jimmy Carter denounced in 1976.

Cutler is one of the very best Washington lawyers, and also one of the most repellent, precisely because he is a liberal Democrat, active in the ACLU and other admirable groups, a generous donor of his talent to the poor and to progressive political causes. A conservative Republican who grew rich helping large corporations to thwart government supervision would be acting in a way consistent with his free market principles. But few of the best Washington lawyers are conservative Republicans. The early giants of modern Washington law were New Deal braintrusters who helped to found regulatory agencies, then set themselves up in practice representing clients before these same agencies. This tradition has continued, for obvious reasons. The more experience you have had in government, the more you'll know about how to protect your client from it. The more contacts you have at an agency, the easier it will be to get help from that agency. The more sympathetic you seem to the general cause of progressive reform, the more sympathetic legislators and regulators will be to your suggestions for "compromise" or "delay" in a particular case. So the best Washington lawyers are ones with long and varied experience in government, lots of friends who are still there, and sterling liberal credentials. Such highly polished souls do not come cheap. But large corporations are rich, and afraid of the government, and they are willing to pay.

Seen from the left, Washington law is a straightforward Faustian bargain. Seen from the right, it is a vast protection racket. Liberal lawyers in the regulatory agencies, on the Hill, and in the executive departments impose troublesome rules and threaten more; then these same people and their friends offer (for a fee) to help evade the present rules and prevent new ones. Lloyd Cutler, oddly, has had no full-time government job since World War II. But his firm regularly supplies lawyers to the government at all levels, and takes many of them back again. A stop or two at an agency or a Cabinet department or a Senate committee is a standard part of the career path at a large Washington law firm like Wilmer, Cutler & Pickering.

A naif observing the practice of Washington law might wonder: How do these liberals-for-hire live with themselves? They are able to do so, with ease, thanks to two important elements in their working lives. First, there is the grand agnosticism of the law. Lawyers are taught not to worry whether the cause they represent is a just one; the legal process will decide that in due course. Nor do they need to worry about consistency. If they are helping to enforce the tax laws one day, then using that experience to help defeat them the next, they are serving the great legal dialectic the whole time. Using your contacts as a former antitrust official to arrange a soft settlement for a corporate client is merely serving the professional standard that everyone is entitled to a lawyer, and every client is entitled to the most vigorous possible representation.

The moral relativism of life in Washington also makes it easier for Washington lawyers to maintain their split personalities without cracking up. Politicians from opposite ideological poles must work together all day, then see each other at parties that night. Election winners and losers run into one another at restaurants after the losers become lobbyists or get executive appointments. In a city where everything is politics, no one is encouraged to take politics too seriously. It's understood that nothing much ever changes anyway, and meanwhile we all have to make a living.

It's almost impossible to overestimate the power of these two forces (along with the more common debilitating effects of age and financial anxiety) in corrupting the morals of otherwise intelligent and idealistic people. I have seen it happen. If a firm is thought of as being "Democratic"—meaning the lawyers, not the clients— young lawyers who think of themselves as liberal or even radical will go to work for it and do the most retrograde things, especially if they think that a few years at the firm will lead to a more sympathetic government job. The promise of a little "pro bono" (public service) work usually is enough to soothe the most sensitive conscience.

The top Washington lawyers not only live with themselves quite easily; they enjoy the company. A man like Lloyd Cutler or Clark Clifford or Thomas Corcoran thinks of himself as a statesman and public servant: practicing the noble profession of the law, advising political leaders formally and informally, "arranging things" (as Dolly Levi put it). There is no conflict; it is all of a piece, and all in service of the nation. It's just a happy coincidence that it also makes you rich, and a forgettable one that it often serves political interests you profess not to share.

Joseph Kraft, in a recent column, and Griffin Bell, in his parting interview as Attorney General, both advised Jimmy Carter that he needed to develop closer contact with the Washington establishment. The Washington establishment has been saying this for almost three years. Carter, desperate and floundering, has decided to take this advice. Lloyd Cutler has made his fortune selling indulgences from the federal government. It is as if the Pope had decided to buy one.

Curse of the Giant Muffins

THE NEW REPUBLIC, *January 28, 1985*

*I*n Washington, after the election is the season for cashing in. The losers need to remake their lives. And, having been rejected, they are in no mood to indulge patriotic fantasies about the selfless idealism of public servants. Both Walter Mondale and Geraldine Ferraro have said unabashedly that their main interest for the near future will be bucks.

Meanwhile, those who've shepherded the winners triumphantly back into office are now, like ripe peaches, at the peak of their marketability. So this is when we hear a lot about laying down the weary burdens of power, goals having been accomplished, children to be educated, and so on. Departing Solicitor General Rex E. Lee was especially poignant in a valedictory interview with the *New York Times*: "I've never thought when I was in law school that . . . I'd have to think twice in the supermarket about buying Giant brand or Thomas's English muffins."

We none of us can choose our moments of epiphany, and it is unfair to mock the Solicitor General for experiencing his in a supermarket. Having been through law school myself, I would never begrudge any fellow sufferer the muffin of his choice. Nor do I sneer at the larger hunger—for affluence—symbolized by Lee's preference in breakfast food. Let him who is without sin cast the first Giant English muffin. But keep three things in mind before expending too much sympathy on our high-level politicos.

First, it may be that most of these people can make more money *now* in private life than they make in government, but many were making *less* before they got their high government posts. There is a Cinderella quality to many Washington careers. It doesn't take the newly discovered starlet long to forget she didn't always have a swimming pool, and it doesn't take the newly appointed assistant secretary (formerly an underpaid research fellow or journalist) long to forget that he didn't always have a car and driver.

Second, having held a high government job is often the only reason these people can expect to make huge incomes when they leave it. Their government connections, reputations, and experience is what makes them valuable. Even among those (like Rex Lee) with valuable independent skills, their former eminence earns them a substantial premium.

Third, when these people talk of returning to "the private sector," they do not mean they are moving to Des Moines to manufacture widgets. They are remaining in Washington to leech, in some way, off the government, usually by peddling influence. James Reston wrote January 6, "Democrats . . . think of politics as a life career. . . . The Republicans, in contrast, seem to think of politics . . . as a temporary adventure or noblesse oblige duty." In fact, Democrats and Republicans alike think of it increasingly as a simple investment.

Cashing in is simply the last act in the standard four-act Washington epic tragedy. Act One is *idealism*. Our hero gets involved in politics because he or she believes in racial equality, or lower tax rates, or baby seals. Act Two is *pragmatism*. Our hero learns that to achieve important political goals, you must compromise and work within the system. Act Three is *ambition*. Success within the political system—by election or appointment—becomes the goal for its own sake. Act Four is *corruption*. Politics becomes merely instrumental once again, this time for personal enrichment instead of an ideological agenda.

It's clear that in recent years more and more people are getting to Act Four, and getting there faster than ever. Why? Several reasons. Washington is increasingly caught up in the Reagan dollar *Zeitgeist*. Power is out; money is in; the exchange window is open. Also, new opportunities have blossomed. The professionalization of political campaigns allows political skills to be marketed retail instead of wholesale, and corporate political activism has created new markets. Yesterday's hack is today's consultant. At a higher level, the growing glamour of Washington has created new possibilities for lucrative speechmaking and corporate advising. And at all levels, any stigma that ever was attached to sheer influence peddling has simply disappeared.

Former Senate Majority Leader Howard Baker is the most interesting recent example, because he is so widely, if inexplicably, admired in Washington. "We're very far from the rest of the nation here," he lectured the *Washington Post* recently. "I wanted to get out of here because I knew I didn't know the country, these people I'm representing." But Baker isn't getting out of here. As another *Post* story put it, without any apparent pejorative implication, he'll be "a lawyer and influence broker" in the Washington office of a Texas law firm, at a reported salary of about $800,000 a year. Two of Baker's former aides have opened up a highly touted new influence-peddling shop of their own. Meanwhile, Baker also is running for President. Being an "influence broker" not only is no impediment; it's considered a great advantage compared to being Senate majority leader, since it's more lucrative, takes less time, and makes you fewer enemies.

Oddly, one reason that influence peddling has become so socially acceptable has been a series of post-Watergate laws attempting to suppress it. These laws have failed utterly. But, like all laws in our law-minded society, they have sapped the power of social stigma. Any behavior not legally proscribed is seen as perfectly okay. There is no way that "influence brokering" can be outlawed. It can only be regulated by the power of stigma. If Howard Baker offers you an English muffin, turn it down.

Welcome to the Power House

THE NEW REPUBLIC, *December 31, 1983*

*L*ast week's announcement that Alejandro Orfila is resigning as Secretary General of the Organization of American States to join the firm of Gray & Company is yet another watershed in the astonishing evolution of Washington's influence-peddling industry.

Robert Keith Gray, a longtime public relations heavyweight and man-about-Washington, founded his own company after co-chairing the festivities surrounding President Reagan's inauguration in 1981. Less than three years later, it is already the largest lobbying firm in Washington. Gray's firm has broken new ground in the brazenness with which it presents itself as selling, not legal services or even public relations, but connections pure and simple. And Gray, in the role of Mephistopheles, has made a dazzling series of conquests.

The induction of former innocents into the coven at "the Power House," Gray & Company's Georgetown headquarters, began with House Speaker Tip O'Neill's top aide, Gary Hymel, who joined soon after the firm started. It culminated, shortly before Orfila signed on, with Frank Mankiewicz, long ago George McGovern's presidential campaign manager and more recently head of National Public Radio.

Alejandro Orfila's arrival at the Power House isn't the definitive proof Washington has been waiting for that there's no one who can't be bought by Robert Keith Gray. After all, we're not talking about Ralph Nader. A 1982 profile in the *Washington Post* "Style" section reported a widespread view about Orfila "that the man most known in Washington for throwing flashy parties is at best a wheeler-dealer public relations specialist." This seems to suggest that he's found his true home. And indeed Orfila and Gray, as birds of a feather, are old chums. Just a few days after Gray's firm opened its doors, Orfila gave a large and well-publicized party in Gray's honor at the OAS headquarters. Why? Orfila told a *Post* reporter, "He knows everyone in Washington. He's introduced me to a lot of people. He's helped open a lot of doors."

So Orfila's is probably not the purest soul Gray has ever reeled in. But his joining Gray & Company (where he will head the International Division and "initiate a commercial diplomatic service for multinational corporations," according to a press release issued in seven languages) is remarkable in two other ways.

First, as head of the Organization of American States, Orfila must be the most eminent, if not the most distinguished, personage ever to go into the connections biz full time in Washington. When necessary, Orfila has styled himself (not very convincingly) as the official voice of the Third World in America's capital. According to the press release (I quote from the English-language version), "Secretary General Orfila has been decorated by the governments of France, Germany, Italy, Spain, the Holy See, Belgium, the Netherlands, Japan, Thailand, Greece, the Dominican Republic and Venezuela," and is a "recipient of honorary degrees from leading universities." Only last year, after the Falklands war, Orfila was being touted, at least in Washington, for President of Argentina, his native land, which he visits occasionally.

But even his eminence doesn't make Orfila unique in choosing to pursue this new career. Prominent U.S. senators with far more real power than the Secretary General of the OAS have given it up and cashed in, and others are planning to do so. Gerald Ford's career since 1977 could be summarized as "The Selling of the Ex-

President." What's really amazing about Orfila's turn to influence peddling—what makes it a significant development in the history of the subject—is that he's *already rich*. Always has been. According to that *Post* profile, Orfila owns a two hundred-acre farm in horsy Middleburg, Virginia, and has "substantial real estate holdings here and abroad and a separate office on Connecticut Avenue with a manager to handle his investments."

What usually drives good people into the world's second oldest profession is a yearning for fleshly pleasures far more modest than the ones Orfila already enjoys. After living on government salaries, surrounded by people who make a lot more, they long for a taste of affluence. But pecuniary motives can't be uppermost for Alejandro Orfila. If he wanted to, he could be a prominent Washington VIP and party giver for the rest of his life and never work again.

When somebody as obviously status-conscious as Alejandro Orfila goes to work for Gray & Company, when he could just as easily do nothing at all, it means that being an influence peddler for hire is no longer merely respectable. It has become positively prestigious. My son the lobbyist. You know, Alejandro, your father and I were really worried for a while. It looked as if you were going to waste your life as head of an international organization dedicated to preserving peace and alleviating poverty. But at last you're doing something your parents can be proud of. Thank goodness for friends like Bob Gray.

Crabgrass Roots

THE NEW REPUBLIC, *August 5, 1985*

The art of lobbying continues to effloresce. Early in the Reagan years it broke out of its prison of euphemism, as influence peddlers stopped pretending they were doing anything else.

Other recent developments include: "one-stop shopping" at firms that employ big shots of both parties; the combined lobbyist/fundraiser, who puts an elected official in his debt and then comes to call for clients; and the combined lobbyist/campaign strategist, who actually works for politicians and twists those politicians for corporate clients at the same time.

Comes now Robert Beckel, former campaign manager for Walter Mondale, who feels these developments have been inadequate. "Even the strongest Washington lobbying team a company can assemble will face powerful, well-connected, and well-funded lobbyists retained by opposing interests," says a handout from National Strategies and Marketing Group, Inc., a new firm founded by Beckel and two other Democratic politicos. "Efforts to influence public policy must employ strategies and techniques far more sophisticated than those used even five years ago."

Although Beckel's firm offers "extensive Washington representation services," its specialty is what it calls "grass-roots" lobbying. Beckel and his colleagues will use the skills and connections they developed in years of Democratic politicking to "*change* public opinion and *mobilize* public opinion" at the local level. For example, "I've got a 76-year-old woman who was a Mondale-Ferraro volunteer. I called her up and said, 'Milly, I've got a three-week campaign and I'll pay you $250 a week,' and she said, 'I'd love to do it; I've got time on my hands,' and I said, 'Okay, you know how to do it, you know the senior citizens.' " Beckel's network then sets up protest groups, organizes petitions, writes to newspapers, demands meetings with congressmen, and so on. In short, the techniques of the antiwar movement and the McCarthy and McGovern campaigns are at last being made available to corporate America.

So far, Beckel's firm has signed up the Public Securities Association, a group of investment banks fighting to preserve the use of tax-free municipal bonds for nongovernmental purposes; a company that wants to prevent the burning of toxic wastes at sea, because its business is burning them on land; and the Professional Golf Association, which wants to save the deductibility of golf tournaments as a business expense, on the grounds that much of the money goes to charity. For his toxic waste client, for example, Beckel created the "Alliance To Save the Ocean."

Beckel and his colleagues are decent people. But the operation they've set up corrupts their own political souls, their party, and the political system.

Beckel bristles at the implication that he's "sold out," and he's surely correct that there's nothing inherently corrupt about wanting to stop living for politics and start earning a decent income at age thirty-six. He argues that the connections he has to offer assure that he'll only be working for progressive causes. He admits he knew and cared nothing about either municipal bonds or toxic wastes before he was hired to lobby these issues. But "my learning curve's been pretty steep," he says, and he's now convinced that he's on the right side of both controversies. He says his liberal principles would prevent him from working for, say, an asbestos manufacturer, but: "In a marginal call, I have to make a living. If I'm out for one company in a fight with another company to see who can make more money, that doesn't bother me."

But when two competing companies hire lobbyists, it's because there's a public policy issue at stake. Neither side may be Attila the Hun, but it will be a remarkable coincidence if the side that hires Beckel is always the same one an intelligent political activist would choose through disinterested reflection. In fact, Beckel is protected by his ignorance. He has no more idea than I do whether toxic wastes should be destroyed on land or at sea. Although he's busy awakening the nation to the perils of a polluted ocean, he says that if the other side had approached him "and said, 'Help us to stop land-based toxic waste disposal because it's polluting the environment,' I'd say yes." That would be "progressive," too.

One of the Democratic Party's problems is that many of the ostensibly progressive programs it's associated with are actually just "social pork barrel," in Dave Stockman's devastating phrase: handouts to politically influential constituencies. Many regulations protect the economic status quo more than they protect workers, consumers, or the environment. Beckel's operation reinforces this dispiriting impression. It's the rich securities brokers, not the urban poor, who've hired Beckel to save industrial revenue bonds. It's fear of competition, not concern about the ocean, that led a land-based toxic waste disposer to finance a campaign against waste disposal at sea.

Beckel and his colleagues speak almost bitterly of the years they spent in the Democratic trenches. Looking at the condition of the Democratic Party now—not just its political condition but its moral condition—it's easy to understand how people would come to feel they'd been saps to waste their youths, energy, and intelligence on it. National Strategies and Marketing Group, Inc., is both a sign and a small cause of the party's continuing decline.

For the political system as a whole, Beckel's operation represents the seepage of Washington's own brand of toxic waste—political cynicism—into the rest of the country. Worse, what Beckel gets paid to do is to aggravate American democracy's biggest defect: special interest gridlock. It's easy enough to organize people in defense of some tax loophole or other; what's hard is to convince them we'll all be better off with a simpler system and lower rates. It's easy to prevent toxic wastes from being treated in any particular place; what's hard is for our society to make a mature decision that they must be treated *somewhere*. Beckel foresees a day when he'll have full-time operatives in every congressional district, ready to mobilize a campaign immediately for any client who walks in the door.

It all might be something to worry about, until you remember that Beckel's last campaign lost forty-nine states.

Access, My Foot

THE NEW REPUBLIC, *April 28, 1986*

*I*t was a big year over at the Office of Government Ethics. According to a special "1985 Year in Review" edition of *Ethics Newsgram*, the OGE newsletter, "The most visible change . . . was the adoption of an office logo." While the ethics cops were admiring their new logo (an upraised hand on a flag-motif background, with the slogan "Public Service—Public Trust"), the most visible change during 1985 in the larger world of government ethics was the final and official abandonment of all restraint by former government officials cashing in on their connections.

The appropriate logo for this development might be Michael Deaver's outstretched hand on a background of cash, with the slogan "$500,000, please." That's a typical Deaver annual fee. Less than a year out of the gate, the former White House deputy chief of staff is billing clients at an annual rate of over $4 million.

Just lately, the newspapers have been filled with scandalized reports that Deaver met with Budget Director James Miller on behalf of the B-1 bomber, produced by his client Rockwell International. This episode surely deserves the 1986 Captain Renault Award (in honor of the character in *Casablanca* who is "shocked, shocked" to discover gambling going on at Rick's Café.) After all, Deaver was just doing what he's paid for. As he himself says, "I wonder what people thought I was going to do when I left the White House. Be a brain surgeon?" Of course not. Why make the financial sacrifice?

It's fun watching Deaver trying to explain how he earns his fees. He is not, he says, "in the business of trying to persuade officials to do something on behalf of my clients." Oh no, he would "never use my relationship [with the Reagans] on behalf of a client." And, "I really resent the suggestion . . . that all I've got to offer is the ability to pick up the phone and get the President."

So that's what he doesn't do. But what does he do? In a *Time* cover story a few weeks ago, he bragged, "There's no question I've got as good access as anybody in town." Now that the heat's on, he denies that he has "the kind of access that's being reported." Why, connections aren't even necessary in his business, because, "What we really are trying to do here is to help a client strategize whatever their objectives may be vis-à-vis Washington, D.C., or the world."

In fact, Deaver has nothing to offer except his connections to the White House. He is forty-seven years old and all he has done in his adult life is (in chronological order) work for Ronald Reagan in Sacramento, run a lobbying firm in Sacramento, work for Ronald Reagan in Washington, and run a lobbying firm in Washington. The value of being friends with the President is not that you can pick up the phone and call the President. It's that you can pick up the phone and call almost anyone else. Fellow citizens, try getting an appointment with Jim Miller to argue *against* the B-1 bomber if you don't believe me.

The current sophisticated view in Washington is that these gold-plated superlobbyists are actually ripping off their clients. That is, they're being paid to corrupt democracy, but they don't deliver. Well, it's undoubtedly true that (like most consultants in every field) these guys expend as much effort hustling their clients as they do hustling others on behalf of their clients. And it's also likely that superstitious corporations and foreign governments are simply paying, in part, for whatever magical properties might rub off from touching the hand that touched the hand of the President. But no one looking at, say, the progress of tax reform can deny that lobbying also works.

The Ethics in Government Act is the product of a distant time— the late 1970s—of what is now perceived as naive moralism in many aspects of government policy. It forbids government officials from seeking to influence their "former department or agency" on behalf of private clients for a year after leaving office, and permanently forbids lobbying on issues where an official "participated personally and substantially" while in government. The original law, passed in 1978, contained a two-year ban on "assisting" in lobbying on matters you'd once been involved with. In 1979, with the high tide of moralism already receding, this was amended to read assisting "by personal presence." In other words, it's perfectly okay to mastermind a lobbying campaign against your own former agency, on an issue you yourself were involved in, as long as you yourself don't pick up the phone.

In every other way, the ethics law is toothless. Deaver's visit to Budget Director Miller didn't violate the rules because the Budget Office isn't considered the same "agency" as the White House. In another controversial episode, Deaver helped to weaken Reagan's resistance to regulations against acid rain, an issue of great concern to the Canadians, then signed up the Canadian Embassy as a client soon after leaving office. The GAO is now investigating whether Deaver's involvement with acid rain was "substantial." The Canadians, justifying Deaver's fee, say they hired him because he was "familiar with the issues." Deaver, denying misbehavior, says, "I don't think to this day I can tell you what acid rain is."

I believe Deaver. The problem with the jesuitical distinctions in the ethics law is not merely that they're easy to get around, but that they fundamentally miss the point. Deaver was Reagan's chief imageer. He probably knows nothing about any serious issue of government. That doesn't make him any less valuable to private clients. Who cares whether Deaver worked on a particular issue before, or whether the White House is or is not the same "agency" as the Office of Management and Budget? The people who are paying him don't care.

Deaver's brazen excess seems to have cracked the carapace of indifference that has protected influence peddling during the Reagan years. Fellow practitioners are worried that Deaver is ruining it for everyone. Suzanne Garment of the *Wall Street Journal* urges lobbyists to "behave with decent self-restraint," which is like telling prostitutes to freshen up their makeup. There is talk of toughening the ethics act.

But no law can ever really control the buying and selling of influence. A renewal of the stigma that once was attached to influence peddling might also help to slow it down and make it more furtive. Our best hope, though, is that image-sensitive clients will decide that hiring these people is counterproductive. This concern should be encouraged. Be forewarned, you corporations and foreign governments looking for Washington "access": from now on, hiring Mike Deaver will be taken as a sign that you might be up to something naughty.

Saint Ralph

THE NEW REPUBLIC, *December 9, 1985*

*H*enry James captured Ralph Nader in his 1886 novel, *The Bostonians.* James called the character Miss Birdseye.

> *She always dressed in the same way: she wore a loose black jacket, with deep pockets, which were stuffed with papers. . . .*

> She belonged to the Short-Skirts League, as a matter of course;
> for she belonged to any and every league that had been founded
> for almost any purpose whatever. [Yet she] knew less about her
> fellow-creatures, if possible, after fifty years of humanitary zeal,
> than on the day she had gone into the field to testify against the
> iniquity of most arrangements. . . . No one had an idea how she
> lived; whenever money was given her she gave it away. . . .
> There was a legend that an Hungarian had once possessed
> himself of her affections, [but] it was open to grave doubt that
> she could have entertained a sentiment so personal. She was in
> love . . . only with causes.

Thus the social reformer, skewered. I worked several years for
Ralph Nader, and he's actually quite warm and funny in person.
Nevertheless, his is the classic zealot's worldview, paranoid and
humorless, and his vision of the ideal society—regulations for all
contingencies of life, warning labels on every French fry, and a
citizenry on hair-trigger alert for violations of its personal space—is
not one many others would care to share with him.

But reasonable people don't move the world. On the twentieth
anniversary of *Unsafe at Any Speed*, his tract against dangerous
automobiles, no living American is responsible for more concrete
improvements in the society we actually do inhabit than Ralph
Nader.

In all statistical probability, at least several dozen of you who are
reading this issue of *TNR* would be dead today if Nader hadn't
single-handedly invented the issue of auto safety. His long campaign
for mandatory air bags may bore most people and enrage a few. But
would even these people want cars without seat belts, padded
dashboards, collapsible steering wheels, and shatter-resistant glass?
On matters ranging from the Occupational Safety and Health
Administration to the Freedom of Information Act (just two of his
monuments), Nader stands accused—sometimes justly—of going
"too far." But without the people who go too far, we wouldn't go far
enough.

Although Nader's personal popularity has diminished, and the
causes he favors are out of fashion, his achievements are as
immutable as FDR's. President Reagan may inveigh against burden-

some government regulation, just as he inveighs against government spending. He may attempt changes at the margin. But he would no more get the government out of the business of protecting consumers, workers, and the environment than he would dismantle Social Security. Americans like clean air and water, safe transportation, open government, honest advertisements, uncontaminated meat. No electable politician would attempt to push back the clock by twenty years.

I wonder how many conservative businessmen, even, would care to return to the days when anyone could light up a cigarette next to you on a long airplane flight, and when an airline could overbook and bump you with no explanation or compensation. No-smoking sections and airline bumping rules—minor bits of Naderism— seemed like quixotic obsessions when first proposed. Now they are taken for granted.

Likes James's Miss Birdseye, Nader knows little of ordinary human appetites. This gives him his fanatic's strength of purpose. But it also sometimes leads him astray by blinding him to the benefits that come with the risks he campaigns against. The pleasure of a hot dog means nothing to Ralph. He tastes only the nitrite. If everyone lived like Ralph Nader, we could dispense with nuclear power and not worry about replacing the energy. In this world of sinners, though, not everyone wants to live on raw vegetables and set the thermostat at 60. Intelligent public policy requires trade-offs that the fanatic is ill equipped and indisposed to make.

Nader's other great weakness as a reformer is that he's a prisoner of the legal mind-set. He believes in the infinite power of lawyers to achieve both bad and good. "The ultimate goal of this movement," says a recent Nader press release, "is to give all citizens more rights and remedies for resolving their grievances and for achieving a better society." But it's open to doubt, to say the least, whether the better society is one where all grievances are thought of as a matter of legal rights and remedies, to be enforced by lawyers and judges.

These days Ralph Nader is something less than a colossus bestriding American society, but still something more than another colorful Washington character. Over two decades he and his ever replenished band of disciples have operated out of a series of ratty offices, generally moving in shortly before the developers arrive to tear the place down and put up another fancy building for fancy lawyers (some of them, no doubt, getting rich off the very laws and agencies Ralph created).

He still wears those awful suits and lives in that same studio apartment. Some cynics think the asceticism is an act. And it's true that his story about wearing shoes bought at the Army PX in 1959 is wearing as thin as those shoes must be. But if a good marketing sense were a bar to canonization, there would be few saints.

At age fifty-two, Nader may be softening a little. He sometimes shows up at those business parties that pass for social life in Washington. I even think I saw him eating a piece of cheese at one a few weeks ago. His narrow lapels, pointy shoes, and skinny ties are now the height of fashion, offering some hope that the day will come when his clothes will be out again and his politics will be back.

For twenty years Washington has been wondering, Where's the catch? Will he sell out for money, or will he run for office? Those are the normal options. But Ralph Nader is not a normal person. Operating on the mental fringe where self-abnegation blurs into self-obsession, Ralph is living proof that there isn't much difference between a fanatic and a saint. I'll bet you Mother Teresa is impossible to deal with, too.

FADS

INTRODUCTION

T he short attention span of Americans is a continuous blessing for journalists and politicians. We can whip up a nice froth of hysteria on any subject we wish, without much fear that the audience will complain, "Wait a minute. We're still hysterical over the matter you were importuning us about last month." The pieces in this section are reprinted in chronological order, since the point (I suppose) is that if it's not one thing, it's another.

From the perspective of the late 1980s, "Nuclear Holocaust in Perspective," a nasty review of Jonathan Schell's 1982 essay, *The Fate of the Earth*, may seem like overkill. Now that the fever of nuclear monomania has passed, it's hard to remember the thrall in which this silly book held the American intelligentsia. The praise was so ecstatic, and so nearly unanimous, that when I and one other reviewer (John Leonard in the *New York Times*) dissented, this affront was considered worthy of an article in *Time* magazine.

This piece was the beginning of the end for me as editor of *Harper's*. The chairman of the board, a pompous investment banker, stormed into my office waving the magazine and thundering, "I have grandchildren!"—his point being that anyone who criticized *The Fate of the Earth* was sentencing his little lambs to nuclear annihilation. And yet, despite the ever-present peril of imminent doom, my former boss has found the courage to complete his new house in the Hamptons (featured not long ago in one of the glossy shelter magazines), and if he has given two seconds' thought a week to nuclear destruction recently, I'd be very surprised.

There's been an amusing role reversal on nuclear matters during the past few years. The Reagan administration launched its strategic defense (Star Wars) program in order to co-opt the millenarian passions of the antinuclear movement—the belief that the end of days is certainly here unless all nuclear weapons are eliminated. I would imagine there have been few converts from antinuke hysteria to pro-Star-Wars hysteria. Instead, the two sides have simply exchanged postures. The right has decided that the very existence of nuclear weapons is simply intolerable and has taken up all the childish rhetoric about wiping them off the face of the earth. Meanwhile the left has gone all sophisticated and pragmatic and rediscovered the strategic magic of nuclear deterrence.

The fad of castrating rapists ("Decisions, Decisions") never took off. Even the South Carolina judge who proposed it never followed through, changing his sentence to a long jail term instead. So far, no state legislature has been persuaded by my endorsement of the Islamic approach to penology.

The irrational hatred of yuppies as a social class ("Arise, Ye Yuppies") continues to fester in our society. When I wrote the article here, the term and the concept were new. Increasingly, though, yuppies must endure the contempt not merely of the older generation but of a rising younger generation who regard us as premature old fogies babbling pathetically about some mythic ancient period called the sixties.

The so-called new patriotism (discussed in "School Spirit Sucks") reached a peak with the 1984 Olympics, faded a bit in 1985, made a comeback with the 1986 Statue of Liberty extravaganza, then collapsed with the Iranamok scandal. Even at its peak, Reagan-style patriotism was all a matter of "what your country can do for you," without a drop of "what you can do for your country." It depended on making no demands, financial or physical, on alleged patriots. Tax cuts and a defense build-up, but no cuts in middle-class entitlements to pay for them; an aggressive military posture but no draft. When the administration tried to tap the patriotic gusher as fuel for popular support of the contras in Nicaragua, there was very little response.

We can test right now my prediction (in "Celebrity Surgery") that nobody would remember who "Baby Fae" was. Who was she? (A: The first human to receive a baboon heart transplant.) Baby Fae survived about a week after this column appeared. Her memory

survived about two weeks. William Schroeder, the artificial heart man, died in 1986. Meanwhile Dr. Robert Jarvik, inventor of the heart in question, has been featured in Hathaway shirt ads. As I write, the nation is obsessed with one "Baby M." She, too, is God's gift to columnists at the moment, though by the time this book comes out you probably won't be able to remember who she was either. (A: The subject of a lawsuit between a surrogate mother and a couple who contracted for her services.)

Missing children and child abuse ("Greasy Kid Stuff"), matters of obsessive concern in 1985, were off the screen within a year. If fewer children are being abused or kidnapped than two years ago, nobody has said so. A topical variant—abuse of the elderly—had a very brief flurry of interest, but never reached the newsmagazine-cover level of intensity.

Former Weatherperson Bernadine Dorhn was not admitted to the New York bar, despite the efforts of her newfound establishment friends. "Dohrn Again" is really a footnote on an ancient fad. I recently had to explain to a *New Republic* intern—born in 1964, I was infuriated to discover—what SDS was. (A: Students for a Democratic Society, leading left-wing student group of the 1960s.)

The occasion for "Tea, Please," reflections on Anglophilia, was the enormously publicized "Treasure Houses of Great Britain" exhibit at the National Gallery, highlighted by the visit of Prince Charles and Princess Di. The disease has gone into remission since then, though there was a brief relapse when Prince Andrew married "Fergie" in 1986.

Sales of the Final Report of the Attorney General's Commission on Pornography have been disappointing, despite my efforts in the *Wall Street Journal* ("Porn Fiends and Porn Hounds") to promote it as a camp classic. (My bit to help reduce the federal deficit.) I have taken the liberty of restoring a few lines the *Journal's* editors deleted in the cause of taste. Don't get too excited. Actually, I was impressed and grateful (as I have been for the two years I've written for the *Journal*) at how much they let me get away with. As is often the case with censorship, though, the distinctions they made were a bit puzzling. It was permissable to describe a photograph of Senator William Roth as "detumescent." It was okay to quote the report's discussion of two women "manually expressing a stream of milk from

their engorged breasts." But the *Journal* drew the line at informing its two million readers that a magazine exists called, "Girls Who Love To Sit on It." Go figure.

As cynical as I may be about such matters, even I was astonished at how rapidly the drug-hysteria balloon deflated. "The Right Spirit" appeared in the fall of 1986. At that time drugs were the biggest issue in the election campaign. Ron and Nancy were about to deliver the first-ever joint marital White House television address on the subject. The media were obsessed. In an open letter from the editor published in June, *Newsweek* compared drugs to the plagues of medieval Europe and declared its intention to cover the drug story as intensively as it had covered the Vietnam War.

By year's end, the drug "crisis" rated two paltry paragraphs in *Newsweek*'s twenty-one-page year-in-review survey. President Reagan, who had pledged hundreds of millions in increased funds for drug enforcement and therapy, was back to proposing huge slashes in these programs. And entrepreneurs who, with true Reagan-era initiative, had schemed to get rich by marketing drug-free urine samples to fool the testers were, well, liquidating their inventories.

Nuclear Holocaust in Perspective

HARPER'S, May 1982

It would be very sad if the world were destroyed in a nuclear holocaust. Jonathan Schell may well feel this sadness more profoundly than I do. His acclaimed three-part series in the *New Yorker*, *The Fate of the Earth*, now rushed into book form by Knopf, is mostly a meditation on how sad it would be. He demands "the full emotional, intellectual, spiritual, and visceral understanding of the meaning of extinction." He asserts that even now, "The peril of

extinction surrounds . . . love with doubt." And, "Politics, as it now exists, is . . . thoroughly compromised." And, "Works of art, history, and thought . . . are undermined at their foundations." Schell cites scientific evidence against any complaisant hope that human life, once destroyed in a nuclear war, might evolve again in a few million years. And don't suppose that humanity might escape nuclear war by fleeing the earth in a spaceship. Schell points out that this would be not only "an injustice to our birthplace and habitat," but futile: "The fact is that wherever human beings went, there also would go the knowledge of how to build nuclear weapons, and, with it, the peril of extinction." I confess, this spaceship business never occurred to me. But, really, I think a nuclear holocaust would be very, very sad.

That said, where do we stand?

We stand where we've stood for three decades, with East and West in a nuclear stalemate that could turn at any moment into mutual annihilation. In addition, we stand with nuclear weapons as the only genuine deterrent to a Soviet invasion of Europe (and of the Middle East, a threat implicitly invoked in the Carter Doctrine). Third, we stand at the edge of a large expansion of the nuclear club, with unpredictable consequences.

Over the past few months a mass political movement—the first in years—has sprouted in the United States and Europe, demanding that something be done about this. Something, but what? On this, the movement is vaguer, because it's hard to think what the Western governments can do to prevent a nuclear war. On the third point, they might stop competing with one another to sell nuclear equipment to the Third World, but it's already a little late for that. On the first point, they might show a bit more enthusiasm for a strategic arms limitation treaty. But the basic balance of terror cannot be dismantled without perfect trust between the world's greatest enemies—an unlikely development.

The West really could do something about problem number two, the dependence on nuclear weapons to protect Europe. That something would be to replace nuclear arms with conventional defense. But a conventional defense strong enough to justify forswearing first use of nuclear weapons would require massively increased military spending for the other NATO countries, and probably a draft for the United States.

The thought of increasing conventional military strength to replace nuclear bombs (like the thought that a successful nuclear ban would increase the chance of conventional warfare) is utterly alien to the mentality of most antinuclear activists. Is the horror of nuclear weapons sui generis, or is the goal abolition of all weapons and war? Are there practical steps that can be taken, or must we await a transformation of human nature? Jonathan Schell's essay well illustrates the confusion of the antinuclear movement.

Perhaps it is lese majesty to call a major three-part series in the *New Yorker* "pretentious," but "The Fate of The Earth" is one of the most pretentious things I've ever read, from the title through the grand finale (which begins, "Four and a half billion years ago, the earth was formed"). "Gosh, is this profound," is about all that many sonorous passages convey:

> *The limitless complexity [of nuclear war] sometimes seems to be as great as that of life itself. But if these effects should lead to human extinction, then all the complexity will give way to the utmost simplicity—the simplicity of nothingness.*

> *Like the thought "I do not exist," the thought "Humanity is now extinct" is an impossible one for a rational person, because as soon as it is, we are not.*

Even funnier are the pompous generalities that come attached to *New Yorker*-style cautionary notes:

> *Human beings have a worth—a worth that is sacred. But it is for human beings that they have that sacred worth, and for them that the other things in the creation have their worth (although it is a reminder of our indissoluble connection with the rest of life that many of our needs and desires are also felt by animals).*

Hannah Arendt "never addressed the issue of nuclear arms," Schell tells us, but of course she is dragged in. "I have discovered her thinking to be an indispensable foundation for reflection on this question." Evil, you know. What is really indispensable is her graphic descriptions of Nazi death camps. They pop up here to illustrate the point (both unenlightening and untrue, on recent evidence) that you can't deny horrors that have already happened. Himmler appears a little later, expressing his desire to make Europe "Jew-free." Schell observes, "His remark applies equally well to a nuclear holocaust, which might render the earth 'human-free.' " In fact, Hannah and Himmler are here for aesthetic rather than pedagogical purposes. This is how you decorate apocalyptic bigthink.

Despite a lot of wacky judiciousness ("From the foregoing, it follows that there can be no justification for extinguishing mankind"), Schell's method is basically bullying rather than argument. The pomp is intended to intimidate, and the moral solemnity is a form of blackmail. Unless you feel as anguished about nuclear war as Jonathan Schell, unless you worry about it *all the time* as he does (allegedly), your complacency disqualifies you from objecting. In fact, you are suffering "a kind of sickness" or "a sort of mass insanity." So shut up.

Much of Schell's essay does take the form of argument, but it tends to be hothouse reasoning: huge and exotic blossoms of ratiocination that could grow only in an environment protected from the slightest chill of common sense. For example, here he is arguing that we should not have an experimental nuclear war in order to see what would happen:

> *We cannot run experiments with the earth, because we have only one earth, on which we depend for our survival; we are not in possession of any spare earths that we might blow up in some universal laboratory in order to discover their tolerance of nuclear holocausts. Hence, our knowledge of the resiliency of the earth in the face of nuclear attack is limited by our fear of bringing about just the event—human extinction—whose likelihood we are chiefly interested in finding out.*

Now welcome please "the famous uncertainty principle, formulated by the German physicist Werner Heisenberg," which makes a brief star turn at this point in the argument. Its role is to escort "an opposite but [not very] related uncertainty principle: our knowledge of extinction is limited because the experiments with which we would carry out our observations interfere with us, the observers, and, in fact, might put an end to us."

The argument is crowned with a portentous aphorism: "The demand for certainty is the path toward death." Then, just to show that he's thought of everything, Schell considers and rejects the idea of holding an experimental nuclear war on another planet, "for if we have no extra, dispensable earths to experiment with, neither are we in possession of any planets bearing life of some different sort." The reader is left convinced that an experimental nuclear war is a bad idea, and that Jonathan Schell possesses either an absurdly swelled head, or a "philosophical synthesis" that is "profoundly new" (Eliot Fremont-Smith, *Village Voice*).

Schell prefaces his discussion of the consequences of nuclear war with a discussion of the difficulty of imagining it. Some of the alleged obstacles are of this sort: "When we strain to picture what the scene would be like after a holocaust we tend to forget that for most people, and perhaps for all, it wouldn't be *like* anything, because they would be dead."

But the main set of obstacles involves a supposed reluctance of people to hear about it. Schell pleads with his readers to make this sacrifice: "It may be only by descending into this hell in imagination now that we can hope to escape descending into it in reality at some later time." He promises to protect their delicate sensibilities: "I hope in this article to proceed with the utmost possible respect for all forms of refusal to accept the unnatural and horrifying prospect of a nuclear holocaust." He flatters their "investigative modesty" as "itself . . . a token of our reluctance to extinguish ourselves." And thence to pages of the usual gruesome description. The horror is lightened only by some *New Yorkery* punctiliousness, as when, having killed off millions in a one-megaton bomb over Manhattan, he adds that newspapers and dry leaves would ignite "in all five boroughs (though in only a small part of Staten Island)."

Schell's posture of reluctant scientific inquiry will be familiar to aficionados of pornographic movies. And there *is* something porno-graphic about the emphasis on grisly details that is the distinguishing feature of the antinuclear movement in its latest manifestation. Perhaps Jonathan Schell is so sensitive that he really does find these disaster scenarios painful to contemplate, and probably we all do withhold true visceral understanding of what it would be like. But others will find such disaster scenarios grimly fascinating (certainly the most interesting part of Schell's book). Is that sick? If so, it is a sickness that is widespread, and one that the antinuclear movement both shares and exploits. So the coy posture is annoying.

But destruction of civilization, or even the agonizing death of everybody in the whole world, would be, to Schell, just a minor aspect of the tragedy of a nuclear holocaust. The greatest crime would be against "the helpless, speechless unborn." Schell brandishes this notion of the unborn as his trump card, in case anyone still thinks nuclear war is a good idea. By "the unborn," he does not merely mean fetuses (though by his analysis—liberals please note—abortion is unthinkably immoral). Nor does he mean the future human race as an entity. He does not even mean future people who might inherit a nuclear-wrecked civilization and environment. He means individual people who will *never be born* if there is no one left to conceive them. "While we can launch a first strike against them," Schell inimitably points out, "they have no forces with which to retaliate."

Schell is *very strict* about what might be called "alive-ism." Having waxed eloquent for pages about the unborn as repositories for our hopes and dreams, he stops to warn that we should not treat them merely "as auxiliaries to *our* needs," because "no human being, living or unborn, should be regarded as an auxiliary." The unborn, he scolds, "are not to be seen as beasts of burden."

Well, my goodness. Do we really have a moral obligation not to deny birth to everyone who, with a bit of help, might enjoy the "opportunity to be glad that they were born instead of having been prenatally severed from existence by us"? I shudder to think how I've failed. For that matter, I shudder for Jonathan Schell—for every moment he's spent banging away on his typewriter, instead of banging away elsewhere.

In solving the problem of nuclear war, Schell cautions, we must "act with the circumspection and modesty of a small minority," since "even if every person in the world were to enlist, the endeavor would include only an infinitesimal fraction of the people of the dead and unborn generations." Yes, the dead count too. So he proposes "a worldwide program of action," involving an "organization for the preservation of mankind." We must "delve to the bottom of the world" and then "take the world on our shoulders." He writes, "Our present system and the institutions that make it up are the debris of history. They have become inimical to life, and must be swept away." What he proposes, in short, is that the nations of the world abjure all further violence—nuclear *and* conventional warfare—and give up their sovereignty to some central organization.

This idea will win no prizes for circumspection and modesty. Other problems come to mind, too. Like, how shall we arrange all this? Schell writes:

> *I have not sought to define a political solution to the nuclear predicament—either to embark on the full-scale examination of the foundations of political thought which must be undertaken . . . or to work out the practical steps. . . . I have left to others those awesome, urgent tasks.*

Good heavens. This sudden abandonment, on page 219, puts Schell's hyperventilated rhetoric in an odd light. Is he just going to head off on a book tour and leave us stranded?

Schell is convinced, though, like the rest of the antinuclear movement, that the main task is education—convincing people of how bad a nuclear war would be. "If we did acknowledge the full dimension of the peril . . . extinction would at that moment become not only 'unthinkable' but also undoable." The key word here is "we." But there is no "we." There are individual actors who cannot completely know or trust one another. That's life. Even if everyone in the world shared Schell's overwrought feelings about nuclear war, the basic dilemma would not disappear; the best defense against an enemy's use or threat to use nuclear weapons is the threat to use them back.

Schell correctly points out the weakness in deterrence theory: since nuclear wars are unwinnable, it's hard to make a potential aggressor believe you would actually strike back once your country was in ruins. "One cannot credibly deter a first strike with a second strike whose raison d'être dissolves the moment the first strike arrives." This may be "a monumental logical mistake," as Schell asserts, but it has prevented anyone from using a nuclear weapon, or even overtly threatening to use one first, for thirty-five years. And in any event, pending his proposed outburst of "love, a spiritual energy that the human heart can pit against the physical energy released from the heart of matter," it's all we've got.

So the first problem with Schell's solution is that you can't get there from here.

The second problem is what "there" could be like. Speaking, if I may, for the unborn, I wonder if they might not prefer the risk of not being born at all to the certainty of being born into the world Schell is prepared to will them.

The supreme silliness of *The Fate of the Earth,* and of much of the antinuclear movement, is the insistence that any kind of perspective on nuclear war is immoral. Schell complains, "It is as though life itself were one huge distraction, diverting our attention from the peril to life." And to Schell, apparently, all considerations apart from the danger of nuclear war *are* mere distractions. He repeatedly asks, What could be worse than the total annihilation of the earth and everything and everyone on it forever and ever? He demands that "this possibility must be dealt with morally and politically as though it were a certainty." We can opt for "human survival," or for "our transient aims and fallible convictions" and "our political and military traditions."

"On the one side stand human life and the terrestrial creation. On the other side stands a particular organization of human life—the system of independent, sovereign nation-states." Gee, I just can't decide. Can you?

If the choice were "survival" versus "distractions," it would be easy, and Schell wants to make it seem easy (though I have to wonder whether he really lives his own life at the peak of obsessive hysteria posited in his writing). In fact, that's not the choice. The choice is between the chance, not the certainty, of a disaster of uncertain magnitude, versus institutional and social arrangements that have some real charm.

Schell suggests at one point that "say, liberty" and other "benefits of life" are relatively unimportant in his scheme of things, because "to speak of sacrificing the species for the sake of one of these benefits involves one in the absurdity of wanting to destroy something in order to preserve one of its parts." But it's clear that he imagines his postnuclear world as a delightful lion-and-lamb affair, no nation-states, no war, free hors d'oeuvres at the Algonquin bar, a place anyone would prefer even apart from the nuclear dilemma. Some of his admirers know better. In a recent column, Eliot Fremont-Smith of the *Village Voice* expressed the general dazzlement *The Fate of the Earth* has induced in the New York literary scene. He called on Knopf to cancel the rest of its spring list in deference to Schell's vital message. But Fremont-Smith did indicate some passing regret for what might have to be given up when Schell's world organization replaces national sovereignty. His list includes "freedom, civil liberties, social justice"—but he is willing to kiss these trinkets away in the name of "a higher and longer-viewed morality." Others may demur.

Actually, if Schell and his admirers really believe that the nuclear peril outweighs all other considerations, they are making unnecessary work for themselves by proposing to convince all the leaders of the world to lay down their weapons. Schell concedes that the people of the Soviet Union don't have much influence over their government, and suggests, rather lamely, that "public opinion in the free countries would have to . . . bring its pressure to bear, as best it could, on all governments." But why not avoid this problem by concentrating on our own governments? Schell is right: the doctrine of deterrence is only necessary for nation-states that wish to preserve themselves as political entities. Nothing would reduce the peril of nuclear war more quickly and dramatically than for the free and open societies of the West to renounce the use of nuclear weapons unilaterally. That would solve the flaw Schell sees in deterrence theory by making the Soviet threat to use them thoroughly credible, and therefore making their use unnecessary. More creatively, we might offer the Soviets a deal: you forswear nuclear weapons, and we'll forswear *all* weapons, nuclear and conventional. They might find this very tempting. So, by his own logic ("the nuclear powers put a higher value on national sovereignty than they do on human survival"), would Jonathan Schell.

In practice, the antinuclear movement *is* concentrating on the free governments of the West, for the obvious reason that these are the only governments susceptible to being influenced. I do not think most antinuclear protesters want unilateral disarmament. But the suspicion that they do is widespread among the political leaders they must attempt to persuade, and is hampering their basically worthy efforts. The glorious muddle of their thinking is hampering those efforts even more. What *do* they want?

Decisions, Decisions

THE NEW REPUBLIC, *December 26, 1983*

A South Carolina judge has stirred the imaginations of a nation by sentencing three convicted rapists to their choice of thirty years in prison or castration. As Jack Benny used to say in his famous "your money or your life" routine, "[pause] I'm thinking. I'm *thinking!*" His Honor Judge Pyle has even one-upped Dr. Johnson: here is a prospect that *really* concentrates the mind.

Indeed, one respondent in an informal poll I've been taking on the subject said that what's most cruel is not the alternatives so much as forcing someone to choose between them. That may be. But this still leaves us as a society with the burden of deciding how we punish criminals. No one is satisfied with the way we're doing it now. Before dismissing a novel alternative as too cruel, each of us armchair penologists might well consider how he (in this case) would decide if convicted of rape and then offered the choice.

An editorial in the *New York Times* condemns the very idea of castration for rapists as "barbarism." Comparing the sentence to sidewalk graffiti, the *Times* describes it as "a sentiment that deserves to be walked on," and sniffs about disfiguring punishment in general (amputation and so on): "If the judge just looks to the right countries and the right centuries, he'll find plenty of precedents for such penalties. He won't, however, find them in the United States."

On most issues, when no more is at stake than the lives of millions of people in faraway lands, I am happy to defer to the judgment of the *New York Times*. On this particular matter, though, it would be especially sad to act in haste and repent at leisure. So before marching through the prison gates, proudly intact, a stack of unread *New York Times Magazines* under my arm, I took the precaution of inquiring a bit about prison in South Carolina. The *New York Times* trumpets what you won't find in the United States. Has it considered what you will find?

First the good news: a thirty-year sentence—which is not unusual for rape in that state, in case you thought (as I did at first) that Judge Pyle is loading the dice—most likely means only about fourteen years of time served. Think of it as now until 1998. How old will you be?

Now, about the accommodations. South Carolina has the most overcrowded prison system in the country. The main cell block at the state's main prison was completed two years after the Civil War, and is so grim that inmates must sign a release before they can be put there. The *Columbia Record* reported recently, however, that there is a waiting list for the privilege of living in one of these five-by-eight-foot cells, because at least you get a cell to yourself. South Carolina is the only state that engages in a practice known as "triple-celling," colorfully described by the head of the state's prison system as "the dehumanizing daily experience . . . of being forced to live in a nine-by-seven-foot room with two total strangers, one of whom refuses to bathe and the other so emotionally disturbed that he cries most of the night." Or you might luck out and be one of sixty men in a thirty-by-fifty-foot dormitory where bunk beds are lined up touching on one side, with an eighteen-inch aisle on the other. Chummy.

There is plenty of opportunity, under such circumstances, to practice your favorite hobby, or have it practiced on you, although it apparently doesn't count if someone merely threatens to kill you if you don't submit. "If he takes his clothes off," explains an inmate, "that's not rape." So just don't take your clothes off for fourteen years, and you'll be fine. Then there's the random violence and murder, a knifing here, an unexplained explosion there. But some inmates say that all this is nothing: what really drives them to despair is the quality of the food and the air.

It could well be that a rapist deserves no better than this. But that hardly justifies dismissing an alternative anyone might sanely prefer as "barbarism." The fallacy is comparing what the Ayatollah Khomeini does in practice with what the United States of America does in theory. The illusion is easy to maintain because our actual practice is hidden away and easy to ignore. A sentence of castration means what it says. A sentence of imprisonment doesn't begin to describe it.

Since the subject of castration is so emotionally fraught (I think I speak for all of us here), consider instead amputation. Several commentators have pointed out that Judge Pyle's sentence misses the point, since rape is a crime of violence, not of desire. It would be quite hard to commit rape with one arm. And who wouldn't prefer to lose an arm rather than lose fourteen years of his life (and God knows what else) in a South Carolina prison?

The purposes of punishment, as taught in law school textbooks, are four: to satisfy society's and the victim's justifiable desire for retribution; to protect society from a repeat of the offense; to deter others by example; and to rehabilitate the criminal. Various of these goals come into and go out of fashion. At the moment, rehabilitation is considered a dead letter, and certainly what goes on in prison is more like the opposite. Top dog these days is preventing criminals from repeating their crimes—or, more accurately, arranging so that they can commit their crimes only against other criminals. And retribution pure and simple is making a big comeback.

By any of these standards except the out-of-favor rehabilitation, the chopping off of body parts (along with branding, whipping, and other antiquarian delights) seems at least as well suited to the purpose as imprisonment, and a lot cheaper too. And who is to say—after reflecting which punishment he or she would take if given the choice—that this style of justice is not more tempered by mercy as well?

And yet, does the heart recoil at the thought of state-sanctioned mutilation? That's good. Just don't flatter yourself that what we actually do is any less barbaric.

Arise, Ye Yuppies!

THE NEW REPUBLIC, July 9, 1984

Now that the Gary Hart campaign is more or less over, perhaps we can think calmly for a moment about yuppies. The specter of a federal quiche stamps program has passed. There will be no transatlantic Perrier pipeline, no National Tennis Elbow Institute, no Department of Life Style. Oh, women may continue to stroll down city sidewalks wearing gray suits, white shirts with little bows, stereo earphones, and running shoes. But this uniform won't be required by executive order. Nor will there be tax write-offs for hot tubs, free government-surplus goat cheese, an FDA ban on frozen peas. The peril is over, at least for four years. What is it, then, about the notion of young urban professionals as a social class with identifiable habits and political attitudes that so many people seem to find alarming, ridiculous, or even contemptible?

There's no denying that the yuppie phenomenon exists. Nowhere in perfect prototype, perhaps (though *People* magazine is probably looking), but everywhere in bits and pieces. Even in Anchorage, Alaska, where I recently spent a couple of weeks, there are fern bars and wine stores and two-lawyer couples who stop for fresh fish on their way back from exercise class. The 1964 earthquake virtually wiped out Anchorage's stock of older houses, but the one or two that remain standing have been gentrified to within an inch of their lives. The business world, characteristically, was on to yuppies long before the political world discovered them. It's not just a media whimsy.

Yuppiedom is the 1980s expression of American bourgeois culture. In the 1950s it was the suburban subdivision with two cars in the garage and wife at home raising kids. In the 1980s it's the working couple in the renovated townhouse sharing the child raising with each other and probably outsiders as well. The 1980s model doesn't describe the way most people actually live, any more than the 1950s model did. But it describes a set of trends affecting a significant chunk of the middle class in this predominantly middle-class country.

What is so offensive about the idea that young and youngish adults should have developed their own version of the middle-class culture that made America great? The offense taken seems to be of two sorts. From the left, there is a sense of irony, verging on outrage, that the generation maturing in the 1960s should have settled into middle-class life at all. *The Big Chill* factor. From the right comes the charge that yuppies are a disgrace to the bourgeois banner—all trivial self-indulgence and consumerist excess, no "middle-class values" of the sterner sort.

Well. Anyone who expected a generation of social revolutionaries to emerge from the 1960s has cause to feel disappointed, though the fraction of that generation who were social revolutionaries even at the time was awfully small. Part of this disappointment, I think, is just the sadness people of every generation must feel as they settle into their thirties and realize that they've made some irrevocable choices about the patterns of their lives. It's only natural that as people approach middle age, their main concern is going to be for themselves and their families. And that's as it should be. Those who expected more of this generation expected too much.

Nevertheless, a bit of the 1960s has rubbed off on those who passed through them. "Middle-class values" of the 1980s include respect for women's equality in both public and private life, concern for the environment, tolerance of human diversity, a healthy skepticism about military adventure. These solid roots implanted in the dominant middle-class culture are surely a more valuable legacy of the 1960s than any number of aging cadres still roaming the land agitating for revolution.

However, these very same new middle-class values can be turned into an indictment. Some polls show that yuppies tend to be conservative on economic issues but liberal on social issues and almost pacifist in their desire to avoid war. The picture is one of unalloyed selfishness: unwilling to tax themselves to help others less fortunate; adamant in demanding a right to sex, drugs, and abortion on demand; and unwilling to risk their own necks in defense of freedom. Yuk! Would you want your daughter to marry one of these specimens?

Based on my own acquaintance with yuppies (some of my best friends . . .), this indictment does not ring true. Selfishness and narrow ambition were not unknown in the 1950s. Yuppies are surely more likely to vote for Walter Mondale than their parents were to vote for Adlai Stevenson. What I find especially unconvincing is the attempt to cast the details of yuppy culture in a Gibbonesque light, as the beginning of the end for America. What, after all, is so terrible about quiche? Are jogging and spinach salad really more decadent than golf and sirloin? Is the journey from an obsession with the perfect martini to an obsession with California Chardonnay really another stage in the decline and fall of American civilization? Many aspects of yuppie culture strike me as clearly superior to what they replaced: small cars versus large ones, backpacks versus briefcases, hanging plants versus curtains, diversity versus conformity. At any rate, these are matters of taste, and nothing a yuppie needs to feel ashamed of.

There is a terminological dispute: Is it "yuppies" or "yumpies"— for "young upwardly-mobile professionals"? I first heard the term "yuppie" several years ago in Chicago's near-north side, an intensely yuppie neighborhood where you're never more than a few steps from yogurt. "Yumpie" emerged after Gary Hart won the New Hampshire primary, followed quickly by victories in Maine and Vermont. Clearly "yumpie" is a local variant which only gained national prominence because Hart's early victories were in predominantly rural states.

The term "yumpie" is doubly inadequate. First, because it misses the genuinely urban flavor of young professional culture, with its emphasis on neighborhoods and restaurants and renovation. Second, because "upwardly mobile" is a misnomer. If anything, yuppie culture is permeated with a sense of *downward* mobility, of couples struggling with two incomes to achieve a middle-class life that their parents enjoyed with one. Statistics do not, in fact, bear out the widespread feeling that things are tougher for today's middle class than they were for the previous generation, except for one aspect of life. But that aspect looms large: housing.

When my family made the big leap to the suburbs twenty-two years ago, my father worried that his children did not fully appreciate this achievement. I remember vividly that he sat me down in our new home and said pointedly: "You know, this is the nicest house I've ever lived in." I'm sure it never occurred to him, and it certainly never occurred to me until much later, that it might be the nicest house I'd ever live in as well.

One theory of yuppie consumption patterns is that pricey comestibles like designer chocolate chip cookies at $1.50 each are "affordable luxuries." They serve as consolation for the lack of unaffordable luxuries like a large house. You may not have a dining room, but you have a dining room table, and everything on it can have a complicated explanation involving many foreign words.

Surely this is more to be pitied than scorned. So be nice. Take a yuppie to brunch.

School Spirit Sucks

THE NEW REPUBLIC, *October 1, 1984*

When I lived abroad in the early 1970s, I discovered, to my surprise, that I was a patriot. Simple homesickness was part of it, along with the revelation that even a civilized country like Britain doesn't share American standards of liberty or plumbing. I also took umbrage at hearing foreigners say things about the United States that I had spent the previous few years saying myself.

Now the whole country is on a patriotic binge, egged on by the media and by President Reagan, who officially christened it the "New Patriotism" in a speech to the American Legion September 4, [1984]. Reagan offered as evidence the new military television show, "Call to Glory," a country-and-western song called "God Bless the

USA," his own invasion of Grenada, and, of course, "those young men and women on our Olympic team this summer."

The President failed to mention the repulsive hit film, *Red Dawn*—"America's Movie," say the ads—about a group of spunky teenagers who take to the hills to resist a Communist occupation of Colorado. Hollywood, nose to the *Zeitgeist*, shows it can swerve right just as fatuously as it swerved left fifteen years ago.

Early in the film, there's a debate between the student council president, who wimpishly suggests taking a vote about whether the kids should turn themselves in, and the former football captain, a charismatic d'Aubuisson of the Rockies, who understands that democracy is mere self-indulgence. Give up if you wish, he says with contempt. But, "If you stay, you're gonna do exactly as I say." They all stay, of course, and proceed with youthful high spirits to blow up the Communists with bombs, shoot them point-blank in the face, and so on. They call themselves the "Wolverines," after the high school team. Oh yes, the wimp democrat also turns out to be a collaborator and is executed.

There are different kinds of patriotism. Which kind is the "New Patriotism"? One kind, the best, is worship of a nation's ideals. The United States is one of the very few nations of the world (Israel is another) founded on a concrete set of noble political ideals. A few others, such as France and England, have democratic traditions ancient enough to be a legitimate part of their citizens' sense of nationhood.

A second kind of patriotism, less austere but far from ignoble, is a love of native culture, folkways, landscape. This kind of patriotism at its best, as in Orwell's writings about England and the English, becomes a celebration of common people that incarnates a fine democratic vision.

Then there's raw, vainglorious nationalism. This can be a harmless matter of "school spirit" (Go Wolverines!), or it can get ugly. The tone of the New Patriotism is perfectly expressed, I think, in the empty bombast of John Williams's theme music for the Los Angeles Olympics. The rhythmic chants of "U-S-A! U-S-A!" and "We're Number One!"—innocent enough during the Olympics themselves—seem more ominous as they continue to echo at public occasions of other sorts, such as the Republican Convention.

For heaven's sake, what is so glorious about winning the most medals in an international athletic contest? Olympic prizes have nothing to do with the values of freedom, tolerance, and diversity that have made America great. Somewhat the reverse, as a matter of fact. If societies are to be measured by their performance at the Olympics, free nations will inevitably fall short of totalitarian regimes, which can organize the whole society in pursuit of such pointless triumphs.

The former top Romanian girls' gymnastics coach, who defected a few years ago, commented recently in *International Gymnast* about the frustrations he faces in America. In Romania, he explained, he had his pick of the girls, and could select those with the best body type. But here, "It's very difficult. . . . You can't [show up at a school and] say, 'Well, I came to do a selection, please present the children.' " What's more, "Over there [Romania]. . . , we had the school program, we had the gym program, and we had the evening study program, and the rest and the relaxation. . . . There just seems to be too much free time over here. . . . It's very hard to control."

The Olympic hysteria is bound to help American coaches overcome these obstacles and dragoon ever-younger children into ever-more-single-minded pursuit of particular sports. For the greater glory of America, parents will send their eight-year-old daughters away to training camps—little islands of Romania—and if they should stumble along the way, like Mary Decker,* they will quite naturally take it badly, having betrayed their country and ruined their lives.

A fourth kind of patriotism, the worst kind, is exclusionary. There's all too much of this in the air as well. In *Red Dawn* we're told that the Communist invasion began with illegal aliens from Mexico blowing up a SAC base—an appeal to nativist sentiment made especially ugly by its complete illogic. But the dominant form of exclusionary patriotism is political, and the main purveyor is the Republican Party. Republicans have taken as a campaign theme that anyone who disagrees with them is un-American.

---

* An American runner who stumbled during a race in the 1984 Olympics and got pouty.

The clearest expression of this theme was Jeane Kirkpatrick's convention keynote address, with its ringing refrain about the Democrats: "They always blame America first." Logic suggests that the main focus of American political debate should be American behavior and options, not Soviet behavior, however heinous. In 1980 Ronald Reagan was blaming America first. But Kirkpatrick does not buy this. Her implied syllogism: if you disagree with Reagan administration foreign policy, if you complain louder about El Salvador than about Afghanistan, you are "blaming America first," and are therefore unpatriotic.

Just as *Red Dawn* is "America's Movie," President Reagan announced in Dallas that the Republicans are "America's party." The Democrats, by implication, are somebody else's party. When Reagan says that his reelection will "make America great again and let the eagle soar," he is indulging in mere foolish vainglory. But when he says, "Our victory will be America's victory," he goes too far. And when he ties his own electoral hopes to American success in the Olympics, when he muddles military victory, athletic achievement, fiction and reality, words and music, into a heady nationalist brew, he is not behaving like a true American patriot.

Celebrity Surgery

THE NEW REPUBLIC, *December 17, 1984*

*I*t was hard luck for NBC News that October's transplant of a baboon heart into a human infant took place at a hospital called Loma Linda. Tom Brokaw, NBC's anchorman, and Robert Bazell, its science reporter, both have serious trouble with the letter "L," which ruined the enjoyment of this surgical melodrama for many viewers. Someone goofed. Humana Inc., the private hospital chain responsible for November's artificial heart transplant extravaganza, would have changed the name of the hospital before letting anything interfere with the publicity.

Surgery has entered the age of celebrity. Doctors have tasted fame before, and even sought it, but never before has hype been so central. The operation on William Schroeder is what historian Daniel Boorstin calls a "pseudo-event." It exists only for the purpose of being publicized. That's why Humana, which does little medical research, put together the artificial heart team and is prepared to spend $35 million on their project. "Humana's large public relations staff has been busy in recent weeks," the *New York Times* reports, and "arranged for cameras to be focused on Mr. Schroeder during the procedure."

Thus the familiar rituals of publicity are reenacted. Journalists encamp. The nation meets and briefly becomes intimate with a new set of faces behind a new briefing-room lectern. (Or is it the same lectern?) *People* magazine runs exclusive interviews. Soon enough, all that remains is another name or two added to the national stock of dim memories. Baby Fae. Wasn't she one of the hostages in Iran?

Sorry, I don't mean to make light. But really. During the three weeks the nation was mesmerized over the fate of Baby Fae, eighteen other American babies (at the rate of about 1 in 12,000 live births) probably died of hypoplastic left-heart syndrome, Baby Fae's ailment. The nation did not grieve for them.

Publicized medical dramas take on a somewhat gruesome aspect in the recurring episodes that involve small children awaiting human organs for transplant. The nation conducts a vigil. Will a "suitable donor" arrive in time to save little Mary? What this amounts to is hoping that someone else's little Mary, preferably in perfect health, will be snatched from life in a freakish accident—hoping, that is, for tragedy to strike, so long as it strikes outside the spotlight of publicity. Sometimes it happens, and prayers of thanksgiving are heard across the land.

Most gruesome of all are the occasions when publicity itself determines who will live and who will die. This happens, for example, when distraught parents who know how to play the hype game beat out distraught parents who don't for scarce organs and limited experimental therapies.

One concern raised by ethicists about the Baby Fae case was that the parents were not offered the option of a human heart transplant or a different experimental operation that has shown some signs of success. This is wildly naive. True enough, Baby Fae was selected for a baboon heart by doctors who were looking for a place to put a baboon heart, not by doctors weighing the best alternatives for Baby Fae. But these other experimental options, like the baboon option, are only available fortuitously. "The conventional therapy," says a specialist, "is to place the babies in a corner and let them die." And the conventional therapy was Baby Fae's real option until the baboon people came along. But the TV cameras changed her situation. Ironically, the doctors were then ready to give Baby Fae a human heart, if one had been available when her baboon heart failed. By becoming famous, she had jumped the queue.

Celebrity patients like Baby Fae and Mr. Schroeder (people who are famous for being sick, that is, not famous people who get sick) are actually participants in a process that is more religious than medical. It is a public sacrament designed to celebrate our society's respect for the value of human life. By going to extremes to extend a few highly publicized symbolic lives, we demonstrate that we value the individual human being above all. Unlike other societies of the past and present, we are not social engineers who subordinate the individual to the perceived good of society as a whole.

Unfortunately, this ennobling premise is essentially false. No society, even the best, can avoid social engineering. You know it's a statistical likelihood that 2.47 workmen will die building a bridge, and you build it anyway because you need bridges. American health care, the most extravagant in the world, is nevertheless full of trade-offs of lives for money and lives for other lives. William Schroeder, for example, couldn't qualify for a human heart transplant because he is two years past the cutoff age of fifty.

The noble premise, in fact, makes sensible social policy much harder. The Baby Fae operation cost $1 million (less, perhaps, than what the media spent publicizing it). Even if the baboon heart could be made to work, and even if the cost were greatly reduced, is this the most efficient way to save human lives? And are these baby lives the ones most worth saving? We find these questions unbearable to ask.

Another example. Our national policy about health care innovations is absurd. New drugs must run a regulatory gauntlet so long and so costly that many useful pills are never developed, or only sold abroad. Medical "devices" such as artificial limbs must be approved before they can be used. New types of surgery—the riskiest, most invasive, and most expensive form of treatment—are virtually unregulated. One reason for this chaos is our collective inability to think rationally about when risks are worth taking that could harm a few or could help many.

From the simple rational point of view, it is hard to justify the effort to save Baby Fae, and even harder to appreciate the public emotion that became engaged in it. As it happens, the simple rational point of view is one of my favorites, and often undervalued, in my opinion. Nevertheless, we are a rich enough society that we can afford a sacrament or two. Radical efforts to save a few publicized human lives are not worthless even if they are merely symbolic. They honor a societal ideal that can't—in fact, shouldn't—always be kept. What distinguishes us from the barbarians is that at least we keep it in mind.

Greasy Kid Stuff

THE NEW REPUBLIC, May 13, 1985

*H*ave you hugged your child today? Careful, it's a trick question. According to the National Committee for the Prevention of Child Abuse, both excessive "fondling" on the one hand and "failures to provide . . . psychological nurturance" on the other can add you to the statistics on the nation's most fashionable social pathology. The "Living" section of the New York Times recently offered an article titled "A Puzzle for Parents: Good Touching or Bad?" as a guide for hug-hungry grown-ups looking to strike just the right balance. Caution: the mere pleasure of hugging a child is not sufficient reason to do so. "If adults are seeking the contact out of their own emotional . . . needs," the *Times* advises, that's "bad touching."

Why, now, has America become obsessed with child abuse in its various permutations: beating and molestation, kidnapping and abandonment? Of course these are tragedies when they occur. Despite heroic efforts by the media and social service agencies to prove otherwise, though, there's absolutely no evidence that they are any worse a problem than they were a few years ago, when everyone was worried about rape and drunk driving, and there's precious little reason to hope they will be less of a problem when national attention has moved on again.

My spies at *Newsweek* tell me that as they were closing their cover story a year ago on sexual abuse of children (a scant two months after their cover story on child abduction), one editor turned to another and predicted that within a year they'd be working on "The Child Abuse Backlash." *Newsweek* hasn't gotten around to it yet, but others are working on that story now. It has two angles. First is the witch hunt aspect. The reputation of a prominent California official was dragged through the mud by a ten-year-old girl who turned out to have made up a story that he molested her at his daughter's slumber party. A Chicago businessman was convicted of trafficking in child pornography when his local drugstore photo clerk turned in snapshots he'd taken of his six-year-old daughter, fresh from her bath, playing innocently with him and his wife in their living room. Lurid tales of pedophilic orgies in a small Minnesota town evaporated before a frustrated prosecutor's eyes as children admitted they'd made most of it up. Episodes like these have given people pause.

A second concern is whether we're raising a generation of paranoids by warning kids from the tenderest age about all the horrible things that might happen to them if they let grown-ups, including their own parents, get too friendly. A special Spiderman comic distributed by the National Committee for the Prevention of Child Abuse teaches kids to watch out for overenthusiastic baby-sitters, to be wary of new acquaintances, and to feel free about reporting Dad to the neighbors if he takes too much advantage. Perhaps unintentionally, the comic also encourages its young readers to open the window if a muscular stranger in a red-and-blue spider mask knocks asking to be let in, and to leap into his arms when he says he's going to take you to see your parents.

What puts me off about child abuse fever is not the concern that useful correctives may go too far, but the way the furnace is being stoked by grown-ups for reasons having nothing to do with the welfare of children. A lot of the graphic horror stories in the press are themselves little more than child porn, published or broadcast because editors and producers want to titillate. And when they're not being salacious, the media are being mawkish, which sells almost as well. It's an established fact, though science has been unable to explain it, that every kid who's ever been abused, molested, or kidnapped is cute as a button and possessed of both an angelic disposition and an equally adorable puppy dog.

Corporate PR departments have eagerly joined in. Southland, parent company of 7-11, used to concentrate on muscular dystrophy, but recently launched an ad campaign on the theme "Child Abuse: It's a Crying Shame." I called the social agency listed in the ad to ask where they had gotten the figure that 1 in 12 children is "in danger of" abuse. (An eager-beaver government study couldn't come up with more than 1 in 100 actually suffering from "abuse or neglect.") A woman said blithely, "Oh, somebody must have gotten it from somewhere. Ask Hill and Knowlton," the PR firm that prepared the ad.

The most shameless exploiters of children, though, have been our nation's politicians. There is now a "Children's Caucus" in the Senate, established on the ludicrous premise that children's interests previously had been ignored "because," says Senator Paula Hawkins, "they have no vote and no lobby." Child abuse is one of those issues politicians love because it's so utterly uncontroversial. No one's for it. So Congress and the President have been having a high old time the past couple of years passing laws against it.

Conservative Republicans who spend most of their political energies denouncing the idea that government can solve any problems at all—including problems it has been solving rather successfully for half a century—forget all that when an issue comes along that the television networks have gotten their constituents all het up about. Suddenly government action is urgent. And none of this state and local near-beer, either. We're talking 200-proof Big Central Government. The Missing Children's Act of 1982 authorized the FBI to search for missing children without any evidence they'd crossed state lines (a requirement that still holds for murderers). Republicans Hawkins and Alfonse D'Amato are the chief backers of a bill called the National Child Protection Act, which would apply all sorts of meddlesome national regulations to day-care centers. There's talk of extending federal regulation to baby-sitters. President Reagan himself proposes a substantial budget *increase* for the National Center on Child Abuse and Neglect, a division of the otherwise-battered Department of Health and Human Services.

For politicians, for the media, for the citizenry, issues like child abuse serve as a substitute for serious politics. It's a problem, sure, and government should do what it can to help. But it's not a systemic problem like unemployment or public education or national defense. Carrying on about child abuse allows everyone to engage in a mock exercise of civic virtue, without engaging the really great questions of government. Unlike child abuse, these are matters on which competing values must be weighed and about which people will tend to disagree.

Dohrn Again

THE NEW REPUBLIC, *October 14, 1985*

> They were careless people, Tom and Daisy—they
> smashed up things and creatures and then re-
> treated back into their money or their vast care-
> lessness, or whatever it was that kept them
> together, and let other people clean up the mess
> they had made.
> —*The Great Gatsby*

Whatever gave Scott Fitzgerald the idea that there are no second acts in American lives? It all depends on who you are and who you know. Consider Bernadine Dohrn and Bill Ayers, former heads of the Weatherman faction of SDS. Dohrn and Ayers emerged from a decade of hiding in 1980, married in 1982, and live with their three children in Manhattan. The papers reported last month that Dohrn, a 1967 graduate of the University of Chicago Law School, is working in the litigation department at the New York office of Sidley & Austin, a prestigious Chicago law firm, and has applied for admission to the New York bar.

Dohrn's attorney, Don H. Reuben, told the *New York Times*: "She's so conservative she's dull. I suspect it's children, the law, life and reading *Time* magazine." He told the *Washington Post*: "She's a yuppie. She has evolved from revolutionary to square." Imagine that.

But this isn't a *Big Chill* saga of lost youthful idealism, or a case of that political aging process known as "drifting to the right." For one thing, Dohrn and Ayers weren't just another pair of student protesters. They were important figures in SDS's move toward violence, which eventually led to several deaths. They believed that protest politics and the youth culture were an explosive combination and were eager to light the fuse. At the crucial June 1969 SDS convention, it was Dohrn who announced the purge of the opposing "Progressive Labor" faction. (PL, lunatic in its own way, favored close-cropped hair, adopted a more traditional Marxist class analysis, and eschewed anarchic violence in favor of organizing American workers for the big uprising.)

The name "Weatherman" came from the Bob Dylan lyric, "You don't need a weatherman to know which way the wind blows." Later, in deference to feminist sensibilities, the group was renamed the Weather Underground. Weatherman's philosophy, as summarized by Ayers, was: "Kill all the rich people. Break up their cars and apartments. Bring the revolution home, kill your parents, that's where it's really at."

Weatherman's big moment came in October 1969, when it staged the "Days of Rage" in Chicago. Although the organizers promised thousands of angry rioters, only 300 showed up (along with almost as many disappointed reporters). These few stalwarts duly set a bonfire of park benches and went on a window-smashing rampage until dispersed by police. On the second day, Dohrn led a special charge of women, wearing helmets and armed with lead pipes, against "that bastion of the imperialist army," a draft induction center. The next month, November, Weatherman tried, with little success, to foment violence at the huge and overwhelmingly peaceful Moratorium-Mobilization antiwar march in Washington.

The leaders of Weatherman soon became frustrated at trying to stage mass rioting without any masses. So at the end of 1969, they met in a "National War Council" and decided to go underground, where they would become "urban guerrillas." Dohrn declared it was time for "armed struggle" and praised the example of the Charles Manson family: "Dig it. First they killed those pigs, then they ate dinner in the same room with them, then they even shoved a fork into a victim's stomach."

Barely two months later, on March 6, 1970, an explosion destroyed a town house in lower Manhattan that turned out to be a Weatherman bomb factory. Three people were killed, including Diana Oughton, Bill Ayers's longtime girlfriend. (When they met in 1965, says Thomas Powers in his book *Diana: The Making of a Terrorist*, "Ayers was boyish, articulate, good-looking . . . not yet a revolutionary but already experienced in captivating girls with a combination of charm and social anger.") The next month police found another bomb factory in a Chicago apartment rented by Dohrn and two other women.

Over the next several years, bombs went off sporadically at the Capitol, the Pentagon, and various other government and corporate offices. One, at New York City police headquarters in June 1970, exploded shortly after a "declaration of war" surfaced from Dohrn, promising, "Within the next fourteen days we will attack a symbol or institution of Amerikan [sic] injustice." Later missives from Dohrn and Ayers claimed credit for freeing Dr. Timothy Leary, the LSD man, from prison in California and for blowing up a statue of a policeman ("pig") in Chicago.

When Dohrn and Ayers resurfaced in 1980, she was unapologetic. She accused the United States of "unspeakable crimes" and said she still believed "in the necessity of underground work." Bombing conspiracy charges against the couple had been dropped in the mid-1970s because of illicit government surveillance. Prosecutions for the bombings themselves were never pursued. As a result, Ayers was charged with nothing. Dohrn was allowed to plea-bargain for three years of probation on charges stemming from the Days of Rage.

In October 1981 Weatherwoman Kathy Boudin, who had escaped the exploding town house and hadn't been seen since, was arrested while fleeing an armed robbery in which three people were killed. Dohrn refused to cooperate with a grand jury investigating the massacre the next year. She accused the government of "illegality, lies, and misconduct." At that time (only three years ago) her lawyer described her to the court as being "intractable in her views and beliefs to the point of fanaticism." The undoubted reason he said this is that you can't be jailed for contempt of court if the judge is convinced you'll never change your mind. The judge wasn't convinced, and Dohrn went to jail. But she was released seven months later, without ever agreeing to cooperate. Now she wants into the New York bar, and the same lawyer who called her a fanatic calls her a harmless yuppie.

You may wonder how on earth a person with this record got hired by one of America's biggest and stuffiest law firms. The explanation is that her father-in-law, Thomas Ayers, is the former chairman of Commonwealth Edison Company and a doyen of the Chicago establishment. Ayers senior led the recently abandoned effort to get a 1992 World's Fair in Chicago. Sidley & Austin was counsel to the World's Fair Authority. Ayers is on the board of the Chicago Tribune Company. Don Reuben, a prominent Chicago attorney, is general counsel. And so on. Even without her radical baggage, a person who hadn't cracked a law book for eighteen years couldn't ordinarily get hired at a place like Sidley. Thanks to her establishment ties, however, the managing partner is terribly understanding. "We're not going to hold her past against her," he says.

The New York attorney who is helping Dohrn get admitted to the bar is Harold R. Tyler, former federal judge, former deputy attorney general, and name partner in the distinguished firm of Patterson, Belknap, Webb & Tyler. "She acts like a perfectly typical lawyer in a big firm," Tyler says. High praise indeed from a man like him.

It's hard to know which sight is more appalling: Bernadine Dohrn embracing the establishment or the establishment embracing Bernadine Dohrn. The entire spectacle reeks of contempt for serious politics. A lot of former radicals have become liberals and not a few have become conservatives, but they remain engaged in the struggle for what they see as a better world. Dorhn, if her high-priced apologists can be believed, is as contemptuous of this struggle as she ever was. (Bill Ayers used to talk of the need to "smash ideas . . . and combat liberalism in ourselves.") For Dohrn, it seems, there is no acceptable purpose in life between violent revolution and corporate litigation.

"The parents of 'privileged' kids [love those quotation marks!] have been saying that the revolution was a game for us," said Dohrn's July 1970 "declaration of war" from underground. She promised to prove them wrong. Now she's proved them right. And, of course, she's proved Dylan right as well.

Tea, Please

THE NEW REPUBLIC, November 25, 1985

*I*t strikes without warning—the disease that every year turns thousands of formerly normal Americans into mental cripples, willing to spend vast sums and travel thousands of miles for a fix. On Sunday evenings, an eerie quiet descends on upper-middle-class neighborhoods throughout the land as millions indulge their shameful habit. One of our nation's most cosmopolitan cities is now so thoroughly in the grip of this illness and its dreadful symptoms that healthy citizens from the rest of the country are staying away for fear of being infected.

The disease is Anglophilia. Washington used to be a carefree town where the natives, in their colorful gray pinstripe costumes, whiled away the days forming PACs, holding hearings, and issuing press releases. Now they drink tea, don their Burberrys, and queue up in the rain to see "Treasure Houses of Great Britain" at the National Gallery.

Despite the reassurances of so-called experts that Anglophilia cannot be spread through casual contact, we all know cases of people who've returned from a ten-day American Express bus tour swathed in tweed, sporting watch fobs, and nattering on about their "shed-jool." But these symptoms often clear up under an intense regimen of merciless ridicule. Lesser manifestations of the disease, such as a weakness for royalty, are widespread in the general population, many of whom have never even been to Canada. While there is no known cure for this, doctors believe it is essentially benign. Far more intractable and worrisome are the insatiable cravings for British scenery, British conversation, British journalism and theater—in the most extreme and pathetic cases, even British cooking—that develop among Americans who live in England for any extended period of time. In my own experience, this virulent form of the disease strikes after about six months of exposure.

The current hysteria over the visit of Prince Charles and Princess Di is less a matter of Anglophilia than of simple celebrity. If a celebrity is defined as someone who is famous just for being famous, then Britain's pea-brained royals are in some ways the original celebrities of the English-speaking world. For generations, their sole function in life has been to attract attention and admiration.

Today the worldwide celebrity machine has grown beyond anyone's control, let alone that of the British royal family, but they remain the ideal grist. *USA Today* recently devoted an entire page (the Gannett equivalent of a six-volume treatise) to questions and answers about Charles and Di. *Newsweek* managed to be scurrilous and sycophantic at the same time by running Diana on the cover, titling the story "Beyond the Fairy Tale," and promoting it on the contents page with this wonderfully hypocritical sentence: "The gossip, which invariably casts Diana (left) as the heavy whose capricious moods have supposedly alienated an increasingly eccentric and subdued Prince Charles, is both inevitable and unseemly." This approach is actually in the great tradition of British journalism, which often strikes a posture of: "Shame on those who say Princess Margaret is having an affair (pictures on page three)."

One level more alarming than royalty mania is the Anglophilia of "Masterpiece Theatre," in which "Britain becomes a sort of theme park, populated by epicene poets, irascible noblemen, loyal retainers,

stiff-upper-lipped soldiers, eccentric authors and likable drunks,"
writes a likable Brit of my acquaintance in a recent issue of *Harper's
Bazaar*. Alistair Cooke is the idealized Briton to many Americans,
who would be amazed to learn that he is the idealized American to
many Brits. He has developed the perfect mid-Atlantic accent,
which sounds British to the audience of PBS and American to the
audience of the BBC, to whom he's been broadcasting a "letter from
America" for decades. He always self-consciously says "we" when
talking of the United States.

From "Masterpiece Theatre," it is only a short step to cream teas,
sherry, subscribing to the *Economist*, touring stately homes, buying
marmalade from Crabtree & Evelyn, and taking baths instead of
showers. The *Economist* makes the whole world seem like a theme
park, where statesmen frolic for the amusement of a wry detached
observer who understands them far better than they understand
themselves. American editorial writers (even *TNR*'s) tend to favor the
furrowed-brow approach: "There are no easy answers to this complicated and deeply troubling question," etc., etc. For the
Economist, any fool can see that "the following three steps must be
taken immediately." I like to think the writer sat down at his
typewriter and decided there should be three steps before he decided
what they were, or even perhaps what problem they were intended to
address.

Of course even the most recidivist American Anglophile recognizes that "Masterpiece Theatre" and stately homes—and even the
Economist's brisk self-confidence—are artifacts of an England that
doesn't exist anymore. That's why the most crippling and incurable
form of Anglophilia is the one that wallows, not in England's former
greatness, but in her current decline: the endearing shabbiness, the
comfortable atmosphere of resignation. The bitter wit of *Private Eye*,
Britain's satire and gossip magazine that makes American journalism
seem paralyzed by gentility, and the jaunty undertones of self-
mockery and unseriousness that run through the *Spectator*, Britain's
leading political and literary journal, are products of a decadent
civilization that I find irresistible.

Doctor, is there any promise of a cure? The French are rumored
to be far ahead of us in research in this field. But the best therapy at
this point is a stable maintenance program consisting of three hours

a week of public broadcasting, semiannual visits to the scepter'd isle, and a large Stilton cheese at Christmastime. When you actually start hanging around with likable British drunks (and not bathing at all), medical science considers you beyond hope.

Porn Fiends and Porn Hounds

WALL STREET JOURNAL, *July 17, 1986*

> Consider a woman shown in a reclining position with genitals displayed, wearing only red feathers and high-heeled shoes, holding a gun and accompanied by a caption offering a direct invitation to sexual activity.
>
> —*Final Report, The Attorney General's Commission on Pornography*

Well, okay. Upon receiving an order like that one from an official government commission, in a report bound in solemn blue and stamped with the Justice Department seal, it is our patriotic duty to take a moment to comply. Actually, the commission serves up this fantasy to illustrate the inherent futility of its own pedantic effort to divide pornography into four categories: violent, nonviolent but degrading, nondegrading sexual activity, and nudity. But it also nicely illustrates the comic failed seriousness of these two fat volumes.

You can picture the commissioners sitting around a heavy table in a wood-paneled Justice Department conference room, gravely considering this hypothetical woman in red feathers and high heels. "With respect to such . . . materials," they sadly conclude, "we were unable to reach complete agreement."

It is easy to make fun of the Attorney General's Pornography

Commission Report. And, what the heck. Like any red-blooded American, the first thing I turned to when I got my hands on a copy ($35 at your local Government Printing Office) was the section labeled "Pictures." A bit disappointing. The first page shows a middle-aged man in a coat and tie, shot from the waist up. "Senator William V. Roth from Delaware, Chairman of the Committee on Governmental Affairs . . . is seen here testifying. . . ," says the detumescent caption. And it's downhill from there.

For the dirty bits, you must turn to a chapter labeled, "The Imagery Found Among Magazines, Books and Films in 'Adults Only' Pornographic Outlets" (pages 1499 to 1802, in case you're in a hurry). As the commission explains with a poker face, "Among the most common inquiries made to the staff . . . was a request for information on the content of currently available pornography in the United States." I bet.

Many have noted the irony of the government selling pornography. You have to read the stuff to appreciate how wildly funny it is ("Wildly funny"—*Wall Street Journal*), especially in the commission's high-toned presentation. The effect is something like a berobed Warren Burger intoning today's flavors at Baskin-Robbins. The telling point is that the porn hounds and the porn fiends share a mystical bond. Or, more prosaically, they have the same screw loose: they take this stuff seriously.

What sane person could read the commission's earnest 108-page alphabetized list of porn magazine and book titles without laughing? It's like a bizarre incantation. Recite after me: ". . . *Big Boobs, Big Boobs #1* and *#2, Big Boobs Bonanza, Big Boys and Their Buddies, Big Bust Bondage, Big Busted Ball Buster, Big Busty Babes . . . Girls Will Be Guys, Girls Who Love Their Toys, Girls Who Love To Sit on It, Girls Who Love to Sit on It #2, Girls Who Love To Sit on It #115, Gym #2, Gym Jocks, Gym Nasty, Hairy & Horny, Hanging Breasts, Hanging. . . ,*" well, you get the idea. Titles range from the hilariously but unquotably literal to the charmingly antique (*Gentleman's Companion, Swedish Erotica #98*) to the mock-bland (*Unisex Shoes and Boots*) to the almost-lyrical (*How To Play the Organ, Roger's Boys out of Uniform*).

After the listings come some sample descriptions, all wonderfully deadpan.

> *Squirt 'em . . . is a four color cover magazine measuring 8¼ x*
> *11 inches. There are 48 pages containing 69 photographs, 12 of*
> *which are four color photographs. The cover of the magazine*
> *features four photographs of two caucasian females, apparently*
> *naked, manually expressing a stream of milk from their engorged*
> *breasts.*

The plot summary of a novel called *Tying Up Rebecca* reads like
a sixth grader's book report, down to the sing-song voice, clumsy
grammar, tense problems, and obvious padding:

> *Chapter One begins on the page numbered 5 and finishes on the*
> *page numbered 25. . . . As Schultz watches, masturbating*
> *himself, Becky urinates into the toilet. Some of the urine splashes*
> *and extinguishes Mr. Schultz's pipe. He ejaculates on his clothes*
> *and Patty enters the bathroom dressed only in panties and*
> *bra. . . . He ejaculated in her, which knocked her half of a foot*
> *backwards. . . . Becky saw Loomis in pain and wanted to help*
> *him, in accordance with her Girl Scout oath, but she hesitated*
> *because she was nude. . . . Chapter Five begins on the page*
> *numbered 80 and ends. . . .*

If no one on the commission giggled at that business about the pipe
and the Girl Scout oath, these people are sicker than we realize.

The sexist convention of referring to men by their last names and
women by their first names continues in the movie summaries. In its
description of the classic *Deep Throat*, the anonymous voice of the
Pornography Commission begins austerely referring to the lead
character, played by Linda Lovelace, as "a female," but soon slips
unconsciously into a chattier mode: "Linda says there's more to life
than just screwing around." (This, of course, is the commission's
own philosophy.) Running the film in verbal fast-forward creates a
dizzy, Keystone Cops effect: "Dr. Young is then shown having
sexual intercourse with the blond nurse. Linda is shown performing
fellatio on Reems. Dr. Young is shown having intercourse with the
blond nurse. Then Linda is shown . . ."

Most of the humor in the main body of the Porn Report comes
from the commissioners' comic judiciousness, their effort to show

that they are not extremists but reasonable people who have thought of everything. In a discussion of how pornography turns sex into a commercial enterprise, they pause to note: "Whether the act of making sex public if done by a charitable institution would be harmful is an interesting academic exercise, but it is little more than that." Struggling with their own self-imposed dilemma of how to oppose portrayals of sex without seeming to oppose sex, they "unanimously" announce their opposition to "a proliferation of billboards displaying [a] highly explicit photograph of a loving married couple engaged in mutually pleasurable and procreative vaginal intercourse"—apparently the only type of sex they could all agree is okay in private. (The multiple elements of this standard are worthy of one of the more complex SEC regulations, and the question of how you would portray a sex act as "procreative" is one the commissioners duck.)

There is a snicker or two to be had, finally, in the commissioners' imaginative search for ways to crack down on porn without seeming to propose new forms of censorship. For example, they suggest making it an "unfair labor practice" to hire people for sexual performances. The products of this practice could then be confiscated under the labor laws. "This recommendation," they avow, "is made only out of an abiding concern for those persons used in these sexual performances. . . . Seldom, if ever, do employers maintain insurance, pay benefits, or provide pension plans to performers."

All right, what about a photograph of a loving married couple, both with employer-paid medical, legal, and 401(k) plans plus free parking, engaged in mutually pleasurable and procreative vaginal intercourse, and distributed to other loving, procreative married couples by a nonprofit foundation? Will that do? Undoubtedly not. Through one far-fetched theory of "harm" or another, the commission manages to disapprove of virtually any portrayal of anything that might offer man or woman a salacious chuckle.

Despite its stagy endorsement of current Constitutional limits, the commission's recommendations would drastically curtail people's freedom to read what they want. The commissioners even buy the absurd theory that traffic in pornography constitutes a violation of the civil right laws—this from a Justice Department dedicated in every other context to narrowing the application of those same laws.

Anyone who thinks pornography is a danger to the Republic should shell out $35 and try to read pages 1499–1802 with a straight face.

The Right Spirit

THE NEW REPUBLIC, *September 8, 1986*

"Between you and me, old man, I'm glad they
got me before it went any further. Do you know
what I'm going to say to them when I go up before the tribunal? 'Thank you,' I'm going to say,
'thank you for saving me before it was too late.' "
"Who denounced you?" said Winston.
"It was my little daughter," said Parsons with a
sort of doleful pride. "She listened at the key-
hole. Heard what I was saying, and nipped off to
the patrols the very next day. Pretty smart for a
nipper of seven, eh? I don't bear her any grudge
for it. In fact I'm proud of her. It shows I
brought her up in the right spirit, anyway."
—*Orwell, 1984*

*D*eanna Young was all of thirteen years old when she showed up at the Tustin, California, police station August 12 [1986] to report her parents for using drugs. She brought with her as evidence a trash bag filled with marijuana, unidentified pills, and $2,800 worth of cocaine. Deanna apparently made her decision after hearing an antidrug talk at church.

Judith Young, thirty-seven, a bankruptcy court clerk, and Bobby, forty-nine, a bartender, were carted off to jail. Although they have since been charged and released, Deanna at last report was still in the

custody of the Orangewood Children's Home, despite her pleas to be
let out to rejoin her parents. According to Deanna's lawyer, parents
and child have met, and "they are very supportive of her."

So we're well on our way toward the conclusion to this story that
everyone is longing for: tearful reconciliation-cum-press conference.
Parents announce that they now recognize the error of their ways,
praise daughter, join drug rehabilitation program. Nancy Reagan
helicopters in from the ranch to present whole family with award for
showing "the right spirit." Music up and out. A spokeswoman for
Dick Clark Productions—one of several Hollywood companies that
have inquired about the film rights—said, "It would be great if the
family got back together again and we could have a happy ending."

We don't know what home life was like for Deanna Young.
Maybe there was no dinner on the stove most nights, no help with
the homework, no one to tuck her in, because her parents were
drugged out all the time. The point is that Mrs. Reagan had no idea,
either, to what extent the Youngs' drug habit was interfering with
their parental duties when she congratulated Deanna for turning
them in. "She must have loved her parents a great deal," Mrs.
Reagan opined. USA Today found a psychology professor at Kansas
State University to declare that it "takes some guts to do something
to help . . . when your parents are unable to help themselves."
Judging from the sepia-washed coverage this episode has gotten in
the press, it appears that encouraging children to spy and rat on their
parents is now an official policy of the war on drugs.

Obviously arresting someone for using drugs is not like arresting
someone for "thought crimes," as in 1984. On the other hand, the
political response to the current hysteria over drugs contains a
genuine whiff of thought-crime thinking. There is more and more
pressure for people to get on board, to have "the right spirit."

Consider the growing fad of "voluntary" drug testing. President
Reagan started the ball rolling by taking the test himself and inviting
seventy-eight top White House aides to follow suit. His Commission
on Organized Crime recommends "voluntary" testing for the whole
federal government. The only point of such a program would be to
set an example for private employers.

In a way, the prospect of widespread voluntary drug testing is even
more ominous than the idea of mandatory testing. By ostensibly

giving you the right to refuse, voluntary testing makes the act of urinating into a bottle a patriotic gesture—a test of your right-mindedness as well as your clean-bloodedness. This is especially true since, as a matter of logic, the notion of voluntary drug testing is nonsense. If you're using drugs and the test is truly voluntary, you won't take it. The test is meaningless unless the authorities are willing to draw some negative conclusion from a person's refusal to take it. And if they are, it's not really voluntary, is it?

Here is White House press spokesman Larry Speakes on this delicate conundrum: "We believe the American people, under voluntary testing, would certainly want to, in many cases, step forward. And those who don't, as in some cases, and are obviously on drugs, would certainly find a certain amount of peer pressure particularly as we make progress in the area of cleaning up the workplace." Pretty comforting, eh?

Speakes's reference to "cleaning up the workplace" points to another insidious aspect of this drug-testing fever: the use of employers to enforce social mores. A treasured difference between an American-style free-market capitalist society and a Mussoliniesque or Japanese-style corporate state is separation of the economic and personal spheres. In America, a job is just a job, and how you lead your life is none of your boss's business if you're doing your job well.

A properly administered drug test must be supervised to prevent cheating. Thus it becomes a classic humiliation ritual: urinating on command in front of a watchful agent of your employer or the government. A free people ought to have an awfully good reason before subjecting themselves to this.

Sure, some jobs offer reason enough. There is widespread and easy consensus that there's nothing wrong with drug testing for air traffic controllers, people with high-level security clearances, and so on. But this is a solution in search of a problem. I'm aware of no evidence of widespread drug use among air traffic controllers or CIA agents. The demand for drug testing of people in "high-risk" jobs is really a response to a more generalized need to do *something*— anything—about drugs. It's part of the effort to put the country in "the right spirit."

That's why the search for excuses to test for drugs is becoming comical. In Hawkins, Texas, high school students must fill a jar before they're permitted to join in extracurricular activities such as the student council and the cheerleading squad.

Conservatives are supposed to believe that society is healthiest when authority is diffuse. Central government power should be minimal. Social control should spring from smaller social units between the state and the individual—most especially, the family. But in the rush to exploit the great drug hysteria, it seems that top-down authority is back in and parental authority is out.

MERITOCRACY

INTRODUCTION

Stated baldly, the proposition that America should be a society where people can get ahead "on their merits" is a hard one to argue with. And indeed, although the word itself was seldom used, "meritocracy" was one of the powerful uniting themes of Reaganism. It brought together, for example, the neoconservative intellectuals infuriated by affirmative action and rich businessmen oppressed by high taxes. Both saw Democratic government policies as thwarting America's meritocratic promise.

As someone who's done okay in the meritocratic game, I am not so selfless that I want to see it ended. Nor am I so stupid that I can't see what has happened in societies that have attempted radical leveling experiments. But the ideology of merit rarely gets poked around the way it should. That's what these articles attempt to do.

At one extreme, among traditional Republican business types, "meritocracy" is just a defense of the status quo. Among the intellectuals who came to conservatism from the left, there is generally still a recognition that American society is not yet as perfectly meritocratic as it might be. In its purest intellectual form, meritocracy consists of the belief—generally advanced by people who were born smart but not rich—that all the natural advantages of being born rich should be eliminated, while all the natural advantages of being born smart should be preserved. It's been eighteen years since the notorious *Atlantic* article by Harvard psychologist Richard Herrnstein, noting that a perfected meritocratic society—far from an egalitarian paradise—would be more rigidly hierarchical than any previous society known to man. But the meritocratic ideal remains strong.

Meritocracy has been much in the thoughts of the American intelligentsia for the past decade because of the debate over racial preferences. Those who say they support "civil rights" but oppose "affirmative action"—or support "affirmative action" but oppose "goals and quotas," or support "goals" but oppose "quotas," or support "equality of opportunity" but oppose "equality of result"—generally have some ideal of meritocracy in mind.

"The Conspiracy of Merit" was my first signed piece for *The New Republic*, written almost a decade ago. It is the product of someone still immersed in the American educational rat race, which shows. It also predates the recent (and generally welcome) fashion for entrepreneurship. The occasion for the article was a special *TNR* issue dedicated to the then-forthcoming *Bakke* case. *Bakke* kicked off a series of Supreme Court decisions on affirmative action that has left the area in a state of almost perfect confusion. Under slightly different procedural circumstances, the same constitutional provision—the equal protection clause of the Fourteenth Amendment—can either forbid you or require you to practice reverse discrimination.

"The Conservative History of Civil Rights" and "Greed and Envy" both concern Reagan administration efforts to build a public ideology that will support their policy agenda, which actually derives from an ideology perhaps better kept private. "Just Dribbling," about Georgetown University's all-black basketball team, is an attempt to test civil rights principles in a novel context. It is also my only attempt since college to write on a sports-related topic. It brought no commissions from *Sports Illustrated*.

Just four months after mocking the MacArthur Foundation's "genius award" program ("What's So Great About Excellence?"), I found myself working for the MacArthur Foundation as editor of *Harper's*, which the foundation had recently saved from folding. Based on my subsequent dealings with the MacArthur family, I may be the only person in America who can say with total confidence that he or she will never win a MacArthur Award. In the years since the "genius awards" program got started, the selections have become a bit less wearily obvious. Every group of winners includes one or two ostentatiously bizarre choices—a magician or a convicted rapist or a dog food manufacturer—just to prove these awards are "unconventional." Most of the winners, though, remain just the type. And the award itself has become one more shimmering credential, to be included on résumés and book jackets and eventually in obituaries.

In the years since "Fate and Lawsuits," about litigation over the pregnancy drug DES, first appeared, the explosion of product liability lawsuits has become an officially sanctioned "crisis." The tort explosion has even made the cover of *Time*, and reform has come close to passing Congress on several occasions. The Reaganites and their business allies would love to see national legislation to limit runaway state-court judges and juries, but are trapped by their own pieties about federalism. Businesses are similarly trapped: they don't like being sued in California, but they do like being able to incorporate in Delaware.

My friend who railed against the cult of alligator shirts ("Dressing Down") is James Fallows, Washington editor of the *Atlantic*. At the moment Jim is living in Malaysia, where, for all I know, they have real alligators wearing shirts with little journalists on them.

The Conspiracy of Merit

THE NEW REPUBLIC, *October 15, 1977*

*F*rom their high perch, the Brahmins of merit view developments all around them with alarm. Society seems on the edge of abandoning its commitment to "equal opportunity." Desirable places in the social hierarchy no longer are automatically dispensed to people "on their merits." Well, why should they be? The notion of "merit" is invoked to justify not only the rules that determine who shall be blessed with various kinds of good fortune but also the social decision to permit and even encourage vast disparities in individual fortunes. Yet the validity of merit as a social ordering principle rarely is examined. Having survived a fair number of society's ordeals of merit (like any other member of the educated elite), I think this country is in the grip of merit madness. This madness possesses four symptoms: an irrational belief that "merit," as commonly defined, is morally praiseworthy; a ludicrous overestimation of how rewarding merit contributes to national prosperity; blindness to the innate unfairness of the merit principle; and an underestimation of how recurring meritocratic ordeals corrode social life and the lives of individuals.

In its decision in the *Bakke* case, the Supreme Court of California expressed familiar sentiments when it refused to endorse racial quotas for medical school admission. To do so, the court wrote, "would call for the sacrifice of principle for the sake of dubious expediency and would represent a retreat in the struggle to assure that each man and woman shall be judged on the basis of individual merit alone, a struggle which has only lately achieved success in removing legal barriers to racial equality." Race, obviously, has nothing to do with merit. Therefore, it follows, race should have nothing to do with determining who gets society's goodies or positions of access to them. Likewise sex, religion, absence of physical handicap. None of these things are meritorious, and therefore none of them deserves to be rewarded with social advantage.

But how do the qualities we define as "merit" differ from these "unfair" advantages? Some are different. The meritocratic ordering principle, operating under laboratory conditions, rewards hard work, dedication to a given task, loyalty to a particular set of values. But it rewards even more intelligence, imagination, education, and a variety of other factors that are either genetic or instilled by environment at a very early age. Everything about the meritocratic system conspires to convince its beneficiaries that success is a function of moral worth, and therefore is justified by it. Some of the most desirable meritocratic plums—prizes, scholarships, etc.—serve no social function except the celebration of "merit" and the praise of those who have it. It is easy to believe—almost impossible not to believe—that worldly success in a meritocratic system is the just result of one's own endeavors. But surely these endeavors play a very small part in most worldly success stories. Or at least if I were about to begin the meritocratic struggle, and if I were told to choose either a generous dollop of innate advantages or the opportunity to exert myself without these, I have no doubt which aspect of "merit" I'd pick.

The apparent unfairness of a system that provides more of what everyone wants to some people than to others, even on the basis of "merit," is rationalized by the concept of "equal opportunity." If everyone has an equal opportunity to exercise merit in the service of ambition, justice has been satisfied and the inequality of result doesn't matter. The job of social reform, therefore, as meritocrats see it, is to eliminate all advantages *other than merit*. The common metaphor is a foot race. No competitor should have a head start or other "unfair" advantage. To be black is like running the race while chained to a ten-pound weight. You have heard all this before.

But in the attempt to create equal opportunity as a justification for meritocratic inequalities in result, the ideologues of merit are hoist on their own petard. One by one the list of officially disapproved handicaps grows: poverty, race, religion, sex, age, physical handicap. Inevitably one wonders, Why not mental handicap? What about stupid people? If "equal opportunity" is what society guarantees to everyone, aren't stupid people as much entitled to it as smart ones? It is as arbitrary a piece of bad fortune to be born stupid as it is to be born poor or physically handicapped. Why should society go to great lengths to compensate for the one disadvantage and ignore the other?

It appears that the pertinent innate differences between individuals can be divided into two categories. On the one hand there are "unfair advantages," and on the other hand there is "merit." Inequalities in the distribution of society's manna based on the former must be ruthlessly eliminated. Inequalities based on the latter are celebrated.

We are ruled by a conspiracy of merit. Those who have it get power, prestige, wealth; those who haven't don't. Those lacking the qualities called merit aren't likely to be able to challenge this system, and those blessed with these qualities aren't likely to want to. People who have risen through merit perpetuate and refine the meritocratic system, smug in the belief that its moral authority is sufficient to justify any degree of social hierarchy, and its mechanics are so refined that any deviation from meritocratic principles for whatever social purpose is self-evidently evil.

Of course there is an important second line of defense for meritocracy. Meritocracy may not be a moral imperative, but at least it is an instance of the general rule of economic efficiency that scarce resources—including human resources—should be priced at their marginal value to society. Rewarding merit assures that merit will exert itself to the maximum possible extent, and society as a whole will be enriched. Paying doctors extravagantly assures that society will have its choice of the most intelligent and dedicated people in selecting its doctors; admission to medical school is the occasion for this choice, and it would be foolish to let the occasion slip by without asserting the principle of merit.

But this rule of economic efficiency, however correct and however important, is simply crushed under the weight of our psychological commitment to meritocracy. It cannot support this commitment. When the reward of merit is seen as something that serves the interest of society in general, rather than as something that is the *right* of the meritorious *individual*, it loses a lot of its moral force. It becomes harder to see why the principle of merit must never be sacrificed to other important social goals, such as integrating blacks and women into the high reaches of the economy. The principle has *no* force, except to the extent it actually does contribute to social efficiency. The traditional method of choosing among candidates for medical school, for example, clearly rewards the standard indices of merit—intelligence, determination, etc. But so what? The question is whether it produces the best doctors. Is each of the 100 students admitted to a class at the Davis Medical School going to be a better doctor than the 5,000th candidate? The 500th? The 105th? In every common field of endeavor, the rhetoric of merit as moral worth disguises the crudeness of meritocratic principles as tools of social efficiency.

Furthermore, once we abandon the idea that merit itself *deserves* to be rewarded, it becomes impossible to justify on grounds of efficiency alone the enormous disparities in wealth and prestige that the meritocratic system perpetuates. Are these disparities really necessary to entice meritorious types into activities where their merit will do society the most good? A recent survey we took shows that the typical *New Republic* reader is a professional making $34,000 a year.* If the jobs of *New Republic* readers and writers carried the same salaries and cachet as those of the people who make their livings cleaning up after us, is it likely that very many of us would say "the hell with it" and pick up a broom? Is it really necessary to pay doctors five or more times the national average income, or would— say—only twice that figure be sufficient to entice enough qualified candidates into a profession they all claim on their med school application forms they are eager to join irrespective of money?

The concept of meritocracy and how it is supposed to work has evolved over the past 100 years. It strikes me as improbable that the meritocratic machinery as it operates in the late twentieth century actually does serve to direct talented people toward productive occupations. The obsession with rooting out, testing, certifying, and rewarding merit may have exactly the opposite result.

The paths to success are much more highly structured and defined today than they were in the more fluid society of the nineteenth century. Success is coming more and more to consist of rising to the top of some bureaucratic hierarchy. Corporate leaders today did not found great industrial empires, they rose through them. The top lawyers are partners in huge law firms. Reaching these pinnacles, or even more modest peaks within a particular occupation, depends less on the direct application of personal merit and more on credentials— official certification that one possesses merit. Merit was once thought of as what people possessed who had gotten ahead. There was no need to define it with any precision, or to make official determinations of who had it and who didn't. Now it is defined as what you *need* to have in order to *qualify* for getting ahead. Once you are certified as having it, getting ahead is virtually assured.

Thus the determination of merit takes on the quality of self-fulfilling prophecy. Instead of a steady progress in which the wheels of the economy slowly but inexorably sift out merit and reward it, life is a series of officially administered meritocratic crisis points: school report cards, admission tests, college grades, graduate school entrance exams, honor societies, professional qualification exams,

---

* Thanks to inflation, and to *TNR*'s tonier image in recent years, that figure is now double.

prizes, interviews, promotions. On each occasion your merit is measured. If it is found sufficient, you pass on to the next meritocratic moment. Increasingly as you rise, your merit is measured by how many hurdles you already have jumped. The connection between the qualities being rewarded and the social goal allegedly being served by rewarding these qualities becomes weaker and weaker.

Inevitably this perpetual formal assessment and reward of merit discourages creative and ambitious people from careers that exploit their merit and drives them into careers that merely confirm it. Instead of becoming inventors or entrepreneurs, they become lawyers or cogs in the corporate machine. The meritocratic process becomes an end in itself, consuming the energy and creativity that it is supposed to measure and then channel into activities where they can be most productive. Too much about today's meritocratic process encourages people to sublimate their own values and interests in order to engage in a Sisyphean struggle through one meritocratic ordeal after another in competition against their colleagues.

No one should be required to run a foot race chained to a ten-pound weight. But by the same token, no one should be required to run a foot race in which he is fatter or clumsier than his opponents. And why should life be like a foot race anyway?

The Conservative History of
Civil Rights

WALL STREET JOURNAL, *June 20, 1985*

"There are some today who, in the name of equality, would have us practice discrimination. They've turned our civil rights laws on their head." So said President Reagan in his radio address last Saturday. This is a familiar story. According to the official conservative history of civil rights, there was an Edenic golden age, circa 1964–1969, when every decent person agreed that the government should exert all its power to prevent discrimination based on race. Let the editors of the *Wall Street Journal* continue the saga (from "The Colorblind Vision," March 11 [1985]):

> *After the Civil Rights Act of 1964, civil rightists made rapid progress toward equality under the law. It was only in the 1970s that the new goal, "affirmative action," was introduced, putting the movement behind a new form of discrimination, racial quotas. . . . [T]he Reagan Justice Department [is] simply trying to return to the original track.*

Trouble is, there was no such golden age. Among those who never shared "the colorblind vision" in the 1960s was Ronald Reagan, who vociferously opposed both the 1964 Civil Rights Act ("a bad piece of legislation") and the 1965 Voting Rights Act ("humiliating to the South"), ostensibly on constitutional grounds. Syndicated columnist James J. Kilpatrick, who recently praised the Reagan administration for being "fervently devoted to civil rights" and savaged its critics for advancing "the Orwellian doctrine that some are more equal than others," was a leading segregationist bitter-ender.

The *Wall Street Journal*'s position on the 1964 Civil Rights bill in 1964 was one of reluctant acquiescence. It complained that the provisions forbidding discrimination by restaurants and hotels were "an abridgement of property rights," which it connected to "the growing contempt for private and property rights" shown by Negro rioters. It defended the Southern filibuster against the bill in the name of "minority rights." It commented after three Northern civil rights workers disappeared in Mississippi and were feared (correctly, it turned out) to have been murdered: "Without condoning racist attitudes, we think it understandable if people in Mississippi should resent such an invasion. The outsiders are said to regard themselves as some sort of heroic freedom fighters, but in truth they are asking for trouble." In the end, the *Journal* did note approvingly that the civil rights bill, however defective, would "affirm a public philosophy on civil rights."

Clearly, though, if it had been up to most of those now bleating about how the civil rights movement has betrayed the Civil Rights Act, there would be no Civil Rights Act. I share most of the practical doubts about affirmative action rehearsed so often on these pages. As a social policy, it's probably a mistake. But the pious complacency of affirmative action opponents, floating on clouds of self-righteous twaddle about "merit," strains my patience. This is especially true of those who have embraced the principle of "old-fashioned," "color-blind" civil rights just in time to apply it in a way designed to achieve exactly the opposite of what was intended.

Bradford Reynolds, the head of the Justice Department's Civil Rights Division, has no record of opposing civil rights. But he has no record of supporting them, either, that justifies Mr. Reagan's description of him as "a tireless fighter against discrimination." It's hard to see how anyone with an ounce of passion about civil rights, in the traditional sense of ending discrimination against blacks, could have attempted to reverse the established government policy of denying tax exemptions to segregated private schools. Mr. Reynolds insists he didn't want to do this, but felt the law required it. He made no effort to change the law, though, until after a public outcry, and the Supreme Court ultimately rejected his bizarre legal interpretation.

Writing in *Newsweek* June 10, George Will praised Mr. Reynolds's civil rights approach. "Reynolds supports affirmative action as initially conceived 20 years ago. Then it meant recruiting and training programs to interest qualified minorities to enter the pool of applicants." Thus a second element of the Edenic myth: that there used to be a good kind of affirmative action morally superior to the "racial spoils system" of goals and quotas.

But why should "recruitment and training" be exempt from the general anathema on favoritism by race? In an ostensibly meritocratic society, every rung on life's ladder is "recruitment and training" for the next. Special recruitment and training for blacks denies opportunity to innocent white victims—simply because of their race—just as surely as does any other form of favorable treatment. No, "reverse discrimination" obsessives must have the courage of their convictions: if they mean what they say, all forms of racial preference and color-consciousness are equally invalid.

They can't mean what they say. Clarence Pendleton, the head of Reagan's Civil Rights Commission, who rails against reverse discrimination, got his job because he's black. Can anyone doubt it? Being a black who opposes affirmative action was a qualification for the job. In this context, his race was part of Mr. Pendleton's "merit," not something apart from it.

What George Will describes as "a bedrock principle of this republic, the principle that rights inhere in individuals, not groups," does not exist. For example, the Supreme Court has been agonizing in recent years over whether affirmative action can override seniority systems in government agencies. (The court ultimately said no.) In one of these cases, involving layoffs at the Boston Fire Department, a footnote revealed that neither race nor seniority was the major factor in layoff decisions. The major factor was an absolute preference for veterans. Veterans' preference may be a good or a bad social policy, but it is an American tradition, and it is a policy based on group attributes, not on individual "merit."

In a nation where people are getting ahead and falling behind for all sorts of reasons—some fair, some unfair; some based on individual attributes, some based on group characteristics; some serving important social functions, some simply arbitrary or actually harmful to society—you have to wonder about an administration whose greatest moral outrage is reserved for people who acquire some advantage because they are black.

Greed and Envy

THE NEW REPUBLIC, February 27, 1984

> There will be those trying to appeal to greed and envy—and make no mistake, that is what they are trying to do—who suggest that our tax program favors the rich. This is the same antibusiness, antisuccess attitude that brought this country to the brink of economic disaster.
> —*President Reagan, January 31 [1984]*

All right, let's talk about greed and envy. Success, too. These are all crucial concepts in the Reagan worldview, reflected in the policies of his administration.

I was surprised to hear Reagan come out against greed. Could this be the handiwork of that nefarious coven of pragmatists we keep reading about—the one the far right claims has taken over the White House? Or is it one of Reagan's famous "gaffes"? No, no, Mr. President, you're *for* greed. Adam Smith demonstrated in *The Wealth of Nations* how the "invisible hand" directs individual greed in ways that produce general prosperity. You're supposed to accuse the Democrats of not understanding this, of killing the goose that lays the golden eggs. Remember?

The claim for supply-side economics is that it can cure a sick economy through the healing power of greed. Indeed, greed is even more central to supply-side economics than to traditional free-market theory. Supply-siders claim to be able to play greed like a fiddle, to ride it like a bronco, to manipulate greed with scientific precision through changes in tax rates. Lower a man's taxes, unleash his greed, and stand back.

The plain fact is that Reagan's tax program *does* favor the rich. The biggest and quickest tax breaks, by far, went to top-bracket investment income, and to inherited wealth. Counting Social Security, most wage earners actually have had a tax *increase* since Reagan took office. True supply-siders make no apology for this. Rewarding successfully applied greed is the whole idea.

Now, envy is more complicated. This subject brings out the conflict within modern conservatism. Old-fashioned Tory-style conservatism prizes stability and social order. Because social order requires hierarchy, disparities of fortune are healthy. Anyway, they are inevitable. The good society is one in which everyone knows, and is contented with, his or her place. From this perspective, encouraging people to compare their stations in life with those above them is corrupt and dangerous demagoguery. It creates insatiable appetites and rends the social fabric. That's "envy," and that's bad.

But Ronald Reagan and the people around him usually claim to be a different and more palatable kind of conservative—the kind sometimes self-styled a "classical liberal." This sort of conservative favors maximum individual freedom and an unfettered capitalist economic system where, as Reagan told the unemployed in his recent State of the Union speech, "Each of you can reach as high as your God-given talents will take you." In this worldview, invidious comparisons are not corrosive; they're healthy. People are *supposed* to be constantly reminding themselves of the heights they've not scaled. And Reagan himself is fond of reminding them by offering success stories in his speeches for audiences to salivate over. Only now it's not "envy": it's "incentive."

What both strains of conservatism agree on is that those who are at the top of our society deserve to be there. And, by implication, those who aren't don't. When Reagan accuses the Democrats of an "antisuccess attitude," he apparently detects some skepticism on this score. I wish I detected more of it. There's nothing wrong with success. In a properly functioning capitalist system, successful people really do enrich society as a whole more than they enrich themselves. This kind of success is important to America's prosperity and strength. It should be prized and nurtured. But the smug Republican assumption that success in our economy is the result of applied moral worth, and that it's therefore immoral and ultimately self-defeating to tinker with success and failure as the economy dishes them out, is wrong for at least four reasons.

Most obvious but least interesting is the fact that many people at the top got there through blind luck, not through any special effort or talent of their own. They inherited wealth, or happened to own land that became valuable or oil when OPEC quadrupled its price. Through policies such as virtually eliminating the estate tax and slashing the tax on oil royalty income, our federal government has made this type of "success" much easier during the Reagan years. (Democrats in Congress, it's only fair to add, share the blame.)

Second, the American economy is not capitalism operating under laboratory conditions, where effort and "God-given talent" are directed by an invisible hand to where they can most benefit society as a whole. There's nothing "antisuccess" about wondering whether society is getting value-for-money from its highly paid investment bankers and lawyers; from corporate executives who run their companies into the ground, then award themselves big raises and "golden parachutes"; from speculators in various markets. Reagan, with his tax cuts, has made success in America more successful, but he's done nothing to make it more productive. If anything, opportunities for unproductive success have increased during his tenure.

Third, if individual talent is "God-given," as Reagan says, why is it so obvious that the individual is morally entitled to hoard all the fruits? Thomas Edison said that genius is "1 percent inspiration and 99 percent perspiration," but surely that's a better definition of failure than of success. Effort helps, of course, but it's not the key. Most of the elements in financial success are "God-given" in the sense that they are the luck of the draw, and have little to do with innate moral worth. So even when riches come through individual talent, productively employed, why shouldn't they be spread around a little bit? One answer is practical: if you don't reward effort by talented people disproportionately, they won't put their talent to work. That's a reasonable justification for some disparities of wealth and income. But it's not a moral imperative, and it doesn't necessarily explain or justify the disparities we've got.

Finally, no one's prosperity in America really comes primarily from individual effort. It comes primarily from the efforts of other Americans, past and present. It comes from the economy and the society that all Americans have built together. Why does a third-generation American barber, say, make four times as much money as his grandfather made, and ten times what a barber makes in some Third World country today? Does he work four times harder? Is he ten times more talented? Of course not. The American entrepreneur who makes millions by building a better mousetrap probably learned science at public schools, tapped into generations of mousetrap R&D, produces and markets his mousetrap in the world's most efficient economy, and sells it to the world's most prosperous consumers. Everybody's "success," however great or modest, however augmented by luck or by grit, is largely a product of society. Is it "antisuccess" for society to claim a share?

What kind of conservative is Ronald Reagan? Denouncing "greed" and "envy," he sounds less concerned about the state of capitalism and individual liberty (both worthy concerns) and more like that other kind of conservative, who prizes wealth and poverty for their own sake, because they're "God-given."

Just Dribbling

THE NEW REPUBLIC, *April 15, 1985*

T he hot topic in Washington lately has been Georgetown University's basketball team. As I write, the Hoyas are on the
verge of winning their second straight NCAA championship.* Not a
hot topic is the fact that even though Georgetown's student body is
disproportionately white, the basketball team (also for the second
straight year) is entirely black, from Coach John Thompson down to
the lowliest benchwarmer. There is no conspiracy of silence; it's just
considered unremarkable. Blacks have come to dominate basketball.
Almost three-quarters of professional players—and even more start-
ers—are black.

Nevertheless, it's interesting. Forty-one of the forty-three tenured
professors at Georgetown's prestigious law school are white. Even
those forty-one probably see this statistic as evidence that blacks are
racially disadvantaged in society as a whole. If there were *no* blacks
on the Georgetown law faculty, this would be taken as strong
evidence of direct institutional racism and could well lead to
lawsuits. But if it's self-evidently wrong that the top of the legal
profession is overwhelmingly white, why isn't it self-evidently wrong
that the top of the basketball profession is overwhelmingly black?
Should there be affirmative action for whites on the basketball
court? Or as some conservatives argue, do examples like this
show that the thinking behind affirmative action is fundamentally
flawed?

After all, making the Georgetown team confers tremendous
advantages. It gets you into a top university. It gets you financial aid,
special academic help, and good jobs through the alumni network.

---

* They lost.

College athletic scholarships are often a cruel false promise for talented blacks, who are used and then discarded without job skills or a degree. But Georgetown and Coach Thompson pride themselves on being different. And for those who do make the pros, the average annual income is $300,000.

So why is it that these advantages go disproportionately to blacks? Many people believe, though fewer will say publicly, that blacks are genetically superior in athletics, especially basketball. A controversial *Sports Illustrated* article fourteen years ago cited evidence that black men on average have longer arms and legs, denser bones, less protruding heels, and what-not. The trouble with this argument (besides the fact that it's never been proved) is that it raises the unnerving question whether genetic advantage can explain the white predominance in most other walks of life—another rarely expressed but widely held belief.

The genetic explanation is not worth reaching for in either case, since cultural explanations are so apparent. Sports like basketball loom large in black culture for several reasons. Most obvious is racial discrimination in other fields, including most sports. Even as opportunities expand, black athletes remain the role models for ambitious black youngsters. But to explain is not to justify. Similar cultural factors can explain why whites are overrepresented in, say, law. But defenders of affirmative action are not satisfied with this explanation in that case.

A better explanation might be that in basketball, unlike law and most other fields, meritocracy demonstrably works. Ability is objectively measured and visibly rewarded. Cronyism and prejudice are harder to disguise. That's why blacks, once freed of official discrimination, have done so well. In *Anarchy, State and Utopia* the philosopher Robert Nozick uses Wilt Chamberlain as his example of morally justifiable inequality.

And yet Georgetown's Coach Thompson has been accused of discrimination against white players in his recruiting. He denies it. But the conservative black economist Walter Williams has written in defense of just this kind of prejudice, when directed against blacks by white employers. Generalizing from stereotypes isn't racism at all, he says, but rather the efficient minimizing of information costs. Williams would say: Black ball players tend to be better. Why look for whites? Most people won't find this an appealing argument for prejudice.

Thompson may not practice racial discrimination, but he would have a hard time proving it to the satisfaction of our civil rights laws as now interpreted. In the photo-negative case, here's what would happen. First, his all-white team would create a presumption of bias. Second, to overcome that presumption Thompson would have to provide objective justification for all his recruiting methods. A newspaper profile of Thompson a couple of years ago quoted Georgetown's president, Father Timothy Healy: "He has rejected players because he does not feel they will fit the team. What I think he really means is that they don't fit his personality." This was intended as praise, but the same words said about the dean of the law school could cost Georgetown hundreds of thousands of dollars.

The great defect in the affirmative action mentality is that it treats life like a scientific experiment. It leaves no room for subjective judgments, cultural preferences, intuitions, established relationships, and all the other messy elements of fate that determine who ends up playing basketball for Georgetown. Rooting out all these elements in the name of eliminating bias is not only a hopeless task but a misguided one.

But the even greater defect in the mentality of affirmative action critics is that they don't see the difference between prejudice against blacks and prejudice against whites. One is an historic injustice that remains widespread, while the other is an occasional anomaly. This may seem like belaboring the obvious, but it's a distinction apparently beyond the grasp of Clarence Pendleton, the head of President Reagan's Civil Rights Commission.

Pendleton is a black former California "consultant" who thinks his race had nothing to do with his appointment. He recently denounced as "immoral" the view of two other commissioners that civil rights enforcement should be especially solicitous of "disfavored groups" such as blacks. This controversy has generated a lot of editorial huffing and puffing about how the civil rights laws are for everyone. Of course that's true. But they're especially for blacks. That is the only good reason why every would-be basketball player in Washington is cheering John Thompson's Hoyas instead of suing them.

What's So Great About Excellence?

THE NEW REPUBLIC, *June 6, 1981*

John D. MacArthur got rich by selling one-dollar life insurance policies through newspaper ads during the Depression. "Dubious" is how *Parade* magazine charitably described this scheme in 1976, by which time MacArthur was a self-made billionaire and self-styled colorful old codger, fond of shoveling leftover food into his pocket at banquets. When MacArthur died in 1977, he left almost the entire billion to a foundation named after himself and his wife. MacArthur's own soft spots were for dogs, trees, and the handicapped. But his foundation's first original venture is a "Prize Fellows Program" designed to "honor a small number of exceptionally talented individuals who have given evidence of originality and dedication to creative pursuits." The first 21 fellows have just been chosen, with the help of 100 secret nominators scattered throughout the country. Each winner will get $24,000 to $60,000 a year for five years (tax free) plus health care and other expenses, so that they all may "devote themselves to their own creative endeavors." The net effect of John D. MacArthur's entrepreneurial life and philanthropic afterlife, then, will have been to take one dollar each from a large number of poor and ignorant people, assemble the money into somewhat larger amounts, and give these piles to a very few members of the prosperous, educated elite.

People, even editorial writers, have compared the MacArthur Foundation scheme to that old television series, "The Millionaire," in which an anonymous financier dispatched one-million dollar checks to unsuspecting ordinary people. But the premises of the two enterprises are quite different. The charm of "The Millionaire" was the spectacle of fate being flouted. Life had dealt these characters a lousy hand, but suddenly they had a royal flush. The MacArthur Foundation, by contrast, sees itself as fate's midwife, combing the nation for life's winners and making sure they are delivered safely into affluence and esteem.

Fate rarely needs such help. The redundancy of the exercise is well illustrated by the names of the first MacArthur Fellows. Roderick MacArthur, son of John D., seems to believe that his selections are more exotic than those of similar exercises that are the stock-in-trade of other foundations, fellowships, prize committees, and so on. "It's a high-risk venture," he told the newspapers," . . . the risky betting on individual explorers while everybody else is playing it safe on another track." In fact, far from requiring 100 anonymous tipsters, putting together a list like this is a parlor game. Given one or two of the names, many people could come up with half a dozen others without even knowing what the list was for. It could be this year's honorary degree recipients at Princeton, or a Presidential Commission on the Future of Values, or the celebrity endorsers for a tony Scotch advertising campaign. Round up the usual suspects; check for diversity of fields, sexes, races; call the press conference.

What philanthropic purpose is served, for example, by conferring yet another honor on Robert Penn Warren, dear old poet though he may be? Warren won a Rhodes scholarship back in 1928. Since then, according to *Who's Who*, he has been the official poet of the Library of Congress, the Jefferson Lecturer of the National Endowment for the Humanities, a Houghton Mifflin Literary Fellow, a Guggenheim Fellow, and winner of the Levinson Prize, the Caroline Sinkler Prize, the Shelley Prize, the Robert Metzler Award, the Sidney Hillman Award, the Edna St. Vincent Millay Prize, the National Book Award, the Irita Van Doren Literary Award, the Van Wyck Brooks Award, the National Medal for Literature, the Emerson-Thoreau Award, the Copernicus Prize, *three* Pulitzer Prizes, and honorary degrees from Harvard, Yale, and twelve other colleges.

Robert Coles, the Harvard psychologist and another MacArthur Fellow, has won many of the same prizes as Warren (though only one Pulitzer), plus others. He accepted five honorary degrees in 1978 alone. The MacArthur list includes two other Pulitzer Prize winners

(Carl Schorske, the Princeton historian, and James Alan MacPherson, the novelist), one other well-known Harvard professor (biologist Stephen Jay Gould), and at least one other Harvard honorary degree recipient (Elma Lewis, who promotes arts for poor blacks in Boston). Even the ones you may not have heard of are identified as having "won honors for her poetry, film-making and plays" (Leslie Marmon Silko, a thirty-three-year-old Pueblo Indian) or having "received a number of awards" (Robert S. Root-Bernstein, a biochemist at the Salk Institute).

Not one of the first MacArthur Fellows is suffering from lack of recognition for his or her talents. What's more, though some probably can use the money more than others, not one really faces financial obstacles to exercising his or her creativity. They are already doing whatever it is the MacArthur Foundation admires them for doing, many are doing quite well at it, and presumably they will keep on doing it, unless this windfall encourages them to stop.

What the MacArthur Foundation really seems to be rewarding is a sort of generalized capacity for receiving honors. In doing so, it has created the ultimate credential in a credential-obsessed society, a *reductio ad absurdum* of meritocracy. Other exercises of this sort, from the Nobel Prize downward, generally require excellence to manifest itself in some concrete form, and/or insist that the honor is contingent on some duty or other. The MacArthur people wish to celebrate merit in the abstract, and seem perfectly content to let it stay abstract. Thus their prize raises most clearly the question of what social function these exercises perform. Why is celebrating excellence considered a legitimate function of charities, and even of the government itself? That is, since the winners of these awards generally are winners in the larger sense, what good do these awards do for life's losers?

For a democracy, we are strangely tolerant, and even enamored, of gratuitous invidious distinctions between people. I once had a fancy fellowship at a time when it was not open to women. A great fuss was made about this and the rules were changed, as they should have been. But I could never get worked up over the notion that excluding women was *unfair*, because the fellowship, like all such institutions, was unfair by its nature. It was restricted to men, it was restricted to citizens of certain countries, it was restricted to college graduates of a certain age. More fundamentally, it was restricted to the sort of people who win fellowships—smart, glib, capable of moderate-to-excessive obsequiousness. All these restrictions but the first remain. The founder of this fellowship, like John D. MacArthur, had made his money by exploiting the sort of people who don't win fellowships. The only way to make the fellowship *fair* would be to dismantle it and give the money back, but I could never get my fellow fellows worked up over that notion. Thank goodness.

Prizes of this sort are considered part of the general incentive and reward structure that makes our society and our economy function. Perhaps some narrowly focused honors really do have this effect, operating on, say, artists or scientists like the profit motive on a business executive. But take something like the Kennedy Center Honors, created three years ago because, according to Kennedy Center Chairman Roger Stevens, "We believe that there is a need in this country for national recognition of individuals who enrich our lives and our culture by their life work in the field of the performing arts." A "need"? The first winners were Marian Anderson, Fred Astaire, George Balanchine, Richard Rodgers, and Artur Rubenstein. Have they really been underappreciated and underrewarded for their contributions to our cultural life? Is there another potentially great hoofer out there somewhere who has considered Fred Astaire's career—the fame, the glamour, the money, the love of millions, the other awards—and who has decided it's not worth it, until he reads that Fred has won the Kennedy Center Honors, and decides not to become a dentist after all? That's what you have to believe in order to suppose that giving Fred Astaire one more award serves any useful purpose.

Here's another one. George F. Kennan recently was awarded the 1981 Albert Einstein Peace Prize. The prize, worth $50,000, was established two years ago by the Albert Einstein Peace Prize Foundation, presumably to encourage peace through the price mechanism. Would George Kennan be any less for peace without the prospect of $50,000 before his eyes? It is a libel even to suggest as much. Have George Kennan's previous efforts for peace been thwarted by poverty and obscurity? It would be hard to say this of the winner of the Pulitzer Prize, sundry honorary degrees, the usual. Is anyone going to work harder for peace on the off chance that someone might give him $50,000? Unlikely. So what has the Albert Einstein Peace Prize done for peace?

Roderick MacArthur said in unveiling the MacArthur Prize Fellows Program, "This program is probably the best reflection of the rugged individualism exemplified by my father." But in fact it reflects precisely the opposite attitude. John D. MacArthur was self-made. He left school in the eighth grade and worked in a bakery, at a gas station, in the army, and at various entrepreneurial schemes. The basic theory of meritocracy is that in a free society the meritocratic virtues—imagination, daring, hard work—will produce their own reward, and in John D. MacArthur's case, for better or worse, they did. But there is no such thing as a self-made MacArthur Prize Fellow. This reward must be conferred. The MacArthur program, with its 100 "talent scouts" and its predictable standards, perfectly symbolizes the spirit of credentialism, in which these same meritocratic virtues are tested for in the laboratory and rewarded from the common fund. The enterprise is not merely silly, but snooty: an exercise in invidious distinction for its own sake.

Fate and Lawsuits

THE NEW REPUBLIC, June 14, 1980

In 1937 a British scientist developed an inexpensive chemical substitute for the female sex hormone, estrogen. This was a great medical breakthrough. In 1947, the Food and Drug Administration approved diethylstilbestrol (DES) as a treatment to prevent miscarriages, thought to be caused by hormone deficiencies. During the next twenty-four years, more than a million pregnant American women took DES on prescriptions from their doctors. In 1971 a Harvard scientist reported a link between mothers who had taken DES during pregnancy and a rare type of vaginal cancer years later in their daughters. The FDA withdrew its approval of DES for problem pregnancies. Shortly afterward, the lawsuits began.

DES, it turns out, causes cancer in about one out of a thousand "DES daughters" in their teens or early twenties. Some have died. When the cancer is caught in time, the usual treatment includes a hysterectomy and removal of the vagina. As many as 90 percent of DES daughters have adenosis, a minor abnormality of the vagina. There is no evidence so far that adenosis is harmful or precancerous, but women who have it are advised to get a special examination every few months. DES daughters have a higher-than-average rate of miscarriages, but this may be genetic, since pregnancy problems are what led their mothers to take DES in the first place. DES is now thought to have been worthless in preventing miscarriages, though that, like everything else about DES, is disputed.

More than one thousand lawyers are involved in litigation over DES, according to Connie Bruck in the *American Lawyer* magazine. Most of the lawsuits involve DES daughters suing the companies that manufactured the drug. There are ninety-five lawyers representing the drug companies. Eli Lilly, the company with the most suits against it, has teams of defense lawyers dotted around the country. There are hundreds of attorneys representing DES daughters. The main function of most of them is to refer clients to one of several attorneys specializing in DES litigation. The original attorney shares the fee. Larry Charfoos of Detroit, leader of the DES specialists, has about four hundred cases and is co-counsel in lawsuits in thirty different states.

The drug companies are scared to death. Lilly's total sales of DES from 1947 to 1971 were $2.5 million. It already has spent many times that amount in legal expenses. Even $10,000 for each adenosis case could add up to billions, and Charfoos claims there already have been some adenosis settlements "in the $30,000 to $50,000 range." He says that recent reports about fertility problems will raise the price of adenosis settlements. No adenosis cases have come to trial yet. In the two cancer cases so far, both last year, juries awarded the victims

$500,000 and $800,000. Until then, cancer settlements had been in the $150,000 to $250,000 range. Now they will be higher.

Joyce Bichler's case is typical. In July 1953 her pregnant mother began to bleed and cramp. The doctor prescribed DES, which she took for less than twelve days. Joyce was born with no apparent problems in January 1954. In the fall of 1971 her cancer was diagnosed and she underwent a hysterectomy and vaginectomy. In 1974 she sued Eli Lilly. The trial began May 19, 1979, and ended July 16. The jury awarded Bichler $500,000.

Five hundred thousand dollars is not an absurd excess of compensation for the loss of all of a woman's reproductive organs at age seventeen, for the pain and suffering she has undergone, for the emotional strain and loss for the rest of her life, and for her medical bills. No one sensible would trade the experience for $500,000 if she had the choice. But almost everything else about the DES litigation is absurd. As an illustration of the law at work, it is a farce. As a way of dealing with the risks of living in a complex and scientifically advanced society, it is inept. As an exercise in doing justice, it is an evasion.

For example, if $500,000 was just compensation for what Joyce Bichler has suffered because her mother took DES, is the $800,000 that Anne Needham got from another jury for the same tragedy more just or less just? How about the $260,000 Cindy Dettelbach settled for last month, before her case went to trial? "That's the nature of our business," Larry Charfoos says cheerfully. "Cancer might have a very different price in a small town in Iowa than in Manhattan, New York City."

Of course Joyce Bichler won't get $500,000. Her lawyer will get a percentage of it as his "contingency fee." The usual fee for plaintiff's personal injury lawyers is one-third of any recovery, plus expenses. And the Bichler judgment will cost Lilly a lot more than $500,000 because it has lawyers too. Top corporate litigators charge by the hour—$150 an hour or more, and as much as $400 an hour for time spent in court. Lilly had three lawyers on the Bichler case, and the trial lasted two months. Before that came five years of research, depositions, preparing witnesses, and so on. Now comes the appeal. Transcripts of trials and depositions, at $2 a page, can cost $15,000 for a several-week trial. Big-time experts can get $1,000 a day for their testimony, which often takes several days. In preparing a case like this, lawyers crisscross the country, often in twos and threes, flying first class and running up hotel and restaurant bills, all of which the client pays for. In the DES litigation, according to Bruck in the *American Lawyer*, all the drug company defense lawyers meet periodically for massive strategy sessions at resort hotels. Charfoos told Bruck that twenty lawyers from other drug companies sat in the audience throughout his DES trial against one of them in Chicago last year, just to watch. All that is what lawyers call billable time.

A 1977 government study of product liability concluded that each dollar paid to plaintiffs costs defendants another 42 cents in expenses, almost all for lawyers, and that about 35 cents of the plaintiff's dollar goes to lawyers too. This means that on the average it takes 77 cents in legal costs to deliver 65 cents to the victim, not even counting the cost to the government of running the show or the time contributed by people drafted for jury duty. Clearly it will cost more than $1 million to get Joyce Bichler about $300,000. And like a traveling road show, the same lawyers and the same hired experts will litigate the same issues at equivalent cost dozens, or even hundreds, of times around the country before the DES saga is over. The victims will get thousands; the lawyers will get millions.

The doctrines of tort law were devised for straightforward moral situations—somebody's misbehavior causes harm to somebody else—and for narratives that observe the three unities of classical drama: time, place, and action. It takes heroics of legal sophistry and that deus ex machina known as the jury to apply tort law where a company makes a pill and twenty years later someone who wasn't even born yet faces an increased risk of cancer. For example, in half the DES cases, no one remembers which company's pills the victim's mother took. About 150 different companies made DES during the early 1950s. Ordinarily they all would be off the hook whenever the other side couldn't prove which one made a particular mother's pills. Joyce Bichler's lawyer, like many others facing this dilemma, chose to sue Eli Lilly, since Lilly apparently produced more DES than anyone else. One jury concluded that the lawyer hadn't proved Lilly made Mrs. Bichler's pill (how could he?), then a second jury ordered Lilly to pay $500,000 anyway, on the theory that all the companies competing to sell DES actually were acting "in concert," and therefore all are individually liable for the harm caused by any DES pill. The California Supreme Court has taken a different tack. That court ruled in March that when the manufacturer is unknown, it is up to the drug company to prove that it *didn't* make a particular DES pill, which of course is impossible.

Two-thirds of the 400 young women known to have developed this very rare form of cancer are DES daughters. But 999 out of 1000 DES daughters don't get this cancer, and some who get this cancer aren't DES daughters. Joyce Bichler's father had recurring cancers that led to removal of most of his prostate and part of his colon. Statistics reveal a strong genetic element in cancer, too. Who's to say that DES caused the cancer in any particular case? The law is indifferent to any sufferer whose cancer was not caused by DES, thus placing great moral and financial weight on a distinction that science cannot make. The law solves this problem by letting the jury decide.

Very few of the plaintiffs in these DES lawsuits have cancer. Most have adenosis, apparently a benign condition. Some have no physical problem at all. To win a lawsuit, you must establish that you've suffered some harm. DES daughters do have to get regular check-ups, but the cost of these is not enough to interest the personal injury bar. So in the noncancer cases, the lawyers are asking courts to find that "fear and anxiety," or the increased *risk* of getting cancer, are themselves harms. Charfoos is asking $2 million each, but has suggested that he would settle eighty of the noncancer cases *en masse* for a total of $3 million or $4 million.

The biggest challenge for the plaintiffs' lawyers is establishing that the drug companies did anything wrong. They produced a drug that they sincerely believed would help pregnant women avoid miscarriages. It was thoroughly tested by the standards of that time and approved by the FDA. The damage took two decades to show up. Until the thalidomide disaster in 1962, there was no known case of a pregnancy drug causing deformities in the offspring, and the discovery of the DES link in 1971 was the first evidence that any pregnancy drug could cause cancer in the offspring. Nevertheless, the plaintiffs' lawyers argue that the drug companies should have foreseen that DES might cause cancer years later in daughters of pregnant women who took it and therefore shouldn't have marketed it for miscarriages.

Sometimes the law helps plaintiffs to avoid this problem by holding manufacturers "strictly liable" for defects in their products, whether or not they were negligent. The reasoning is straightforward. As the chief justice of California put it in March, "From a broader policy standpoint, defendants are better able to bear the cost." By making producers liable whether or not they've done anything wrong, "the risk of injury can be insured by the manufacturer and distributed among the public as a cost of doing business."

After all the legal and factual issues have been spun out for a couple of months, they are turned over to the jury, which has been chosen for its previous ignorance of both. The jury is told the law and is supposed to apply it to the facts. The Bichler jury was told to answer a long series of unanswerable questions such as whether DES caused Joyce Bichler's cancer, whether a reasonably prudent drug manufacturer in 1953 would have tested DES on pregnant mice, what such a test would have revealed, whether the drug companies acted "in concert," and so on. It was told various rules of evidence, such as "prior statements are not legal proof of the facts stated therein." It was asked to compute the exact dollar value of Joyce Bichler's troubles, based on how long it predicted she would live. The jurors were expected to ignore irrelevant matters such as Lilly's size and wealth, which the plaintiff's lawyer referred to frequently, but only (of course) in reference to a minor issue in the trial. Jurors were told about Mrs. Bichler's medical bills, but not about her legal bills. The law, for its own reasons, assumes that plaintiffs don't have to pay their lawyers, which they do, and that they do have to pay their doctors, which very often (if they're insured) they don't. Five days of deliberations produced the figure of $500,000.

The hundreds of suits over DES are the law's ham-handed way of dealing with two tricky questions: What risks are worth taking in an uncertain world? And who should bear the loss when the risks turn out badly? In dealing with both these questions, the law tends to overlook the fact that taking risks brings benefits as well as harms. For example, a DES class action filed recently in Maryland asks the court to rule "that, if without DES a class member would not have been born, she may, under Maryland law, maintain an action for injury from exposure to DES." The law, by its nature, abhors a loss more than it values a gain. Therefore the law discourages taking risks whenever hopes of benefit must be weighed against unknown dangers of loss. This is exactly the situation created by scientific advances such as new drugs.

Whether or not the drug companies were careless about DES, no degree of care will prevent occasional disasters of this sort. Under present arrangements, any such disaster will produce many lawsuits. And no matter how exquisitely the legal doctrines about "fault" and "unavoidably unsafe products" are refined, the enormous costs of defending these suits and the natural sympathies of juries assure that drug companies will pay heavily for all their disasters. The potential human cost of failure, however blameless, thus enters their calculations of whether it is worth marketing a new drug. This sounds fair enough, if you forget about the lawyers' costs for a moment. But the law does not help the companies to absorb all the benefits of health and happiness that come when one of their drugs works well. All they get in that case is the price of the pill. So the law works as an influence not against irresponsible risks, but against any risks at all.

There is a gruesome futility about the law's loathing of risks, its celebration of hindsight. Right after the DES-cancer link was discovered in 1971, some DES daughters with adenosis submitted to partial vaginectomies to avoid getting cancer. This is now regarded as unnecessary, because adenosis does not seem to lead to cancer, but the victims are suing the drug companies over this loss even while other DES daughters are suing over the fear that adenosis might lead to cancer after all. The doctors who had to decide, in the early days, whether to operate for adenosis may well have been influenced by fear of lawsuits if they failed to operate and cancer did develop. Some of the most important evidence about the effects of DES comes from a controlled experiment at the University of Chicago in the early 1950s. Three of the women involved in this experiment are now suing the university for having put them at this risk. The university and others will be more careful in the future, thus increasing the risk that new cancer sources will go undetected. Meanwhile the fear of lawsuits is making doctors and hospitals reluctant to help track down DES daughters, thus increasing the risk that some of them will get cancer that isn't caught in time.

Science makes trouble by presenting us with apparent boons that have unpredictable consequences. That is what Dr. Dodds did at

Oxford in 1937. But science also makes trouble by discovering causes and connections that formerly were thought of as just fate. That was what Dr. Herbst did at Harvard in 1971. For most of its victims, cancer remains just fate. But all cancers are caused by something. Is it any less fate to get cancer just because the cause becomes known? The extravaganzas of recrimination staged by our legal system on such occasions help to avoid facing up to the fate problem directly. Sometimes the recrimination is justified. Yet the technical somersaults the law performs to assure that the victims can recover suggest that fate itself is what's really bothering us. There's nothing to be ashamed of in this. In fact, the insistence on finding human responsibility, so that fate can be exonerated, before the victim will be given alms, is an illogical and expensive conceit.

Advanced legal thinkers accept this reasoning, up to a point. They see products liability litigation as a social insurance program. Even if no one's at fault, manufacturers should absorb the cost to the unlucky few and share it among the lucky many who use their products without harm. Seen this way, litigation makes sense only to lawyers and judges. The costs that get spread around to the lucky many are far greater than what reaches the unlucky few after the lawyers are done. The amounts the victims receive vary arbitrarily over a wide range, and the process of getting any money to them takes years.

Some legal thinkers even acknowledge this and go one step further. By analogy to no-fault auto insurance, they propose a no-fault products liability system. A government program would pay set amounts of compensation to victims of defective products and collect a small tax on all products covered by the program to pay the cost. This would spread the risk equitably while avoiding expensive litigation, in theory.

But even this lawyer's version of justice seems cramped. The logic of socializing risks is a slippery slope. If no one is at fault, why socialize the cost of getting cancer from DES and not the cost of getting cancer from sources unknown? Why not socialize the cost of being handicapped, or even of being poor? That is to say, why not socialism? Socialism, in this sense, doesn't refer to public ownership of the means of production. It merely means an underlying assumption that there is no moral basis to fate as nature dishes it out.

Under the influence of lawyers, society goes to great lengths and costs to undo the workings of fate in specific transactions, while ignoring workings of fate in the general injustices of life. Someone who gets cancer because of DES will be reimbursed (minus lawyers' bills) for her physical pain and suffering, her mental anguish, her reduced sexual satisfaction. Others will get thousands of dollars for benign physical defects, or for the fear that they might get cancer. Meanwhile someone who gets cancer for no apparent reason can't even get her medical bills paid for. And what about someone who has to spend her life mopping other people's floors, or who can't get a job at all? That is a misfortune, too, but no one is proposing a "no-fault" compensation program for her.

There are limits, of course. Should we compensate people for being ugly? Should we spread the risk of being slothful? Should we insure against being unhappy in love? Probably not. Fate is too capricious and imaginative for any society, no matter how generous, to make up for the ways fate can find to make people miserable. Furthermore our own society believes, correctly, that a market economy works best for everyone involved, and such an economy requires a dose of inequality and risk in order to work at all. But *how much* inequality and risk such an economy requires should be a more pressing question than it is.

A society that doesn't guarantee high-quality health care, a satisfying job, and a decent minimum income to all its members is kidding itself to suppose that justice is satisfied, or even served, by devoting billions of dollars to lawsuits over specific misfortunes. Ritual triumphs over fate in ceremonies of litigation make it easier to ignore fate's own triumphs in everyday life.

Dressing Down

HARPER'S, *February 1983*

A friend of mine, writing in another magazine, argues that America is rife with snobbery and obsessed with status, and offers as evidence the fact that people will pay extra for a shirt with a little alligator sewn on it. He may be right about snobbery and status, but I think he's got it wrong about the alligator.

My friend and I come from similar backgrounds, have similar tastes and a similar view of the world, and neither of us owns any shirts with alligators on them. Why not? It is tempting to say that we are free of such petty snobbery and would rather save a dollar or two than gain whatever status is available from displaying an alligator on the chest. On reflection, however, the truth is different. If offered two shirts, one with an alligator and one without, I, at least—and he too, I think he would admit—would pay at least a dollar or two *more* if necessary for the shirt without the alligator.

Analyzing my motives in this imagined exercise, which I pre-sumptuously impute to my friend as well, it seems to me that they bear more of the indicia of snobbery than the motives of people who pay extra *for* the alligator. After all, the instinct that longs for the alligator is *inclusive*, a desire to embrace and be embraced by the alligator-wearing crowd. The instinct that rejects the alligator is *exclusive*, a desire not to be associated with the sort of people who wear alligators. Speaking for both of us, I can assert confidently that this latter desire is not based on modesty. It does not derive from any sense that we are not worthy of the alligator and those who wear it. By process of elimination, then, the awful truth: we feel superior to people who wear alligators. We are snobs.

But what kind of snobbery is it? I see three possibilities. One is conventional snobbery of a more sophisticated sort. Seeking status through the wearing of alligators is a mug's game. There are too many alligators by now plastered on too many things to confer any status anymore. Alligators are passé. Serious prestige freaks moved on long ago to shirts with little polo players embroidered on them, and no doubt are onto something else by now which I can't inform you of. Anyway, it's been pointed out often that all the brazen consumer status symbols that have sprouted in recent years—initials on luggage, signatures on jeans, and so on—are basically déclassé because they are too obvious. Real status clothing is unlabeled and reveals itself only in a subtle code involving placement of buttons or shape of collar or a certain kind of stitching—and only, therefore, to others who know the code.

A second possible interpretation of anti-alligator snobbery comes from the famous distinction first promulgated in a 1956 book by the British aristocrat and novelist Nancy Mitford. Mitford divided all forms of behavior into two categories: U (for Upper Class) and non-U (non-etc.). Anything self-consciously affected or refined is non-U. It's non-U to say "home" and U to say "house," non-U to say "odor" and U to say "smell," and so on. Under this dispensation, any badge of status as blatant as an alligator on your shirt is definitely non-U. An unmarked tennis shirt is better, but the ultimate U torso covering would be a torn old flannel undershirt. Of course, the U and non-U distinction is every bit as self-conscious as the stratagems of the straightforward status-seeker, or more so. The true aristocratic attitude, held by someone truly convinced of his superior place in the scheme of things, would be one of complete indifference to whether his shirt had an alligator on it or not. Few people have that kind of insouciance. This U/non-U business is for those who wish to fake it, and can be quite convincing if executed with panache.

But there's a third possibility, most treacherous of all. If my friend really thought that alligator shirts had become utterly commonplace and therefore a sign of low status, or if he thought that aristocrats wouldn't be caught dead in them, he'd go out and buy a dozen. As a matter of fact, the sport shirts I've seen my friend wearing are not unmarked. They have a little fox on them, which indicates to the cognoscenti that they were bought at J. C. Penney's. My friend is a reverse snob.

Far from being rare or eccentric, reverse snobbery is, in my experience, by far the most common kind of the slice of American society occupied by people who worry professionally about things like snobbery and social class. In fact, and perhaps this sounds complacent, I sometimes wonder where all this alleged snobbery of the traditional sort is. There is racism, of course, and far too much economic inequality. Favoritism and unfairness are everywhere. It is better to be rich, as Sophie Tucker said. But social class snobbery? Among people like me and (if I read *Harper's* demographic studies correctly) people like you, it seems a pretty spent force.

My adult life began when I arrived at an elite Eastern university from the Midwest, a second-generation American-born ethnic (Jewish), upper middle class—poised, in other words, after about seventy years of climbing by three generations, for a final assault on perfect respectability.

In the world of snobbery as portrayed by Henry James and Edith Wharton, a person like that ought to feel the slings and arrows of invidious distinction from above most exquisitely of all. Maybe I'm insensitive, but I've never felt a thing, never to my knowledge been a victim of anti-Semitism, never been excluded from anything I wanted because of my background. There may be clubs and social sets that I can't get into, but they exert no appeal and no influence beyond themselves.

A journalist moving in generally meritocratic circles makes friends and has associates from widely different social backgrounds. No WASP aristocrat has ever pulled rank on me without seeming ridiculous, and none has put me on the defensive for being who I am. On the other hand, even very good friends from working-class backgrounds often manage to make me squirm. I've never been made to wish I'd gone to Groton, but I'm often made to wish I hadn't gone to Harvard. That's reverse snobbery.

The mechanisms of snobbery, it turns out, work perfectly well when turned upside down. Fine distinctions can still be made about one's parents. Which is more humble: an outer borough of New York City, a small Midwestern farming town, or an Appalachian coal mining community? Not finishing college is good; not starting is better. The most amusing parallel between reverse snobbery and the ordinary kind is the way some people will hide their pasts in order to remake themselves, or shade the truth to make their backgrounds look more modest than they really are. A friend of mine used to brag that his father was a Chicago cop; it turned out his father was a police administrator, and his mother was a professor at the University of Chicago.

The nastiest feud I ever had was with another close friend who prides himself on being proletarian. I accused him—accurately—of belonging in the top 10 percent of income distribution in America. He virtually called me a bounder and challenged me to a duel.

The political uses of reverse snobbery are various. Inverted social attitudes among left-wingers are Tom Wolfe's favorite subject. However, reverse snobbery is also a central theme in the writings of neoconservatives, who claim (somewhat implausibly, in my opinion) that they are in touch with the wisdom of the common people, whereas liberals operate in effete, affluent isolation. The two leading neoconservative reverse snobs are Michael Novak, who makes a market in blue collar ethnics, and Thomas Sowell, the black economist, who charges that the civil rights movement has been dominated by light-skinned blacks.

Of course, reverse snobbery is less offensive than the other kind. It's a natural enough expression of pride (or, to be a bit subtle, it's overcompensation for insecurity) on the part of people who've jumped a lot of hurdles to get where they've gotten. Even among reverse snobs who haven't really faced so many hurdles and are just putting on downscale airs, it's in some ways an expression of the egalitarian spirit.

On the other hand, there is something not egalitarian at all about reverse snobbery among successful people; there is something truly snotty. Reverse snobbery is really the U and non-U game of traditional aristocrats adapted for use by the meritocratic elite of our own society. Call it M and non-M. It is M to write a book. It is non-M to wear fashionable clothes. The more other status systems, however artificial and ridiculous, are undermined, the more the status system of merit will predominate. The most noticeable class snobbery of modern America is people who think they're better just becaue they're smarter. Like U players, serious M players are only faking indifference to status as a way of establishing their own.

This game of one-upmanship is exhausting, but probably unavoidable. The true egalitarian, I suspect, is as rare as the true aristocrat. One piece of evidence here is the way those who criticize the status obsessions of others pride themselves on mastering all the subtleties of the status rankings they object to. A more convincing display of genuine indifference—and therefore genuine superiority—would be to misunderstand the system completely. Actually, come to think of it, maybe that's exactly what my friend was trying to establish by getting it all wrong about alligator shirts. Rats. Okay, Jim, you win this round.

GRUMPS

INTRODUCTION

People tell me I'm a grump. Maybe so. This last section consists of miscellaneous grumps that don't fit in any other category, even by the low standards of relevance I've set in this book.

"A Gaffe Is When a Politician Tells the Truth" is about a long-forgotten controversy of the 1984 election campaign. But the very fact that such a forgettable matter dominated the headlines for several days illustrates one point of the piece. In the 1988 campaign there will be more real issues to talk about than in 1984, but there should be plenty of entertaining gaffology as well.

While a gaffe can ruin a politician's career, certain forms of lying are so integral to the modern political campaign that nobody even notices they're going on. My favorite example is the routine dishonesty of direct mail fund raising ("Fibbing for Dollars"). For years a standard accusation against the Democrats was that the "party of the people" relied too heavily on large donations from the rich while the Republicans, ironically, had developed a mass base of small givers. So now the Democrats have built up their own direct mail operations, using all the same shoddy devices to snooker money out of people. Great.

Part of the self-righteous image farmers have created for themselves is that they slave away from dawn to dusk. The movie *Country* (discussed in "Buying the Farm") hews to this traditional line. Why is it, then, that—as any journalist who has written about farmers can tell you—farmers seem to have more time than anybody else (except possibly the elderly) to write you long, haranguing letters whenever you dare to dissent from their orthodoxy Why is that? Hmm?

During the 1984 campaign I wanted to write a column urging

people to lie to pollsters. Rick Hertzberg, then editor of *TNR*, dissuaded me. He apologized handsomely when Mike Royko made headlines with a column pushing the same idea. In "Vox Pop Crock," I lamely urge that people approached by pollsters refuse to talk.

To this day, more than five years later, whenever I am introduced to someone who then says, "Aren't you the guy who wrote. . . ," the reference that follows is usually to "The Race Is Not to the Swift," a short *New York Times* op-ed piece about trying to find an apartment in New York. Many journalists have had a similar experience. The articles you slave over for weeks sink without a trace. Something you dash off turns out to be your bid for immortality.

The other journalistic lesson I learned from this article is that the real scum are beyond insult. The point of this piece, or so I thought, was that New York rental agencies are awful places run by awful people. But at least one agency pinned this article on the wall, just to intimidate customers. As for me, I lasted less than two years in New York. I endorse the philosophy of a friend who says: "If I can't make it there, I'll make it somewhere else."

A Gaffe Is When a Politician Tells the Truth

THE NEW REPUBLIC, *June 18, 1984*

We have reached a political nadir of some sort if the Democratic Party candidate for the leadership of the free world is chosen on the basis of a casual remark about New Jersey. Yet is seems possible history will record that Gary Hart lost his chance to be President when he stood with his wife, Lee, on a Los Angeles terrace and uttered these fateful words: "The deal is that we campaign separately; that's the bad news. The good news for her is she campaigns in California, and I campaign in New Jersey."

The TV networks played this incident very big, the analysts of the print media went to work on it, and it appears to have blossomed into a gaffe. This could cost Hart the New Jersey primary—and therefore, everyone agrees, any hope of the nomination.

The "gaffe" is now the principal dynamic mechanism of American politics, as interpreted by journalists. Each candidacy is born in a state of prelapsarian innocence, and the candidate then proceeds to commit gaffes. Journalists record each new gaffe, weigh it on their Gaffability Index ("major gaffe," "gaffe," "minor gaffe," "possible gaffe," all the way down to "ironically, could turn out to be a plus with certain interest groups"), and move the players forward or backward on the game board accordingly.

Hart's Jerseyblooper contained both of the key elements of the gaffe in its classically pure form. First, a "gaffe" occurs not when a politician lies, but when he tells the truth. The burden of Hart's remark was that, all else being equal, he'd rather spend a few springtime weeks in California than in New Jersey. Of course he would. So would I. So would Walter Mondale, no doubt, along with the vast majority of Americans, including, quite possibly, most residents of New Jersey. This doesn't mean that California is more important than New Jersey, or even a better place to live and raise a family. It certainly doesn't mean that people who live in California are superior to people who live in New Jersey. Quite the contrary. Just as youth is wasted on the young, California is wasted on Californians. Hart's remark just means that California is more appealing than New Jersey as a place for someone from neither state to spend a few weeks.

The second element of the classic gaffe is that the subject matter should be trivial. Political journalism has evolved in somewhat the same direction as literary criticism, which is now dominated by de_____tructionists. Deconstructionist criticism is indif-_____ry value of the "text"—novel or poem or _____zing. The "text" is just grist for arcane and _____s. A work of no special merit is even preferable _____n't distract from the analysis, which is the real

Similarly, political journalism dwells in its own world of primaries and polls. If necessary, journalists can take a significant fact—such as Jesse Jackson's continuing embrace of the repellent Louis Farrakhan—drain it of all its moral implications, and turn it into a gaffe. But campaign mechanics make for preferable subject matter. And the ideal "text" for political journalism to chew on is an episode of no real meaning or importance—such as a small joke about New Jersey—which can then be analyzed without distraction exclusively in terms of its likely effect on the campaign. The analysis itself, of course, is what creates that effect: a triumph of criticism the deconstructionists can only envy.

Once the press certifies that a gaffe has been committed by any candidate, the rules call for a quick round of lying by all of them. Here too, Jerseygate followed the classic pattern. Walter Mondale, in his patented serial-monogamy style, proclaimed "I love New Jersey" and swore there's no place on earth he'd rather be. Hart asserted preposterously that all he'd really meant to complain of was having to fly across the country to meet his wife in California, rather than allowing her the pleasure of flying across the country to join him in New Jersey.

Journalists—stern enforcers of political etiquette—require politicians to tell these whoppers in order to put the campaign back on its proper course. Should a politician fail to lie at the first post-gaffe opportunity, the punishment would be headlines on the order of HART COMPOUNDS JERSEY GAFFE or MONDALE SPURNS JERSEY TOO.

So you can't blame Mondale for following the script. But you can blame him for a repeat performance the next day, when he began by saying he was "not going to press the point" regarding Hart's insufficient love of New Jersey, then repeated Hart's remark, repeated his own demand for an apology, and spent several minutes doing variations on the theme.

Mondale happened to be in New Jersey at the moment of Hart's gaffe. But Mondale is spending nearly twice as much time in California as in New Jersey in the period leading up to both state primaries. What a sacrifice! And what should we make of what Mondale told a group in San Francisco in mid-May? "I saw th̶ eautiful morning," he said, "and for one sane moment I th̶ would withdraw from the race and spend the rest of my life right here." Right here? In California? Mondale seems to be saying that if he were sane, he would never step foot in his beloved New Jersey again. I think he should apologize. Sounds like a gaffe to me.

Fibbing for Dollars

THE NEW REPUBLIC, *September 3, 1984*

CAUTION: shrieked the envelope in bright red. THE ENCLOSED INFORMATION IS EXTREMELY DAMAGING TO THE STATE OF ISRAEL. Oh my gosh! My first thought was to dash to the bathroom and douse it in a tub of water. Instead, I took a deep breath and opened what turned out to be a fund-raising appeal for North Carolina Governor Jim Hunt, who is trying to knock Jesse Helms out of the Senate. The letter described Helms's copious anti-Israel activities.

This "package" (as they're called in the direct mail business) was prepared by a Milwaukee firm called AB Data, which specializes in raising money on Jewish themes. The owners claim to have developed a unique computer program which can find the Jews in any mailing list. The process—they call it "ethnication"—uses surnames, zip codes, and comparisons with other lists.

For cynical manipulation, deception, and sheer malarkey, political mailings make even the wildest TV commercials look li _____ scourse. Many of these techniques _____ zine industry. Having been involved o _____ siness sides of magazines, I'm so _____ trast between what you assume ab _____ and what you assume about your c _____ a journalist, you assume your intelligent, rational, discerning. As a businessman in search of those readers, you assume that they will really believe they've been specially selected to receive this limited offer; that they need a package full of little items to play with, such as a reply card that's too big for the return envelope unless they tear off a pointless stub; that they'll respond better to a long form letter with the word "you" several times in the first paragraph, occasional passages framed by little stars, and at least one "P.S." at the end. These are just a few standard tricks of the trade.

Richard Viguerie, the king of the new right, pioneered the use of direct mail for political organizing and fundraising. Conservative Republicans still lead the field. But liberals and Democrats are catching on and catching up.

Here is a package AB Data prepared for the reelection campaign of Michigan Senator Carl Levin. It's directed at people who've already contributed once, and the envelope says, "You have to be a little meshuga. . . ." Meshuga means crazy in Yiddish. The pitch, signed by Levin, is that he knows it's crazy to ask people for money a second time, but he's doing it anyway. Bruce Arbit of AB Data explains the theory behind claiming to be crazy while asking to be reelected to the U.S. Senate: "You're dealing with a man of incredibly high integrity, unflinchingly honest, and I think his donors appreciate that."

This nicely illustrates the difference between "honest" in the political consultant's sense of projecting an image and *honest* in the more traditional sense of telling the truth. Carl Levin is an honest pol, for a pol, but this letter is hardly proof. For one thing, he didn't really write it. For another, whoever did write it knows perfectly well that, far from being "meshuga," repeated dunning of people who've already given once is the essence of political direct mail. The first letter is called "prospecting," and almost always costs more than it brings in. The payoff comes when you hit up givers again. Roger ver, the dean of Democratic mail mavens, says that in a typical aign he hits a proven donor once a month until six months the election, then two or three times a month until voting then, like chattel slaves, the donors are rented out to ne and causes.
oudly showed me his portfolio of fund-raising p

for the Democratic National Committee. Some of them are festooned with imitation rubber-stamp messages such as OFFICIAL BUSINESS or RUSH—MAIL WITHIN TEN DAYS. Several use the popular gambit of seeking the reader's opinion. OFFICIAL 1984 PRESIDENTIAL STRATEGY BALLOT, says the outside of one, and inside there's a letter from DNC Chairman Chuck Manatt: "You have been individually selected from among the qualified voters in your state to participate in an important national project. . . ."

Craver denies that these are gimmicks. "There's a difference between a gimmick and the effect of a mailing piece." Well what, in Craver's opinion, is a gimmick? He showed me a package from a fundamentalist church in which a woman claims to have seen Jesus in her napkin, and actually includes a paper napkin with Shroud-of-Turin-type markings on it.

Okay. There's a difference between harmless mood-setting devices and outright deception. But how much difference is there between the holy napkin and this mailing from Craver for the DNC? The outside envelope is an official-looking gray and says, URGENT! FEDERAL ELECTION COMMISSION DATA ENCLOSED. Inside, along with a letter from Manatt, is what appears to be a green-and-white computer printout from the FEC, complete with little holes up the sides, reporting how much money the Republicans are raising. A footnote confesses that these are "figures compiled by the DNC." But, apart from this, every effort has been made to make the sheet look like an official document. "Document 441104-001-XBN," it proclaims. "Page 79. Summary Sheet: PC50114."

The phony FEC report is included in the package, Craver amiably explained, "to give it credibility." Once again that "credibility," in the sense of conveying an impression, as opposed to *credibility*, in the sense of being worthy of belief.

As people become inured to each new gimmick, maintaining "credibility" requires ever-higher levels of guile. A recent fund-raising package from the Mondale campaign, for example, begins with a letter from Timothy Finchem, the campaign finance director. "Dear Mr. Softtouch:" it says. "Mr. Mondale asked me to send to you a copy of the attached campaign memorandum." Attached is an ostensible memo from Finchem to Mondale (INTER-OFFICE

COMMUNICATION), urging Mondale to overcome his reluctance and ask "our generous longtime supporters" for more money. Scrawled across the top in blue ink are the words, "Boss—Can we distribute this? Tim."

So far, standard B.S. But how about this? There's another message scrawled at the top in what appears to be handwriting: "Tim—cc: Mr. Bob Beckel, Mr. Jim Johnson, Mr. Stanley Softtouch, Mr. John Reilly—Fritz." The other names are top Mondale campaign officials.

It's hard even to count the layers of artifice here. Finchem didn't really write either the cover letter or the alleged memorandum for Mondale. The memo is not an "inter-office communication"—it was created specifically to mail out. Mondale's direct mail consultant, Robert Smith, told me it was "a rewrite" of a real memo, then, when pressed, said, "I don't recall . . . it might have been a couple." Of course, Finchem never asked Mondale's permission to distribute it, and Mondale never asked Finchem to send a copy to Stanley Softtouch, whom he's never heard of.

Yet Smith seemed genuinely dumbfounded by my suggestion that the package could be considered "deceptive." "People increasingly want to be dealt with one to one and more personally," he said sincerely. "Technology permits you to do that."

Buying the Farm

THE NEW REPUBLIC, December 10, 1984

"Jewell and Gil Ivy are decent, hardworking people," explain the ads for the current movie, *Country*, about farm life in Hollywood's vision of North Dakota, where Jessica Lange fries sausages in lots of grease and serves them up on white bread, and so on. "The Ivy's [sic] way of life is an American tradition—a tradition intelligent, rational, discerning. As a businessman in search of those readers, you assume that they will really believe they've been specially selected to receive this limited offer; that they need a package full of little items to play with, such as a reply card that's too big for the return envelope unless they tear off a pointless stub; that they'll respond better to a long form letter with the word "you" several times in the first paragraph, occasional passages framed by little stars, and at least one "P.S." at the end. These are just a few standard tricks of the trade.

Richard Viguerie, the king of the new right, pioneered the use of direct mail for political organizing and fundraising. Conservative Republicans still lead the field. But liberals and Democrats are catching on and catching up.

Here is a package AB Data prepared for the reelection campaign of Michigan Senator Carl Levin. It's directed at people who've already contributed once, and the envelope says, "You have to be a little meshuga. . . ." Meshuga means crazy in Yiddish. The pitch, signed by Levin, is that he knows it's crazy to ask people for money a second time, but he's doing it anyway. Bruce Arbit of AB Data explains the theory behind claiming to be crazy while asking to be reelected to the U.S. Senate: "You're dealing with a man of incredibly high integrity, unflinchingly honest, and I think his donors appreciate that."

This nicely illustrates the difference between "honest" in the political consultant's sense of projecting an image and *honest* in the more traditional sense of telling the truth. Carl Levin is an honest pol, for a pol, but this letter is hardly proof. For one thing, he didn't really write it. For another, whoever did write it knows perfectly well that, far from being "meshuga," repeated dunning of people who've already given once is the essence of political direct mail. The first letter is called "prospecting," and almost always costs more than it brings in. The payoff comes when you hit up givers again. Roger Craver, the dean of Democratic mail mavens, says that in a typical campaign he hits a proven donor once a month until six months before the election, then two or three times a month until voting day. And then, like chattel slaves, the donors are rented out to new candidates and causes.

Craver proudly showed me his portfolio of fund-raising packages

would withdraw from the race and spend the rest of my life right
here." Right here? In California? Mondale seems to be saying that if
he were sane, he would never step foot in his beloved New Jersey
again. I think he should apologize. Sounds like a gaffe to me.

Fibbing for Dollars

THE NEW REPUBLIC, *September 3, 1984*

CAUTION: shrieked the envelope in bright red. THE
ENCLOSED INFORMATION IS EXTREMELY DAMAGING
TO THE STATE OF ISRAEL. Oh my gosh! My first thought was
to dash to the bathroom and douse it in a tub of water. Instead, I took
a deep breath and opened what turned out to be a fund-raising appeal
for North Carolina Governor Jim Hunt, who is trying to knock Jesse
Helms out of the Senate. The letter described Helms's copious
anti-Israel activities.

This "package" (as they're called in the direct mail business) was
prepared by a Milwaukee firm called AB Data, which specializes in
raising money on Jewish themes. The owners claim to have
developed a unique computer program which can find the Jews in
any mailing list. The process—they call it "ethnication"—uses
surnames, zip codes, and comparisons with other lists.

For cynical manipulation, deception, and sheer malarkey, political mailings make even the wildest TV commercials look like
models of Socratic discourse. Many of these techniques were
developed by the magazine industry. Having been involved on both
the editorial and business sides of magazines, I'm sometimes
unnerved by the contrast between what you assume about your
readers as a journalist and what you assume about your customers as
a businessman. As a journalist, you assume your readers are

that is now being threatened by bureaucrats. But when the government moved to take away the Ivy's land, they picked on the wrong people. . . . Outraged by bureaucratic injustice, they are going to fight."

A nice, all-American story line, ideal for a season that has also seen the release of *Reagan II: The Administration Continues,* and made even more archetypal by the presence of Sam Shepard—the Gary Cooper of the 1980s—in the role of the lean and independent, poor-but-honest farmer being driven off his land by squat bureaucrats in suits. "I've never been on any damn *list* in my life," he snaps, when told he's on a list of troubled debtors compiled by the hateful Farmers Home Administration (FmHA). *Country* (a product of the Walt Disney studios) was inspired by a newspaper photograph of farmers protesting at an FmHA foreclosure auction of a family farm.

In fact, *Country* does tell an all-American story, though not the one its producers think. Like most Americans who imagine they want the government to get off their backs, what the fabled Ivys really want is to nurse unmolested at the government teat. All across the country last month, people voted Republican—not just farmers, but oil producers, doctors, Social Security retirees, and other feisty, independent types—under the illusion that they're sick of burdensome government.

In contrast to their self-image as hardy freemen and stoics, no group in America is more coddled by government than farmers, and none is more whiny and self-pitying. The situation of the Ivys, as the film reports it (with "the sharp edge of informed journalism," according to Vincent Canby in The *New York Times*), is this. They own a farm that has been in her family for one hundred years. At the peak of the 1970s farmland boom, their land was worth $450,000, but now, early 1980s, it is worth only half that. Including equipment, their assets are worth about $300,000. But they have a $100,000 long-term loan from the FmHA on which they are behind in the payments, and another $52,000 short-term FmHA operating loan which they soon must repay entirely. After expenses and debt payments, the Ivys scrape by on "about $9,000 a year, depending on medical bills."

It is the evil bureaucrat's position that this does not make sense. If, after getting subsidized research and development, subsidized electricity, subsidized crop insurance, subsidized water, subsidized storage, subsidized export promotion, and above all subsidized price supports, the Ivys still cannot pay off their subsidized low-interest government loans, the government is entitled to collect its collateral, even if this means putting the Ivys, at long last, out of the farming business. That is the merciless government policy the film protests against.

Putting the Ivys out of farming does not mean putting them on the street. They have a net worth of at least $150,000. (The average farmer's is more than double this.) Placing this sum in tax-free bonds would bring the Ivys more than they now live on, without all the early mornings with the cows and late nights with the pocket calculator the movie portrays. If their farm is indeed worth $225,000, it must be because someone thinks he can run it more profitably than they have done. And one reason their farm is so valuable is the plethora of subsidies and tax advantages associated with farming. Studies have shown that all these favors quickly get capitalized into higher land prices, making the farm life an unattainable dream for poor boys who, unlike Sam Shepard, can't catch the eye of the farmer's daughter.

During the recent election campaign, the Reagan people put out a position paper bragging: "In 1983, over $35 billion of federal resources . . . went to farmers. Net farm cash income is expected to reach a record level of over $42 billion in 1984." This ostensibly free-market, antigovernment administration was unabashed at the boast that a major industry is on welfare to the tune of five-sixths of its net profits. Not that the Democrats hastened to point this out, of course. The Mondale campaign promised to protect and even expand all those subsidies and price supports (to stop those nasty foreclosures, for example), but to save money by doing it more efficiently.

Thirty-five billion dollars is more than the government spent last year on Medicaid and food stamps put together, the two principal government programs for those we now call the "truly needy." Commodity price supports, the principal program for farmers, are like a special tax on the "truly needy," since, in addition to the direct government expense, they raise the cost of food. The government estimates that consumers pay four dollars in higher food prices for every one dollar of direct subsidy.

The point is not merely that the government wastes a lot of money on agriculture—billions to increase production, then billions more to reduce production and/or dispose of the excess—but that the whole extravaganza takes place in a political never-never land, unconsciously well captured in *Country*, where the beneficiaries think they are rugged individualists in the best American tradition. Farmers have achieved a level of dignity in dependence beyond the dreams of the most radical "welfare rights" activist.

Vox Pop Crock

THE NEW REPUBLIC, *September 30, 1985*

*F*erdinand Marcos, president of all the Philippines, decided last month to put off holding a presidential election. According to him, a public opinion survey had shown that most people don't want an election. Marcos provided no details of this remarkable poll. But even if he made it up, this is the ultimate triumph for opinion poll democracy: an election canceled on the ostensible authority of a poll.

The usual complaint about polls is that they lead to democratic excess. They put representative government on too short a leash. Perpetually informed of what the voters think on every issue, politicians follow instead of leading. My complaint is different. Polls undermine democracy, even here where we have real elections. That's because polls don't measure public opinion. They create it, often with building blocks of ignorance, prejudice, and simple muddle. Worse, they reinforce the impression among voters and politicians alike that untethered opinion is what democracy is about.

Some polls solemnly report people's opinions about the unknowable. A *Washington Post*/ABC News poll in July revealed that 54 percent of Americans don't expect President Reagan's cancer to recur before he leaves office; 33 percent think it will recur; and only 12 percent have no opinion. According to a poll taken by *Newsweek* in August, 52 percent of the public now believes that an AIDS epidemic among the general population is either "very likely" or "somewhat likely." The more you know about cancer or AIDS, the more you know that the correct answer to these questions is "don't know." Yet only a few courageous citizens dare to have no opinion. It seems almost unpatriotic.

Equally silly and more nefarious are questions like: "Do you think most poor people are lazy or do you think most poor people are hard-working?" Thus a *Los Angeles Times* poll last April. Perhaps it's reassuring that 51 percent said hard-working and 26 percent said lazy. But only 23 percent got the right answer, which is "not sure." How can you be sure about such a preposterous generality? Yet the very act of taking the poll and publicizing the results gives legitimacy and weight to empty prejudices.

At the other extreme are polls asking people's opinions about indisputable questions of fact. According to a Gallup poll this month, 11 percent of taxpayers are of the opinion that their taxes will go up under Reagan's tax reform plan. Forty-six percent believe their taxes will go down. In fact, the vast majority of people's taxes will go down. Perhaps more seriously, a recent Cambridge Reports poll concluded that almost one person in five believes, incorrectly, that few if any cancers are treatable.

Pollsters profit from the ignorance of their subjects. Are they under no obligation to correct it? Shouldn't pollsters inform the people who have donated their time to answer questions that, yes, most cancers *are* treatable, and they should see a doctor right away when they find a lump? Don't they have some kind of obligation to correct the widespread misapprehensions they uncover about tax reform, or AIDS, or the state of the economy, rather than leaving the impression that these are all simply matters of opinion?

No poll allows you to express reasoned views. You're not allowed to ask, "What do you mean by 'lazy'?" or "Does 'somewhat' mean more or less than 20 percent?" There is no answer category for "This question makes no sense" or "I reject your premises." That is because polls don't seek reasoned opinions. Vague attitudes are what they want, and what they impose on the political system as reflections of "public opinion."

Even the granddaddy poll question about presidential popularity is essentially unanswerable. The classic formulation is, "Do you approve or disapprove of the way President Reagan is handling his job?" I think Reagan has done brilliantly at "handling his job." I just disagree with him about nearly everything. What am I supposed to say?

At their sleaziest, polls take a subject on which the vast majority of people are completely ignorant, implant a prejudice, call it an opinion, and serve it up as a basis for policy. The insurance industry hired the distinguished pollsters Yankelovich, Skelly and White to study public opinion about the proposal in Reagan's tax reform plan to tax the so-called "inside buildup" in whole life insurance policies. The poll showed that 49 percent had never even heard of Reagan's tax reform, let alone this "inside buildup" business. But the pollster read a long description of the "inside buildup" provision, explaining that "taxes would be paid whether or not the person actually obtained any money" and that "a typical 35-year-old man" would owe $5,800 in increased taxes. People were asked their reaction to "this new tax" (actually, of course, part of a general tax cut for individuals). Surprise, surprise, 72 percent opposed it.

Near the beginning of the survey, 62 percent said they were familiar with the concept of whole life insurance. By the end, 71 percent were "aware that you can borrow the cash surrender value of a whole life insurance policy," and even more were dead set against the government's monkeying around with whole life's current tax advantages. Eighty-three percent said that ending the tax advantage would make whole life insurance "less desirable." The insurance people hail this recognition of a mathematical truism as proof that Americans are against closing their loophole.

It's ridiculous to suppose that anyone can form a valid opinion about an issue like the taxation of "inside buildup" in whole life insurance policies based exclusively on information supplied by a pollster. There is no loophole in the tax code that Yankelovich et al. couldn't manufacture a majority in defense of, for their usual fee. It's time to stop listening to these people. Better yet, it's time to stop talking to them.

The Race Is Not to the Swift

NEW YORK TIMES, *January 9, 1982*

*I*t was the second day of my search for a place to live in my new hometown, New York City. I was examining a one-bedroom apartment with "loft" (about three feet of airspace on stilts above the kitchen) that could be mine for only $1,350 a month, plus an agent's fee of about $2,500.

My friends' advice had been unanimous: Yes, the market is very tight, but don't go to an apartment-rental agency—they're a high-pressure ripoff. So I spent a day riding the subways with the classifieds.

The next day, I went to an agency. With my agent paying for the taxis, we visited half a dozen apartments—one bedroom, $1,250, two bedrooms, $1,495, and so on—and while my agent was calling in for more listings I tried to estimate whether a mattress and box spring would clear the ceiling of the "loft."

Suddenly, my agent burst through the door, breathless, and shouted: "Come on quick! There's a two-bedroom near your office for only $1,080, but it's already been listed for five minutes!" As if on cue, another agent from the same firm, who happened to be in the room, declared stagily: "Oh, my goodness. That sounds like a much better deal than this. But you'd better hurry, because five minutes is an old listing in this business."

Well, I wasn't born yesterday. It was evident to me that the whole day had been a set-up designed to soften my resistance to the absurdity of paying more than $1,000 a month for an apartment. Slowly and deliberately, I said I'd be happy to see the place, but I refused to be railroaded. My agent said: "Oh, forget all that. This is New York. Let's go." He dragged me down to the street and waved frantically for a cab. In the cab, he lectured me that he had seen people lose apartments by as little as two minutes.

We arrived at the building, got the apartment key, and were waiting for the elevator, when my agent suddenly went pale. I follow his glance to the front door, where a woman was walking in. "It's another agent!" he hissed, as in a spy novel. Someone from his own office, in fact. "We'd better hurry!" We went up to the apartment. I took about forty-five seconds to look around. It was huge. It was modern. It had a window in the kitchen. My blood began to race. "I'll take it!" I shrieked. "Of course you'll take it," said my agent, "but first we have to beat her back to the office." But couldn't we just telephone? Oh no, my agent said. The rules were that the first one back in the office with a client in hand got the apartment. I charged ahead of him into the street and waved frantically for a taxi.

The taxi driver said, "You want me to take First Avenue or FDR Drive?" It was rush hour. My agent couldn't decide. "What do you think?" he asked me. "It's your city," I said. He bounced up and down in agonies of uncertainty, like the contestants on "Let's Make a Deal" trying to choose between what's in the box and what's behind the curtain where Carol is standing. Finally, he blurted, "FDR Drive." We entered the drive and immediately were caught in traffic. "Oh, nooooooooo," my agent sobbed, "I *knew* we should have taken First Avenue. Now she's sure to beat us."

We crept along, while my agent rocked and moaned. About a quarter mile from the exit, traffic stalled completely. My agent sprang back into action. "Hey," he said, "you're a jogger." (I'd asked about jogging paths.) He paid the driver and yanked me out of the cab in the middle of the highway. We trotted through the traffic, up the exit ramp, and on to the agency's building. We lunged through the lobby, and he began jabbing madly at the elevator button. Then, suddenly, he turned calm and said, "You know, maybe I'm getting carried away." We proceeded in a more dignified fashion up to the agency's office.

As we entered, the phone was ringing, and as we approached the main desk, the receptionist was writing something in a notebook. My agent glanced at it, turned bright red, and screamed, "That's my apartment! That's my apartment! She can't do this! You know the rules!" And so on. The manager raced up and shook him back and forth, other agents offered water, but my agent was out of control. "That's my apartment!" he whined.

The manager explained that because the other agent had unfairly lost some deal the day before, he'd bent the rules for her, saying that she could have the apartment if she phoned in with a client before anyone else physically showed up to claim it.

My agent argued hysterically that we had crossed the office threshold before her phone call had been answered. But the manager was in no mood for Jesuitical distinctions. We'd lost the apartment by twenty seconds—a new record.

My agent turned to me and shouted, "I can't believe *you're* not upset!" But I was too dazed to be upset. I wandered off into the night.

And perhaps the whole adventure was a hoax after all, because I met my agent the next morning and rented the very first place he showed me. No second bedroom. No loft. No window in the kitchen. Small. Dark. But under $1,000 a month! What a deal!